CLANLANDS
IN NEW ZEALAND

CLANLANDS
IN NEW ZEALAND

Kiwis, Kilts, and an
Adventure Down Under

SAM HEUGHAN
& GRAHAM MCTAVISH

with Charlotte Reather

RADAR

First published in Great Britain in 2023 by Radar,
an imprint of Octopus Publishing Group Ltd
Carmelite House
50 Victoria Embankment
London EC4Y ODZ
www.octopusbooks.co.uk
www.octopusbooksusa.com

An Hachette UK Company
www.hachette.co.uk

Distributed in the US by Hachette Book Group
1290 Avenue of the Americas, 4th & 5th Floors, New York NY 10104

Distributed in Canada by Canadian Manda Group
664 Annette St., Toronto, Ontario, Canada M6S 2C8

ISBN 9781804190760, ISBN 9781804191897, ISBN 9781804191910

A CIP catalogue record for this book is available from the British Library.

Printed and bound in Canada.

The authors and publisher have made all reasonable efforts to contact copyright-holders for
permission and apologise for any omissions or errors in the form of credits given. Corrections
may be made to future printings.

Typeset in 12/14.75pt Adobe Caslon Pro Std by Jouve (UK), Milton Keynes

Illustrations by Paul Tobin (paultobinart.com)
Map by Peter Liddiard at Sudden Impact Media

10 9 8 7 6 5 4 3 2 1

This FSC® label means that materials used
for the product have been responsibly sourced.

To those of you who accompanied us on the first trip . . .
and a warm kiwi welcome to those joining us for the
first time . . . Buckle up!

– Sam

This one is for Garance,
With love.

– Graham

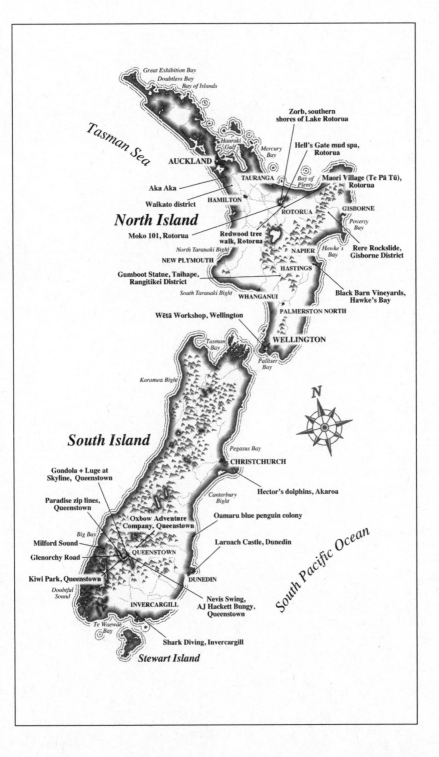

Great Exhibition Bay
Doubtless Bay
Bay of Islands

Zorb, southern
shores of Lake Rotorua

Hell's Gate mud spa,
Rotorua

Hauraki
Gulf
Mercury
Bay

AUCKLAND

Tasman Sea

TAURANGA
Bay of
Plenty
**Maori Village (Te Pā Tū),
Rotorua**

Aka Aka

Waikato district
HAMILTON

GISBORNE

North Island

ROTORUA
Poverty
Bay

Moko 101, Rotorua
**Redwood tree
walk, Rotorua**

North Taranaki Bight
NAPIER
Hawke's
Bay
**Rere Rockslide,
Gisborne District**

NEW PLYMOUTH

HASTINGS

Gumboot Statue, Taihape,
Rangitikei District

South Taranaki Bight
WHANGANUI

**Black Barn Vineyards,
Hawke's Bay**

PALMERSTON NORTH

Wētā Workshop, Wellington

Tasman
Bay

WELLINGTON

Palliser
Bay

Karamea Bight

South Island

Pegasus Bay

CHRISTCHURCH

Gondola + Luge at
Skyline, Queenstown

Hector's dolphins, Akaroa

Canterbury
Bight

Paradise zip lines,
Queenstown

**Oxbow Adventure
Company, Queenstown**
Oamaru blue penguin colony

Big Bay

Milford Sound

QUEENSTOWN
Larnach Castle, Dunedin

Glenorchy Road

Kiwi Park, Queenstown

South Pacific Ocean

Doubtful
Sound

DUNEDIN

INVERCARGILL
Nevis Swing,
AJ Hackett Bungy,
Queenstown

Te Waewae
Bay

Shark Diving, Invercargill

Stewart Island

N

Foreword

When Graham McTavish initially asked me to write this foreword, I was reluctant. To be honest, I didn't really want to read this book.

This has nothing to do with Graham; quite the contrary, I've always held Graham in high regard. We had both served in the trenches together during the making of *The Hobbit* trilogy, and we've stayed in touch ever since. Our friendship is based on a mutual love of history and an uncannily similar sense of humour. I watched the first season of *Men in Kilts* and enjoyed every minute of it, welcoming the news that a second series was on the horizon.

My problem was about the country they had selected for their second series. The Men In Kilts could have gone to some place in Europe, fumbling their way through multiple countries with unfamiliar languages and questionable cuisine. Or perhaps the Middle East, with its exotic foods and where wine and scotch are prohibited in many regions. Imagine them trying to smuggle hip flasks across a border and ending up in prison. That would be funny! They could even have opted for Australia, where men wearing skirts are not merely accepted but celebrated. I've heard they have the odd good wine too.

But no . . . they came here, to my country. To New Zealand. And this triggered a reaction that has been hard-wired into me since birth.

To explain what this is, I will try to paint a picture of the New Zealand I grew up in – a country largely ignored by most of the world. We exported lamb to Britain and had a great rugby team, and that was it. Oh, and we mustn't forget New Zealander Ed Hillary who had conquered Mt Everest in 1953. But that was about it, the extent of our global significance.

We were painfully aware of our humble status. Many Americans, we were informed, had no knowledge of New Zealand, and those who did often mistook us as part of Australia. Whenever a movie or a TV show presented a scene with a world map, Kiwi eyes instinctively darted to the bottom right, searching for our homeland, only to find it missing most of the time. World maps often reached the east coast of Australia and stopped there. We were simply too insignificant for the world to care about. Sceptical? Play Risk and try to invade New Zealand, or better yet, search 'World maps without New Zealand' online.

The only positive thing we could think of was that, with the Cold War at its peak, our obscurity might offer us safety. We hoped that the Kremlin was also using these incomplete maps. But overall, this insignificance had us feeling like the weird kid who's always left out when picking teams for sports.

When I was a kid, *Coronation Street* was New Zealand's favourite TV show. We were all too aware that the episodes we avidly watched every night (on our one and only channel) had actually aired in Great Britain five years earlier. It gave us a sense of being not only thousands of miles from the rest of the world, but also years behind. On the rare occasion that an uncle or aunt would make the long journey back to the Mother Country to 'visit the family', they were also on a secret mission. While in the UK, they would watch the latest episodes of *Coronation Street* and return with valuable intelligence about the soap opera's future plot lines. Uncle Frank would be bombarded with questions, 'Do the Ogdens still run The Rovers Return?', 'Does Ken Barlow get a girlfriend?', 'Ena Sharples does what . . .?? Oh my God!'.

Our sense of isolation did foster self-sufficiency and resourcefulness. Back then everything came into the country by sea, so if anything broke down, or needed repairing, it took forever to ship a replacement part in. We had no choice but to fix things ourselves, and the entire country developed a 'do it yourself' mentality. Anything from a car or bus to a dishwasher, had to be fixed using whatever materials we could find. Fortunately, New Zealand farmers built their fences with something called eight gauge wire, and it proved to be a versatile part of any makeshift repair. It was amazing to see this humble fencing wire used in so many inventive ways. I've used it myself. Even today, if something breaks down, you're likely to hear somebody mutter 'No worries, mate. I'll fix it with a bit of No.8 wire'.

Despite the confident resilience that Kiwis developed, an inferiority complex also became part of the Kiwi psyche. We were incredibly sensitive about what people 'from overseas' thought of our country. I remember, in 1976, when the majority of us flocked to cinemas to watch *Sleeping Dogs*. Roger Donaldson's movie was the first feature film shot in New Zealand in many years, featuring New Zealand actors on the big screen, speaking like us. It was unsettling to hear our own accent. The audience I saw it with squirmed in their seats – 'No! We don't really sound like that . . . do we??'

Allow me to apologize for this long-winded explanation of my hesitation in reading this book. I'm almost there. Please bear with me . . .

Every so often, a book or TV series by a foreigner who had visited New Zealand would appear, in which they gave the rest of the world their opinion of our country. It was horrible, like reading your school report. We would collectively react in one of two possible ways:

- If they spoke highly of us, we could hardly contain our pride. In our minds, New Zealand had suddenly gained the official status of 'the world's greatest country'.
- If they criticized us, or worse, ridiculed us (I'm looking at you, John Cleese), it would ignite a defensive instinct ingrained in most Kiwis. Some of us would feel the urge to hit back (this 'stuff you' attitude probably kept our rugby team, the All Blacks, fuelled for decades, as they continually triumphed over teams from much larger and better resourced countries), but many Kiwis would descend into a bleak embarrassment.

Reading this today, it might be difficult to comprehend the intensity of this embarrassment. Picture this: your child is performing in a school play. They've practised for weeks, mastered their song, and on the big night, they yearn to make their parents proud. Then, mid-song, their voice cracks, going off-key. They forget the lyrics. As sniggers break out among the parents, your child stands frozen . . . and loses control of their bladder. That's somewhat how we felt.

That is why I was reluctant to read this book. I didn't want to trigger the insecure 'fight or flight' impulse that many Kiwis still feel, whenever our country is under the spotlight – however deeply embedded that is.

However, I didn't want to let Graham down either . . .

Times have changed and I had to ignore my instinctual reactions, put my big boy pants on, and read the damn book that Graham had written with Sam Heughan . . . this book.

So, that's what I did . . . and I loved it.

The New Zealand that Graham and Sam explore is no longer the country I grew up in. We're now in a world interconnected by the internet, where international travel is commonplace. New Zealand has become a popular tourist destination, and our sense of isolation has largely evaporated.

Graham's obvious affection for New Zealand and the sense of wonder that Sam clearly experiences during his first trip here, makes this book not only easy to read – it's also immensely entertaining.

Their exceptional sense of humour shines through even when they recount less than positive experiences. I found myself laughing out loud many times – and this was often when they try to grapple with one of New Zealand's many . . . er, eccentricities.

This book is an extensive account of Graham and Sam's adventures while filming their *Men in Kilts* series in New Zealand, but it's much more than that. It reads like a commentary track on a DVD, a parallel narrative, jam-packed with behind-the-scenes stories, amusing anecdotes – and the occasional intelligent observation (these are pretty thin on the ground).

As they travel from place to place, they occasionally delve into the history of a particular location or person. These are my favourite bits. Traditional historians often present such information in a dry, self-important manner. But Graham and Sam skilfully deploy satire and irony to bring these historical accounts to life in a refreshing and entertaining way.

Most importantly, it documents one chapter of the peculiar friendship between Graham McTavish and Sam Heughan. I must admit I thoroughly enjoyed Sam's persistent roasting of Graham, and I think you will too. Knowing Graham quite well, but never having met Sam, there were some moments when I thought, 'Oooh . . . Sam might have crossed the line this time', and yet there's plenty of times when I'd think, 'Yep, bang on! That's exactly the Graham I know'. But rest assured, Graham gives as good as he gets, and this constant banter makes the book a delight to read.

But you don't need to take my word for it . . . you're about to find out for yourself.

Sir Peter Jackson

Wellington, New Zealand
July 2023

Prologue

*'And I looked, and behold a pale horse: and his name
that sat on him was Death.
And then I had another quick look, and behind the really scary
guy on the pale horse there was a camper van, and the name
sat in him was Samwise, and I beheld he was Ginger . . . and
Hell followed with him . . .'*
(with apologies to . . .) The Holy Bible, Revelations 6:8

GRAHAM
New Zealand. Aotearoa – 'the land of the long white cloud'.
Interestingly, it was in fact only the North Island Māori who called
it that. The South Island *iwi* (tribes or clans) preferred to call
it 'Te Waipounamu' after the precious green stone (Pounamu)
that was only found there. They don't like it when people call
it Aotearoa.

In older maps you see New Zealand described as North Island, Middle Island (Middle-earth, anyone?) and South Island, with the tiny and delightful Stewart Island dangling off the bottom, like a comma. On others it is marked as New Ulster, New Munster and New Leinster respectively – clearly an Irish cartographer.

A new land. The newest on the planet. Rising from the oceans like a perfect jewel that lay undiscovered by man for millennia until a group of migrating Pacific Islanders, in probably the 14th century, saw that long white cloud, after many weeks of travel, and knew that cloud signalled land.

It is a child's conjuring of a perfect land. Like Peter Pan's Neverland where you are never far from an adventure. There are volcanoes, alps, fjords, lakes, beaches, subtropical rainforest, and even a desert. I first came to New Zealand in 1994 touring my own play about Vincent Van Gogh called *Letters from the Yellow Chair* with my good friend Nick Pace. I returned several times with my first wife, Gwen, who is from New Zealand, but didn't imagine I'd end up here. When I came in 2010 to film *The Hobbit*, I knew immediately that I would want at least one foot always planted in this magical faraway land, so in 2014 I bought a house.

SAM

As someone new to New Zealand, I had always imagined it as two 'Treasure Islands' (South Island – Te Waipounamu, and North Island – Te Ika-a-Māui) in the Pacific Ocean at the bottom of the world. A country filled with hobbits and flightless birds, the best rugby players in the world and the home of one very grumpy Scottish actor. I imagined a landscape uncannily similar to the Scottish Highlands, equal in beauty but more heightened in drama and pristine wilderness, basically MUCH bigger than Bonnie Scotland. I guess that's why Academy Award Winning director Peter Jackson filmed *The Hobbit* and *The Lord of the Rings* here. But the truth is, my friends, the true appeal of the New Zealand archipelago, its two main land masses stretching 268,000km^2 (103,000 square miles), is . . . IT'S ADRENALINE COUNTRY!

[Graham: Oh God!]

Oh yes! Everyone here is crazy for extreme, endorphin-inducing, bum-clenching, eye-watering, lung-busting ACTION! Yes, Graham, your hobbit hole is nearby, and you filmed here in this astonishingly beautiful land, but do you think I'd agree to go on an adventure with you because of that? No, no, no, it's because of the wild, extreme and very dangerous activities, Grey Dog, and we're going to dive right in!

WELCOME to the land of Zorbs, zip lines and bungee jumping . . . these are MY people!

[Graham: You forgot to take your medication again, didn't you?]

GRAHAM

It was very possible that the whole journey may never have happened. The fact that it did is nothing short of a miracle. Admittedly, this particular miracle may have been conjured by the forces of Beelzebub, those ones that really love inflicting suffering on bald, bearded sexagenarians. (And no, Sam, that's not the name of an exclusive online dating site.) More will be told of the shenanigans and hurdles that we had to overcome to get Heughan into New Zealand but suffice to say, for now, that it was almost as if New Zealand herself didn't want him there. This shy, remote country at the bottom of the world was shouting in protest at his arrival. Pleading with the universe to preserve her dignity and keep the bounding be-muscled one away from her shores. How did this journey begin? To understand that, let's go back to the beginning . . .

We first met in the sweaty casting office in Soho, both Sam and I auditioning for acting roles in a time travel show set in Scotland called *Outlander*. (If this is the first you're hearing of this, then you've likely not read our worldwide bestseller, *Clanlands*, and must immediately start there.) I was up for the part of Dougal Mackenzie and Sam was going for the lead role of Jamie Fraser. Even though he had little TV experience, he landed the part, making me immediately hate him. However, on set, we strangely bonded, in the way that people who are thrown into an alien world bond. Filming *Outlander* in Glasgow and the wilds of Scotland was, in fact, an amazing time for all of us, especially our merry band of thespian Highlanders, comprising me, Sam, Gary Lewis, Stephen Walters, Grant O'Rourke, Duncan Lacroix, and, of course, Caitriona Balfe (who plays leading lady Claire Beauchamp/ Randell/Fraser and recently graced the big screens in the film *Belfast*). We had no idea what the show would be like and for Sam and Caitriona, it was their first major job on TV but we all shared a sense of mutual, strong support towards one another. Then, sadly, it was ruined when Sam and Caitriona murdered me in Season Two (spoiler alert!), their 'characters' thrusting a ruddy great dirk (dagger) deep into my chest, their twinkling eyes suggesting this was something more than acting!

Somehow our relationship survived this trauma (lots of soul-searching and primal-scream therapy), and Sam and I reunited in the even more clammy environment of a camper van in the Highlands of Scotland in 2019, when our idea to travel around Scotland together in 'the Fiat Flatulence' camper became a reality, leading to a *Clanlands* book and the first *Men in Kilts* TV series. The *Clanlands* idea had been conceived by Sam and me in between takes (and lattes) on the set of *Outlander* and was born in my kitchen in New Zealand (well, that's where I was standing when Sam rang).

[Sam: I'd say it was born in a parking lot just off Great Western Road in Glasgow, where I had arranged for a crew to film our adventures. I just needed a grumpy companion for the ride.]

In August 2019, we jumped into filming a *Clanlands* teaser over several insane whisky-fuelled weekends in the Scottish Highlands before we headed to Los Angeles to present the aforementioned tangled footage to the assembled executives of Starz (the American cable and satellite television network that makes *Outlander*). That they agreed to fund an entire season of *Men in Kilts* right there in the room still amazes me, but they did. But before we made it to Scotland to start filming, dear old Covid put a halt to the world and Sam and I found ourselves writing the *Clanlands* book. That first book was written (well, my contribution) in, you guessed it, New Zealand. The release of Season One of *Men in Kilts* followed, after which our thoughts naturally turned to where we could go next. We considered Scotland again. I remember Sam was very keen on travelling by boat around the Hebrides and across to Ireland – I think he even mentioned Scandinavia. *[Sam:* Men in Kilts – *in boats! Who wouldn't love that?]* But considering what happened to me at sea just before Sam arrived in New Zealand . . . I'm glad we didn't. More on that later. I always suspected the island-hopping boat idea was some Captain Bligh ruse to keep me constantly at the point of being swept overboard, or at least vomiting regularly on camera!

However, fate kept pushing us towards the Antipodes, and with Britain bouncing in and out of various Covid lockdowns in 2021, with no guarantee of being able to film without being shut down at any moment, New Zealand looked a very attractive prospect indeed. Seemingly Covid-free by dint of pulling up the national drawbridge, strict quarantines, and stopping anyone with a runny nose from entering the country, life was carrying on as normal. And owing to busy schedules, our only combined free time was December 2021 and January 2022, because ten years on, Sam was still busy frolicking on Fraser's Ridge in *Outlander*, plunging naked into icy streams! And meanwhile, I was terrifically busy clanking around in a suit of armour in a land called Westeros (actually a very large film studio called Leavesden), filming *House of the Dragon*, the blood-soaked prequel to *Game of Thrones* in which I play Ser Harrold Westerling, pretty much the only morally upright character in the entire show. *[Sam: Did you ACTUALLY do any filming, or just sit around drinking lattes, recounting tales and anecdotes of filming with yours truly?]* *[Graham: Actually, I save the anecdotes of working with you for my therapist and legal depositions.]*

And, crucially, for the purposes of our *Men in Kilts* follow-up, over 20 per cent of the New Zealand population are of Scottish descent, many arriving during the Highland Clearances (1750–1860), which started after the Jacobite Risings, when the *Outlander* TV drama was set, and effectively how Sam's and my journey began. Scots continued to settle here after that, even willingly – with assisted passage between the 1940s and 1950s and the creation of the

'Ten Pound Pom' (the amount of money charged for passage by the New Zealand government). Because, if you fell asleep in Scotland and magically didn't wake up until you got to New Zealand, you would, in fact, believe you were still in Scotland.

[Sam: Welcome to Scotland, down under!]

CHAPTER ONE

The Prison Diaries

JANUARY 2022

<u>Location: Top secret MIQ (Managed Isolation and Quarantine) hotel, somewhere in Christchurch, South Island, New Zealand</u>

SAM

What day? The time? Who knows? I'm jet-lagged on the other side of the world and am in purgatory.

The 1970s air con above the bed buzzes angrily at me every 64 seconds. I time each interlude. 73 . . . 45 . . . (?!) . . . 66. Clearly, the machine, like me, has lost track of time. But the random hisses and vibrations disturb my thoughts. I look around the bare room for something else to distract me. A worn grey carpet. Double bed, single thin sheet that doesn't fit and two pillows that have given up the fight and resigned themselves to their sentence. One side-table. One box of sealed water. A phone. A flat-screen 24-inch TV mounted opposite the bed, the cables making their escape through a hole in the wall. A writing desk. One chair. All the items would be appropriate on a film set where the brief was '1970s faded motel'. I stare out of the double-glazed window with no handles or levers to open it; even if I wished to break through, I couldn't. I consider how painful it would be to take a run at the thick glass. 'No, think happy thoughts, imagine yourself outside.' The view was of a man-made fence covered in thick black gauze, which obscured anything other than the sky and the tops of a few tall trees, waving to me in the light summer breeze. The sun breaks into my cell and illuminates an angular patch of the worn carpet, heating its synthetic base. I lie on this little blanket of sun and wonder if people will ask, 'Where did you get your tan?' I imagine there are birds outside singing, but I can't tell. I can't hear anything other than the occasional 'BUZZZ . . . tick, tick, tick' of my air-con companion.

Peering through the security keyhole, I spy an empty white corridor and a grey door, like mine, opposite. I wonder if its inhabitants are staring back.

'Yes, buddy, come see New Zealand, you'll love it, mate! It's so outdoorsy, with INCREDIBLE views, and the people, they're really, really nice . . .' Graham had enthusiastically convinced me, long before I started my journey here. I curse him as I pace between the viewless window and the door. 'Seven . . . eight . . . nine . . . nope,' I sigh. Almost nine medium, average, passable steps. Why had I come all this way, halfway around the world, to be locked up and losing my mind for seven days? No. Ten days!

[Graham: That was an extract from The Prison Diaries *by Sam Heughan, the forthcoming harrowing and brave account of an actor's life during the Covid pandemic, to be published in 2024, all rights reserved.]*

Due to the continuing uncertainty of the pandemic and perhaps Graham's insistence we shoot close to his house, we had decided the second season of *Men in Kilts* would feature New Zealand in all its grandeur. But the process of getting me there had been an adventure in its own right. With a strict entry policy and border control, a crew of ten including Squeezy, our 'safety officer', line producer and quarantine captain, had all applied for a place in the lottery system to gain access to the country. Uncertain times and a demand for locals to return home meant that we didn't want to take up vital places on the scheme but we had been advised and aided by New Zealand's Ministry of Business, Innovation and Employment, who considered our show would begin to revitalize and restore tourism, which had been all but exterminated by Covid-19.

'Congratulations, we did it, you're IN!' read Squeezy's glowing email. I would be arriving to experience Managed Isolation and Quarantine (MIQ) on 24 December 2021, arranged like an early Christmas present from Graham.

So, with tight schedules, the holiday season was the only time we could fit the shoot in. It meant missing my family over Christmas but at least I'd be out in time to celebrate New Year with my bearded travel companion. He may even share some of his most cherished bottles of New Zealand vino with me from his vast wine collection. I imagined he had a huge underground cavern beneath a sparkling villa, filled with countless barrels – hogsheads, tuns and perhaps even the odd barrique barrel – all filled with oodles of luscious Sauvignon Blanc . . .

However, fate took a different turn and my Christmas vacation in New Zealand's finest isolation facility was, at the very last minute, well and truly scuppered. Seventy-two hours before I flew, I was required to provide a negative test, which I passed. But then the rules changed. Ah, of course they did. Now, the powers-that-be required a negative test 24 hours before a flight, as well as proof of double vaccination and a place in the MIQ system.

'I'm not sure about this,' I remember saying to Alex-the-German (the executive producer of *Men in Kilts* and my long-suffering business partner) a couple of days before Christmas and a day before I was supposed to fly. 'I don't feel . . . normal.'

Alex (Persian with a German accent and now living in LA) laughed, 'Ja, ja, when are you EVER normal? Imagine if you had Covid and had to quarantine in LA over Christmas!' *[Graham: Alex's German accent is so extravagantly thick and over the top I sometimes think it's a complete pretence – like my superb equestrian skills – and he is, in fact, from Iowa.]*

Well, he soon stopped laughing and nearly choked on his schnitzel when I, in fact, *did* test positive and had to quarantine in his house in the Hollywood Hills. Luckily, he was staying elsewhere for the holidays and could enjoy a proper *fröhliche Weihnachten* with his family. I, however, was miserable. Away from friends and family, stuck indoors and – more importantly, given the precision planning – unable to fly to New Zealand to start filming our new show. Christmas Day came and went. I morosely managed to roast a chicken, open a bottle of Alex's glühwein from the secret stash and raid his fine whisky collection, comprising superior Sassenach spirits, of course.

[Graham: Even while recounting his harrowing ordeal he can't help advertising his whisky. I'm convinced that if Sam were facing a firing squad, he would offer them a sample of Sassenach and a 10 per cent discount on future purchases.]

I Zoomed my New Zealand Father Christmas, McTavish, to break the news. No longer the Grinch, he appeared on screen, wine bottle in hand, a full house behind him, munching on something he had no doubt *not* made himself. 'Don't worry, mate, we will make it happen!' Usually the more sober of the two of us when it comes to plans and arrangements, we had switched roles and he was unusually optimistic. 'We'll just ask Starz for more money, they won't mind!'

The screen froze as McTavish was in mid-flow, his beard filling the screen and a festive paper hat glued to his head. I shuffled over to the kitchen counter and picked at the carcass of the unlucky yuletide bird. To add to the dire straits I was in, I had fractured my knee and torn my MCL (medial collateral ligament) only a few weeks before. *[Graham: Is that next to your LOL or your OMG?]* I had been cycling back from a mega CrossFit gym session – and no, Graham, it doesn't mean to train in a bad temper! – when I suddenly hit black ice on the road and the bike went right and my leg went left. I found myself on the ground, my leg at a 90-degree angle to my body. Somehow, I managed to cycle home, which was when I realized it was rather serious. I was due to fly to Los Angeles and on to New Zealand and I couldn't place any weight on my left leg! With the combination of injured leg and now Covid, I was beginning to lose hope.

'Don't worry, we will make it work, whatever you need,' Karen Bailey, Executive Vice President of Starz, assured me. She even popped over with some Christmas goodies and left them outside Alex's house. 'When you get to New Zealand, you must try some of that famous wine Graham talks about!' Karen shouted as she sped off.

***

Sauvignon Blanc . . . my mouth started to water. I open the hobbit-sized fridge in my quarantine room: nothing. An out-of-date pint of New Zealand milk, gone off and slowly turning to cheese. A loud knock at the door informed me dinner had finally arrived. It was day one and I'd been travelling for around 24 hours and was ravenous. The thirteen-hour trip from LA had been relatively painless. I had even managed to stretch out on a business-class flight, and I imagined arriving at Wellington airport would be a breeze.

'Put your mask ON!' screamed an irate airport official when I removed one side of my mask to record a cheeky voice note for Graham.

'Pshhhhht, the Eagle has landed.' I repeated, 'The EAGLE has landed, over.' I looked at the official, who glowered back at me from behind his Perspex helmet and N95 mask.

'Put it on and stand in the box. Do NOT move!' I jumped back, having not noticed the floor marked with a number of spaces in the hallway, each containing a groggy passenger awaiting further instruction. It was now a day later than it was in LA. Or was I behind? My jet-lagged brain tried to do the maths, the fluorescent lights disorientating me and burning my dry contact lenses into my eyeballs.

At Wellington airport I was held along with other nervous passengers for a couple of hours in a large room. Eventually, we were separated into groups and put on another plane. An hour later I was told I would be 'held' in Christchurch, on the South Island.

***

BUZZZ . . . tick, tick, tick. The air con woke me from my tormented dreams. Day two; or was it three? I tried to remember. Was the first day 'day one' or 'day zero'? Ten days' quarantine was all I needed to do; I'd just done ten self-enforced ones in LA. Karen had been true to her word and had found not only the finances to extend our shoot, but also, I had managed to win another place on the MIQ lottery, having had to apply for a second time. 2021 finished strongly at the last minute; the plans were finally falling into place and we were all set to go in early January. *Men in Kilts: New Zealand,* here we come . . .!

BUZZZ . . . tick, tick, tick . . . tick . . . tick . . . BUZZZ . . . BUZZZ. Air con, my ass. After pressing every button repeatedly, I stood on the edge of the crumpled bed and tried to rip the machine off the wall. Failing that, I turned it off at the plug. 'Surely fresh air is healthier than piped air!' I yelled at the machine. Its air ducts smiled back, refusing to answer. My air-con-versations (sorry) had been all one-way since I'd arrived and I was now officially losing my mind. After a set period of time and special permission, guests (inmates? prisoners? isolators?) were given 45 minutes a day to leave their room and GO OUTSIDE. But when was that going to happen? I was desperate. I needed something more than these four walls. The phone was my only connection to the outside world. I avoided Zoom calls – I didn't want anyone to see my dishevelled demeanour and pale skin. I'd totally lost it, already.

[Graham: From my personal recollection of the FOUR times I did MIQ (that's three more than one, twice as many as two, and four times more than once), they do a daily mental health check. I have a feeling Sam's room was under suicide watch. Or perhaps they only checked on MY mental health? Hmmm . . . hadn't thought of that.]

[Sam: You had your lovely, long-suffering fiancée with you to help 'break the boredom'.]

[Graham: It's true I did spend one of my FOUR times in MIQ with my then fiancée.]

Meals were delivered three times a day; a knock on the door and then the delivery person would vanish, avoiding all contact. The food was edible *[Graham: define edible]* but so unhealthy – fries, burgers, cans of Coke and sweets. Delightful for a day but I couldn't sustain it over ten. I called the security desk. 'How long?!' I gasped, as if seeking air. 'How long until I can escape outside?'

'Ahhh, yeah, well, I've spoken to the military doctor, he'll make a decision tomorrow.' TOMORROW? I screamed in my head, that's 24 hours, 50,000+ steps to window and back, 1000+ buzzes and . . . and . . . I won't survive.

[Graham: This is the moment, if it were a movie, that Sam would break out only to find empty corridors, an empty hotel, a desolate post-apocalyptic landscape, and perhaps the odd zombie. Actually, come to think of it, THAT IS a description of MIQ.]

I must have gulped loudly or perhaps the air con made a noise but the kindly voice on the end of the phone answered, 'Yeah, see, you may have to stay 14 days, you tested positive.' I became a man possessed. I jumped on Zoom, on my email, I contacted everyone in LA. We had to prove that I'd just had Covid; it wasn't that I was infectious, it was just that the proteins and antibodies were still in my body. In fact, if anything, I was possibly more immune than anyone in the facility! I was shielded, impervious, I was resistant to disease, I was in fact stronger, leaner, more mentally resilient; they couldn't beat me! I would beat them! I needed to be an MIQ SUPERHERO.

[Graham: COVID MAN! I can see the poster now: Sam's even-more-muscular-than-usual body bursting from a Spandex hazmat suit wearing matching plastic gloves and booties, wearing a mask OVER his mask, and armed with fistfuls of syringes.]

No more steps, no more bad food, no more losing my mind. I'd prove to them I was a champion isolator; I would thrive! I found the documents I needed, searched for workouts online, spoke daily to the *Men in Kilts 2* crew, and began to regain control of my destiny.

Cue Rocky theme tune – duh duh duhhhh duh duh daaaah – 'ADRIANNNNNN MCTAVISH!'

By day four, my plea for justice had been heard. The Military Commander had reviewed my case and confirmed my status as Covid-free; I only needed to remain for six more days AND I WAS ALLOWED OUTSIDE! I shielded my eyes from the midday sun, the warm breeze wafting over my mask; I could almost feel it. Birds chirped, cars and people passed by, almost in reach behind the ten-foot barriers.

I was OUTSIDE!

I stopped, allowing a sprinkler, ill-placed to water the trees and unseen gardens beyond, to cover me in a fine mist, cooling my pale skin. The exterior of the Christchurch hotel didn't look so bad; despite being completely cordoned off from the rest of the world by the large barriers, it had a small garden in the centre and a large car park, which I was now standing in for my 45 minutes of daily exercise.

Standing on the car park sidewalk, Christchurch appeared to be a peaceful and quiet town and I could just make out some shops and restaurants nearby and a large replica of a Spitfire aeroplane several blocks away. It reminded me of Graham, strangely, our propeller plane flight in Scotland from Islay to Ben Lomond and his ancestral home, the McTavish caravan park. 'Roger Roger, chocks away, watch out for your kilts, put the kettle on . . .'

Then I smelt it, faintly. The mask blocked my nose, but yes, there it was, a familiar delicate fragrance: lavender. It was a scent which would have sent Jamie Fraser into a frenzy and a quivering mess because it was an aroma favoured by his arch nemesis, Black Jack Randall, Jamie's tormenter and abuser. A beautiful spray of purple flowers by the entrance to the hotel. I reached down and snapped off a twig. Lifting it towards my mask, I edged it down and inhaled deeply . . . 'PUT YOUR MASK ON. NOW!' The sunlight was blocked out by a silhouette. I dropped the sprig and pulled at the elastic of my mask, which slipped out of my fingers and slapped me in the face, covering my eyes. 'Oh God, no, sorry, I didn't mean to, I was just smelling the . . . ' I stammered, fumbling with the face covering.

'The lavender? Yeah, most of you Poms do.'

'Poms?' I thought. Hardly a Kiwi expression and his accent wasn't the same as the cheery staff I had encountered on the phone. Then I recognized him: the security guard from the airport who had shouted at me in my imaginary box; I thought I had detected an accent then. He was Australian, I was sure of it. 'Uh, yeah, well, we have it in Scotland too, I've had some . . . er . . . strange experiences with it.' I smiled with my eyes, hoping my Aussie jailer would warm to me and perhaps extend my exercise time, or perhaps slip me some contraband. 'Ah, you're from Scotland? My folks are from the UK, maybe you know the name Randall?' I froze. YOU'VE GOTTA BE KIDDING ME. (*Outlander* images flashed through my brain – of Tobias Menzies, the actor who played Black Jack Randall, flogging me with unbridled delight, the daily two-hour application of Jamie's leather welts to my back and the terrifying prison ordeal with Randall.)

'Well, I better be getting on.' I made my excuses and tried to sneak away, keeping my back to the wall. At all times.

[Graham: Was he wearing a red coat and a tricorn hat worn at a jaunty angle . . . no pants? Asking for a friend.]

Randall the security guard eyed me, his hands in his pockets. I couldn't help noticing he had some sort of blunt instrument hanging on his hip. 'Yeah, well, walk clockwise. Make sure you stay two metres away from everyone else. You've got five minutes left and leave the lavender alone.' He stared at me until I rounded the corner of the car park into the safety of the garden. 'I'm going to have to make sure my door is *locked* tonight,' I thought as I quickened my pace. That night, under my single sheet, I made a plan for how to tackle my days in quarantine; even the smallest triumphs in this place would help my mental health.

The next day I received a set of dumb-bells from the kind staff and an exercise bike. Each day, I woke up and did 45 minutes of spin, followed by a 30-minute weights session. I ordered healthy food and had regular fresh deliveries left by my door – porridge for breakfast, salmon and salad for lunch. I'd hit 10,000 steps in the 45-minute period outside, powering past other guests, under the watchful eye of Mr Randall.

[Graham: During my times in MIQ, I was often shackled to the wall, flogged, waterboarded; Leonard Low even paid me a visit with his witchy instruments of torture. (Mr Low featured prominently in Clanlands *and our first season of* Men in Kilts *as an authority on witchcraft and the tortures endured by the accused, which he happily recreated on me with his own deeply disturbing personal collection of torture paraphernalia.) I was also shown endless pictures of Sam Heughan, which did the real damage. Okay, maybe only the last bit is true. Maybe.]*

After nine days in Christchurch quarantine, it was finally the last night in the cell which had become my home, where I felt comfortable and had a routine; I almost felt apprehensive about leaving. On my last morning, I rose with the sun, the light spilling over the barriers. I was allowed out now for a whole hour at 7am and my release would be at midday. I quickly hit 10,000 steps and decided to relax for the last few minutes before returning inside to pack my belongings and finally enter New Zealand society as a changed man, forever altered by NZ MIQ. I stopped by the bush of lavender and picked several flowers.

'What are you doing?' Caught in the act, I spun around but no officious officer approached me; instead, a young woman smiled at me from behind her mask. 'Does it smell good?' she asked.

'Oh my God, yes, you must have some for your room,' I replied. 'It smells great and will send you to sleep.' I thrust out my hand and offered her the illegal bouquet. She slid it into the pocket of her workout gear. 'I'm Sophie,' she said. 'It's my last day.' We talked and walked in a circle, two metres apart, and I found out she had been here the whole time but we had missed each other due to different exercise scheduling. She was a yoga teacher and had occupied her time in solitary confinement by stretching, reading and, like me, occasionally talking to the faulty air-con system. She was witty, walked fast and had a great laugh, stifled by the plastic mask material.

Randall appeared. 'TIME'S UP!' he yelled. I wondered how he didn't swallow his mask, each time he announced the end of the session. Sophie and I shared a look, next to the lavender bush. 'Good luck out there,' she said. 'New Zealand has so much to offer, amazing scenery and flowers.' She winked and strode back into the hotel, the lavender sprig waving from her pocket. I choked and started to follow her. 'WRONG WAY, POM!' The Aussie slur echoed across the empty car park. He pointed silently in the other direction. I walked towards the exit to collect my belongings and reluctantly left the Covid detention centre.

Life is all about the timing.

GRAHAM

MIQ stands for Managed Isolation and Quarantine. Like TGIF without the fact that, in there, Friday feels like every other mind-numbingly tedious day. Acronyms like this make me think about language, and the impressions words form in our minds. Managed Isolation and Quarantine is like saying Strongly Recommended Prison or Pain-Free Spanish Inquisition. I can testify that it is, indeed, an odd and disconcerting experience. I remember the first time I did it, when we pulled up in the bus that we had been herded on to . . . well . . . like sheep, at Auckland airport. The hotel was surrounded by metal fencing and we were greeted by soldiers. The woman next to me commented that she'd never stayed at such a nice hotel before, which prompted me to wonder what other kinds of hotels manned by soldiers and police she had stayed in prior to that. For those that have wondered what such a place is like, I will try and give you the short version. You are processed, handed your room key and told where to go. It's at this moment that any similarity with a leisure hotel ends. From that moment you are kept in your room, with corridors patrolled by the police and the army, and allowed out for between 30 to 40 minutes a day for 'exercise' in the area designated as 'safe' to do so. This area is then patrolled by eagle-eyed policemen while you are 'strongly encouraged' not to communicate with any other 'guests' (just in case you planned to build a glider in your room or dig a tunnel). This exercise time is cheerily described as a 'privilege'. *[Sam: I believe Graham used MIQ as a rehab facility. He stopped drinking, worked out daily and even took up meditation . . . McTavish meditating! He really must have lost his mind.]*

The privileges are extended to you once you have returned a negative PCR test result. You are then given a blue plastic wristband to distinguish you from those 'guests' who might try and go for a stroll without one. These tests are administered three times during your stay. I've never actually HAD a frontal lobotomy (despite claims to the contrary) but if I ever do, I think MIQ is what one might feel like. Food is left outside your room in brown paper bags, and you are treated to periodic announcements blasted into your room through the PA system telling you how committed everyone is to your safety. You are allowed to leave exactly 14 days from when your plane landed in New Zealand, to the minute. Then you are 'released' into a parallel world of complete normality.

It's at this moment that I feel compelled to refer you, dear reader, to other famous accounts of incarceration:

- *Letter from Birmingham Jail* by Martin Luther King
- *Conversations with Myself* by Nelson Mandela
- *De Profundis* by Oscar Wilde, written while in Reading Gaol

And last but not least, *Justine*, by that notorious libertine, the Marquis de Sade (come to think of it, this last one is probably strangely similar to Heughan's).

I can't help thinking that Sam drew comfort and inspiration from these giants of history as he exercised on his specially supplied exercise bike. Perhaps he browsed the free internet looking for solace in the writings of Alexander Solzhenitsyn. Alas, we may never know. I leave it to you, dear reader, to draw your own conclusions from Sam's time in a four-star hotel in Christchurch, New Zealand and ask yourself, what would Nelson Mandela say?

CHAPTER TWO

Perilous Beginnings

GRAHAM

New Zealand typically features on many people's 'bucket list'. Often when I say that I have a home there, the response is, 'I've always wanted to go! One day I will!' With the borders reopened I urge anyone who doesn't mind a 27-hour flight to Auckland (located on that bit of a globe you have to get on your hands and knees to get a peek at) to book right away and visit.

If you leave the northern hemisphere during winter (something I would generally recommend anyone to do as frequently as they can) and arrive in the southern hemisphere's summer, you instantly forget the man snoring across the aisle, the child repeatedly kicking the back of your seat, and the delights of airport security. The flood of sunshine and the long days awaken your soul and, by the time you leave, you yearn to return.

However, for those Scots in the late 18th century and 19th

century who came here, it wasn't so much that New Zealand was on *their* bucket list, it was more that they travelled there *in a bucket* (albeit, a large one). Undertaking such a trip wasn't for the faint-hearted, nor probably for those capable of rational thought. To go there by ship in 1850 took between 75 and 120 days of hell. Which makes MIQ look quite frankly pathetic in comparison. Peering through a soft modern lens, it is difficult for us to imagine what was going through the minds of these pioneers. For us, the journey they were contemplating would be the equivalent of us planning a trip to Mars. As they departed the shores of Scotland, England, Ireland or Wales, they were almost certainly saying goodbye to the land of their birth with no hope of return. In the days of modern travel, it's hard for us to comprehend this combination of heartfelt grief and steely resolve. Like those pioneers on the Oregon Trail in the early 19th century in America, they faced a perilous odyssey, knowing with certainty that there would be those among them who would not survive the journey. Imagine stepping on board an aircraft nowadays knowing that some of your fellow passengers would almost certainly be dead by the time you arrive.

[Sam: I've had those thoughts sometimes.]

[Graham: Yes, but thinking of murdering fellow passengers doesn't count.]

It took a special person to make such a choice and to follow that through with action. From the comfort of our modern lives, we can look back on those ancestors who migrated from their place of birth to undertake a perilous journey to New Zealand, as well as other far-flung corners of the globe. The generations that followed owe their lives to those brave souls who came before them. Sometimes families travelled together – some multigenerational – others left family behind or even travelled alone. What would they have made of how we travel today? What would they say to those of us who complain about the movie selection on board the long-distance flight, or are disappointed by the catering, or who resent the sound of a baby crying? I think we can imagine exactly what they would say . . . it would involve a lot of expletives. *[Sam: Which – little does Mr McT the history don know – are exactly the same ones he'll be shouting/screaming/shrieking later on in our adventure . . . hehe!]* The charming accompaniments of a jaunt to New Zealand in those days were the risks of fire, shipwreck, and that jolly apocalyptic horseman, pestilence. Even the easier voyages treated people to regular gigantic brawls aboard ship, and if you were unlucky enough to go in steerage, you slept in bunks like sardines. You also had plenty of fellow travellers on board in the shape of verminous pests. One ship, the *Charlotte Jane*, was nicknamed 'the Cockroach'. (Coincidentally, the same name I gave to our camper vans both in the Highlands and New Zealand. What are the chances?)

You can imagine the onboard announcement: 'Welcome on board. We at Pestilential Voyages know you have a choice of carrier and welcome your business. Just a couple of short safety announcements: there is a strong likelihood of disease on board as well as fire, shipwreck, continual fighting, starvation and, well, death. In the event of an emergency, it's every man for himself. So, strap yourself into those tiny bunks and good luck. You'll need it!'

To add to the all-round sense that you were on board a floating prison, you were subjected to the eye-watering smells from the latrines and the animals on board. When you weren't gagging from the noxious air and praying for the sweet release of death, you were being half drowned in your beds during storms. The mattresses (kindly supplied by the shipowners) were almost constantly wet. You lived on salted and preserved meat, ship's biscuit, flour, oatmeal and dried potatoes. *[Sam: No lattes, protein bars, seven-course tasting menus or bottles of expensive plonk, dear boy.]* I don't imagine many people arrived overweight in New Zealand, and I'm guessing veganism wasn't uppermost in people's plans. The meagre water supply often became undrinkable within a couple of months, which meant passengers attempted to catch rainwater, probably with their frozen, calloused bare hands. Departing from Scotland in the late 18th century, they'd go south-west towards Brazil before lurching to the south-east and sweeping under Cape Horn and then desperately following the 39th parallel towards Australia and beyond, through nerve-shredding storms and icebergs, the sounds of screaming and fervent prayer echoing across an indifferent ocean.

I'm pretty sure that, if it had been available, Sam would've opted for such a journey to get us to New Zealand! But if the journey was harrowing, it was still better for many Highlanders than what they were leaving behind. The infamous Highland Clearances left many with no option, a sort of 18th-century version of 'dinnae let the door hit your erse on the way oot'. Desperate families huddled on the shores of the Highlands and looked for an escape from their greedy, sheep-loving Scottish landlords.

[Sam: Actually, there was a point in the middle of my Covid debacle when we considered flying to Australia and the crew and I taking a boat over to New Zealand, the voyage lasting about ten days. The time spent on the boat would have acted as a maritime MIQ, thus mitigating the need for quarantine on arrival. But I think the rules changed again!]

[Graham: I would've LOVED to have seen that!]

There is a place in the north of New Zealand, the quaint village of Waipu, which possesses a strong sense of Scottish heritage. I want to take you back to the 1770s, when there were many folk old enough to remember the Battle of Culloden, where the second Jacobite rebellion marked the final defeat of those Highland clans, with the people all too painfully aware of the punishment against the Highland people that would follow, when their way of life was essentially proscribed (no more tartan, weapons, etc).

Anchored in the harbour at Greenock sat the *Hector*, destined to transport 200 Highlanders to a new life. Their first choice was the Canadian province of Nova Scotia, because, well, it was closer. They arrived in 1773 with one of their leading local figures, Reverend Norman McLeod. He, along with 40,000 other Highlanders, settled in Nova Scotia, Prince Edward Island and Cape Breton in Canada. The ball-freezing winters were like a comforting old friend and Norman worked hard and built the largest church in Cape Breton, no doubt using only his teeth and his bare hands. But, like a lot of people who were starting a new life away from the familiarity of home, religion became a controversial point. You see, for Norman, the Church of Scotland just didn't possess the right amount of discipline and fervour. And when I say the right amount, I mean LOTS and LOTS of discipline and PLENTY of fervour. Unfortunately, all this discipline and fervour wasn't helping with the supply of food, and the shocking winters, potato blight and struggling fishing industry meant a visit from another apocalyptically inclined horseman – famine.

So it came to pass that the son of Norman-the-fervent-disciplinarian, Donald, suggested another epic voyage, this time to Australia. One can almost imagine the chit-chat around the McLeod dining table:

'What's for dinner, Dad?'

'Clear soup . . . and the back of my hand!'

'Sounds delicious. Any actual food?'

'You spineless weakling! Tell your brother to pass the gruel.'

'He died.'

'What?!'

'Of starvation.'

'What a pathetic toe-rag!'

'I think we should think about moving somewhere else, Dad.'

'Where?'

'Australia.'

'You're an idiot. Time for a beating,' etc. *[Sam: An insight into my evenings spent in the Maui camper van with Graham.]*

Happy nights around the fire, dividing up the one potato, singing hymns until they passed out. *[Sam: Yep.]* But Donald prevailed, and along with the McKenzie brothers (I'm not making this up), they built two ships: the *Geillis* and the *Treacherous English Wife of my Bastard Nephew*. Okay! They were actually called the *Margaret* and the *Highland Lassie*, but I couldn't resist. The *Margaret* set sail with 141 people, including the 71-year-old patriarch Reverend 'Pray Till You Fall Over' McLeod. The other ship took 136. The journey took five months, except for the *Highland Lassie*, which got stuck in the ice and took another five months.

'Where's the *Lassie*?'

'Got stuck in the ice, Dad.'

'What a bunch of pansies!'

On arrival in Melbourne, Norman sold the ship. Unfortunately, he did this just moments before he noticed that there was a huge typhoid outbreak running rampant in the city. Three of Norman's sons died of disease (probably while he was negotiating the sale) and everyone else had to live in tents while being subjected to unspeakable acts of violence, and not just from Norman. Deciding that this was not the kind of disciplined life he was hoping for, the Reverend contacted the New Zealand Governor, Sir George Grey, whom he must've had on the 19th-century equivalent of speed-dial.

'We're coming over! Tell New Zealand to brace hersel'.'

The McKenzie brothers bought another ship, the *Gazelle*, and 90 *Highland Lassie* folk and 33 from the *Margaret* set sail again, finally sailing up the River Waipu on 18 September 1853. Norman once again led the Gaelic-speaking community in their fervent worship until his death in 1866. He was 86 years old, no doubt clutching a Bible in one hand, with the other wrapped around the throat of a sinner. More followed from Nova Scotia, about 1,000, and Waipu now has tens of thousands of their descendants thanks to the iron will of Norman McLeod, and his crew of bampots! Among them, no doubt, a few Dougal MacKenzies . . .

***

DAY ONE, LATE AFTERNOON/EVENING

Location: Wellington – capital city of New Zealand, south-west tip of the North Island

Wellington, the world's southernmost capital, is situated between Cook Strait and the Remutaka Range. Kupe, the legendary Polynesian explorer, navigator and great chief, is acknowledged in Māori oral history as the first person to discover New Zealand, exploring Wellington in the 10th century. It was settled by Europeans in 1839. Population (2022): 213,100.

SAM
All right, so my journey to New Zealand hadn't been anywhere as perilous or as brutal as the 18th- and 19th-century Highland settlers had endured, but it had messed with my head and enabled me to binge-watch Netflix more than is medically advisable. But it was FINALLY time to start our journey in earnest. So, after being released, I took a plane to the capital city, Wellington, and hailed a cab to Graham's gaff . . .

The Desolation of McSmaug

'My armour is like tenfold shields, my teeth are swords, my claws spears, the shock of my tail is a thunderbolt, my wings a hurricane, and my breath death!'

The Hobbit by J R R Tolkien, Chapter 12, 'Inside Information'

McSmaug is considered to be one of the last great dragons of Middle-earth. An ancient creature, obsessed with the passings of old, he rests in his high tower surrounded by the great gold and precious things he's collected over the centuries (mostly per diems and unpaid hotel bills). He was drawn to the enormous wealth amassed by the dwarves of the Lonely Mountain, but decided to move to a suburb of Wellington, New Zealand instead. He laid waste to the dwarves and drove those surviving into exile, though some say, at one time he may even have been one of them. Walking among them, he wore false arms and a beard as a disguise, but nothing could hide his disdain for modern trappings and mobile phones, his loud grumblings of 'Latte! All I want is a caffè latte, is that too much to aaaaaaaaassssssk?!' echoing from the belly of the mountain.

With trepidation and great excitement at being released from my prison sentence, I was now free among the good people of Middle-earth. To my disappointment, however, they did not resemble elves or dwarves, though their accents may have resembled a small faction of hobbits from a distant island.

I showed the driver my destination on Google Maps. 'Chur,'

the driver grunted. Barely able to see over the steering wheel, with his impressive beard and bushy eyebrows, I suspected I had finally met a dwarf of Khazad-dûm, now moonlighting as a Kiwi taxi driver. We made our way east, following the shoreline and, due to my diminutive friend's enthusiasm for speed, we were soon out of the city. There in the distance, akin to the Misty Mountains, was an area called Wainuiomata, from the Māori words *wai* = water, *nui* = big, *o* = of, and *Mata* = a woman's name. Whoever the woman was, Miss Mata was not the only famous resident. For, living a bit further round the coast, in a palatial manor house – in my mind something like Downton Abbey down under – lived Mr McTavish, the Hugh Hefner of the Kiwi Hollywood Hills. I had been cordially invited to visit him at his residence to celebrate my arrival into the country, the beginning of our shooting of *Men in Kilts 2* and my release from incarceration. I had detoxed since my MIQ_day-two epiphany; no alcohol or unhealthy food had passed my lips and I was ready for a feast. The cab finally turned up a winding road that climbed into the subtropical mountainside and we started to crawl slowly up the steep road. The trees crowded in, threatening the car and its passengers, suggesting the driver turn back before the pass became impossible to navigate. My sturdy companion in the driving seat was sweating, gripping the steering wheel tightly with his huge hands as the car gave a final dying cough and shuddered to a stop on a narrow bend. 'Bugger. I can't go any further. Won't be able to turn around. You're tramping from here,' he grumbled, as I climbed out of his exhausted ride.

'Um, is it much further? I called out as he spun around and began the steep slalom down the hill. 'Yeah-nah,' he called out in a cloud of exhaust fumes, and my mini chauffeur was gone. I looked up the hill, expecting to see the towering spires of McTavish Manor ahead, but all I could make out was more greenery and the tall trees beyond.

Some twenty minutes later, breathless and drenched in sweat, my temperature as high as the New Zealand sun, I was standing outside a rather modest door of a faceless bungalow. 'This can't be it . . .' I muttered to myself. Shielding my eyes from the glaring sun, I scanned the horizon from my vantage point. I'd climbed some way and thought I'd be able to spot McTavish's sprawling estate from here.

Nothing. Large homes and villas were dotted over the mountains like the dwellings in the hills of North Hollywood, but nothing that resembled the palatial manor of a man born to be king of the southern hemisphere.

I looked at the simple door and then it hit me: I'd arrived . . . in Hobbiton! Gandalf the Grah(am) must be inside. I hammered on the door and waited for my friend to appear. Silence, except for the sound of crickets – or some Kiwi equivalent [*Graham: cicadas*]. The Doors of Durin remained closed. 'Ah, there's a password, like in the movie,' I exclaimed. I winked at the door, all-knowing. 'Speak friend and enter,' a riddle from *The Lord of the Rings*; all I had to do was say 'friend' in Elvish and the door would open to the kingdom beyond. 'What is the Elvish for "friend"?' I muttered out loud, turning to look for inspiration. 'Maybe Scottish would be better? Chief! Open Sesame, pal! Buddy! Big man? Big Yin!?! Ach, ya dobber!' Nothing. Then, I spotted it. A large shape, hidden by a turquoise blue cover, partially obscured from view by the side of the house. I skipped over and slowly raised the tarpaulin to find myself blinded . . . by gold. Here it was! McSmaug's stash. The fortune hoarded and accumulated by my ancient friend – a 1970 classic Ford Mustang glimmered in the fading sunlight.

[*Graham: It's a 1967 Chevrolet Camaro, but what can I expect from a man whose idea of a classic car is a three-year-old Audi?*]

The silver bumper and gold rims dazzled my eyes; the classic-car emblem of a galloping stallion sparkled before me and caught my breath. 'It must be worth a fortune,' I stammered, dropping to my knees before this priceless treasure. I reached out a sweaty palm to caress the forbidden beauty, 'My precioussss,' I gargled, eyes like fishbowls, desiring what could not be mine . . .

'Get your bloody hands off my car, you cretin!' McTavish's booming voice broke my reverie and I turned to see his hulking frame stooped in the hobbit-hole doorway. 'What the fuck are you doing on your knees?' he said, his beard bristling in every direction. 'Get in here, quick, before the neighbours see you,' and with that I was ushered inside to the dark halls beyond.

'Get heem a glass of wine, mon cher,' said Garance, Graham's chic and classy girlfriend (now wife). 'Allez, ee looks like ee is going to pass out.' *[Graham: If that's your version of a French accent I recommend never visiting France.]*

Graham opened the fridge door and I realized there was a collection of his precious things. Not quite the vast wine cellar I had expected but a collection of delicious Kiwi wines and perhaps the odd bottle of sparkling water.

'I'll, ah, take that, thank you!' He grabbed the offering I had bought from the local liquor store, the most expensive bottle of plonk I could find, and he stashed it at the back, barely glancing at the label. 'Here, try this, I think you'll like it,' he said, eyeing me suspiciously. 'You DO drink wine, don't you?' he added. 'Oh no, wait, you drink anything,' he grumbled and before I could reply he thrust a sensible-sized glass of chilled rosé into my sweaty hands. 'Let me show you around while dinner is cooking,' he said over his shoulder as he led me towards the living room. Garance winked at me. Clearly, she was in charge of the catering tonight and I relaxed, knowing that I was in for a gastronomic treat.

As I followed McRavish, I couldn't help noticing his outfit was somewhat different than I was used to. Gone were the 'special blue sneakers' he'd worn in the first *Men in Kilts*, and there was no blazer or collared shirt. He was wearing a floating, billowing white shirt, in an Ibiza-chic style, open to the sternum and revealing his tanned and impressive chest hair. I don't recall if he was wearing Birkenstocks but wouldn't be surprised if he had been, or perhaps he was barefoot. Chilled, arabesque house music emanated from some high-spec speakers and I felt I'd stepped into an alternate reality. The house was so nice; Scandi modern furniture made the house feel relaxed and homely. I gawped at how cool it was, almost spilling my drink on his luxurious yet stylish sofa. 'Watch where you're going!' he growled, half an eye on me, wary that I may pilfer his precious things or graffiti the fine art.

'I never realized, Graham,' I whispered. 'You're so . . . cool.' I gagged, downing the expensive wine in one shot to lubricate my throat. I couldn't believe it. 'Who ARE you? What have you done with Lady McTavish?' He stopped and turned back at me. There was a glint in the sly dog's eye, or perhaps it was a tear, and the suntan contrasted with the whiteness of his shirt. 'Oh, you know, I've just always been like this. To a wise and good man, the whole of Middle-earth is his fatherland,' he smirked, his perfectly trimmed beard settled into an exquisite line. But then, just as I was beginning to think the man had changed, that he had shed his skin and transformed into *GQ*'s Man of the Year, I spied a room behind him. McTavish positioned his body, hoping to redirect me outside, thus camouflaging the entrance to his secret chamber. 'What's in there?' I asked and tried to peer over his dedicated gym-built shoulders.

'Oh that? No, nothing for you. Best go outside, the *poisson en papillote* will be ready soon. Oh look, more wine, you like wine, don't you? Here, why don't you follow the bottle?' he waved me away, as if thrashing at an annoying insect. I moved towards the garden and the bucket of chilled wine, then, quick as a flash, I doubled back, slipped under his arm and through the secret cellar door.

'Got you!' I crowed. I suspected something, but not THIS! The light flicked on and McTavish's dark secret was revealed. No, not a model railway set, or dolls that he could play dress-up with; something much, much worse . . . Classic Subbuteo!

'Yes, I like to play it with my daughters,' he tried to explain.

'Uh-huh, your teenage girls like to collect and paint little statues of football players, then flick them around a tablecloth, pretending they're at the World Cup?' I jeered, delighted with my find and knowing Mr McChic's demeanour was changing before my very eyes. I could almost see the Aran sweater and tweed hat materializing before me.

His beard drooped. 'They do, actually, and they're in vintage boxes, I collect them,' he murmured, his hand raised in anticipation of me dropping one of his prized possessions. 'Pleeeease put it down, leave it on the table and we can go have all the drinkie-winkies your cretinous little heart desires,' he pleaded.

'Only if we play. And if you lose, I'm telling everyone you're an antique toy collector,' I replied. This was turning out to be one of the best reunions I've ever had. Then I spotted the Lego village. 'It's the girls' – not mine. I promise,' he jabbered. 'I don't play with it, they wanted to, um, well, it's Hollywood Boulevard . . . made out of Lego.' I marvelled at his creation. The man had truly spent time and money creating this miniature brick version of the Walk of Fame, complete with Chinese Theatre and . . . wait . . . wait . . . there, standing in the centre, before the brick Kodak Theatre, a Lego man, all in white. No, not Gandalf, the figure was bald, bearded, holding a tiny little Oscar trophy. 'That's not meeee!' he squeaked. 'And it's just a pretend Oscar!' I returned the miniature McTavish to walk the gold star-studded street and escaped the man-cave, sporting the biggest grin in the southern hemisphere.

'Good to see you, buddy! Can't wait to start our road trip,' I said, settling into the comfortable garden furniture and helping myself to another glass of wine. 'Will you be bringing any of your other toys on the trip?' I sniggered.

GRAHAM

Throughout history there have been many celebrations of a returning hero, an upswell of public joy at the homecoming of a long-absent traveller. The crystalline epiphany that perfectly captures a combined sense of relief and elation, perhaps surprise, even 'How did this individual survive?', bafflement maybe, but mostly unbridled delight. One thinks of those who return from war. Families who had given up hope but NO, there he is, marching up the path to your door . . . alive!

[Sam: I think I know where this is going . . .]

We remember those impossible stories of survival: Shackleton, the American guy who amputated his own hand, Poon Lim, a Chinese sailor who survived 133 days adrift alone on a raft, and Mauro Prosperi, an Italian who got lost on a six-day ultra-marathon in the Sahara Desert and ended up drinking his own urine and sucking out the insides of bats that he had discovered and decapitated. Sam is probably searching the internet as he reads this, enthusiastically signing up for this Darwinian death-trap. But let us not forget

Odysseus (boy, did he have a hard time of it) and, of course, the biblical account of the return of the prodigal son.

Which brings me to Sam's eventual arrival at my door in Wellington after his time in quarantine. Similar to those I just listed? I shall let the reader decide. My invitation to dinner had been long-standing, long before we even thought of doing *Men in Kilts*. I love showing people New Zealand, and I fondly imagined Sam coming for dinner at my house, just as Duncan Lacroix (who played Murtagh in *Outlander*) had done three years earlier.

I was slightly disappointed to discover that, far from making my house his first port of call, on release, Sam had already been out the previous night in Wellington, crawling from one pub to another, being barred from entry because he didn't have a vaccine pass. I think he may have ended the evening with a jolly group of the local homeless, passing a bottle of Sassenach between them while he read passages from his autobiography, *What's the Point?!* [*Sam: Actually, it's called* Waypoints *– ahem, a* New York Times *bestseller! Looking forward to your memoir – can I suggest* Greypoints *as a title?!*]

But arrive he did.

I had told my children, Honor and Hope, that Sam was coming and they were VERY excited. It's long been a point of mild irritation that both of my children adore Sam. They think he's funny, charming, handsome, generous and kind. Why, I hear you ask?

[*Sam: Because I torment you?*]

A quick note about my road. It is a little treacherous. [*Sam: A little? I'm surprised you're able to navigate its steep incline and sharp turns in your pimped-out granny wagon!*] It's a single winding steep uphill road (little wider than a goat track), with hairpin-blind bends and no street lights. Many of my neighbours treat it like a racetrack, hurtling down it in a continual game of chicken with unsuspecting visitors. In short, the kind of road Sam would LOVE to live on!

I opened the door and, incredibly, there he stood. He had brought about three bottles of wine. (Never underestimate the generosity of a career booze-hound.) I think there may even have been flowers, no doubt stolen from my own garden. It was genuinely great to see him. So many times, over the past two or three months, I thought this moment would never transpire. So, to see him, in the flesh, in the same city as me, smiling in his open-hearted way, really did make me happy. *[Sam: You must have started early.]* I can't remember what he was wearing. Probably a sleeveless top, and a pair of budgie-smugglers, but in fairness it was a warm night.

I cooked. Well, some of the meal. My fiancée (now wife), Garance, cooked quite a lot of it. Well, she IS French! Now, I do not profess to be a good cook – my cooking style is basic and non-toxic, which I consider a culinary triumph! Maybe I roasted something, I'm not sure. *[Sam: You put a tray in the oven.]* Possibly because the main roasting that evening was of ME at the hands of the ginger revenant. Oh, how my children laughed. So did my lovely partner, her laughter pealing out as Sam dropped another roasting bomb at my expense. Even my neighbour, Andrew, who joined us for dinner, laughed. I think they got short of breath such were their wild hoots of hysteria. My only solace was that I don't think Andrew had the vaguest notion who Sam was (he doesn't watch TV, preferring melancholy classical music), but perhaps, weirdly, that actually made it worse.

Booze was cracked open. We settled in for a long evening on the deck, looking out across Wellington harbour, with the lights twinkling like diamonds on the far shore.

I gave him a quick tour of the house. I have two offices, which I like to call my man-caves, but other unkinder individuals refer to them as my 'Halls of Him'! In them I have photos, mainly from my theatre days, memorabilia from jobs, my collection of dwarf noses from *The Hobbit*, weapons I've accumulated *[Sam: i.e., stolen]* from my work, axes, .44 Walker Colt pistols, swords, as well as books, stuff from my parents, paintings done by my kids, and my comic book collection. In short, evidence of a giant nerd trapped in an endless childhood.

I've never been to Sam's house; I've never been invited. I imagine it to be quite roomy, with gardens that he never personally tends, perhaps a moat, various pilfered *Outlander* memorabilia, his Batman costume from that S&M touring production he once did, his collection of rugby shirts celebrating the sport he has never played and, of course, a VERY well-stocked whisky cabinet. *[Sam: Correct!]* I've never seen it but I imagine its sheer scale and volume would almost hurt the eyes. The Helen of Troy of whisky collections. Pride of place would no doubt go to that whisky he makes, the name escapes me, it begins with S . . . Sasquatch? *[Sam: Sigh.]* And, of course, let's not forget the rail upon rail of sleeveless tops. One day I hope to visit, or at least to stand outside, in awe of the Home of Heughan. I wonder if it has a name? You know, nothing so dreary as a street number. Something like Lavender Heights, with a wrought-iron gate with his initials monogrammed into the ironwork, perhaps a bronze fountain statue of him peeing from under a kilt? *[Sam: I have two cast-iron Sassenach unicorns on my gate.]*

By dessert, the table was littered with empty bottles; I think we then started on the whisky. My children refused to go to bed, and after several drams – not the children, for God's sake – my neighbour tottered home next door, and we bade a fond farewell to my soon-to-be travelling companion as he climbed into the cab he'd ordered, to begin the perilous descent down the goat track. I suspect the evening was only just beginning for Sam. The bars were still open, the budgie-smugglers were getting restless, and he had some freedom to celebrate . . . even if it was with his homeless WhatsApp group.

SAM

Sunlight broke through the curtains. 'What is that?' I wondered, being unaccustomed to sunlight in the depths of winter. 'And where am I . . .?' It took me a few moments to realize I wasn't at home in Scotland but 20,000 miles away, on the other side of the world, in a hotel room in Wellington. I felt something. 'What is this sensation? I've felt it before . . . oh God . . . my head!' A hangover, only Antipodean. Ten days of enforced sobriety in MIQ, then last night at Maison McTavish, I had broken the seal. Several times over. After a terrific night of fish baked in a bin bag and oodles of Sauvignon Plonk, I had escaped the clutches of Sauron the

Sozzled and his army of wine-pushing companions, and navigated my way out of the man-caves of Mordor and back down Mount Doom. I recall thinking, 'Oh what a good idea! Just ONE more drink . . .' and off I went to frequent some of the more welcoming establishments of Wellington. The Muggles were indeed friendly. A photo taken in a cocktail bar at 12.38am shows that I was enamoured with the bar's interior design and in particular a hanging bottle of Buckfast (a Scottish delicacy) that adorned the ceiling in one insalubrious joint. The barmaid was friendly, although perhaps because I insisted on buying her (and the other customers) any drink their hearts desired. I stared into her emerald eyes and was completely taken by her Kiwi accent, tattoos, wry smile and ability to pour exceptionally strong drinks. After staggering out of the cocktail bar sometime later, promising my new amour I'd return the next day for more bottomless punch, I zigzagged my way back to my lodging on the waterfront, only to be ushered into another lively establishment on the famous Cuba Street. The barman was Scottish and I was a Scot. In fact, the whole bar appeared to be Scottish and we drank, laughed and reminisced and I bought rounds and . . . and . . .

***

I studied the hotel room. The contents appeared to be upside down. Or perhaps everything was, down under. 'I need water!' I gasped, instinctively reaching for a bottle by the side of the bed, only to quickly pull back when I saw my hand was covered in blood! I squeezed my eyes shut and looked again. Not only my hand, but as I drew my arm away, I examined the sheets and they too appeared to be covered in litres of thick, red blood.

'Oh my God, I'm dead!' I gasped. 'Or maybe I was bitten by a great white shark?' I lifted the sheets gingerly to see what remained of my torso and in doing so dislodged the half-eaten remains of a luxury shish kebab onto the floor, the thick red spice sauce having spilled all over the sheets in my slovenly slumber. 'I wonder if you can get *kebab en papillote*?' I mused. 'Ah well, at least I'm not bleeding out . . . just yet.' I yawned and rolled out of the large double bed (silently thanking Starz production for the pleasure, it being twice the size of our trusty camper van's single bunk beds) and stumbled over to the bay windows to examine the view. The first sunrise in the world happens in New Zealand and that morning I watched the sun imperceptibly rise over Wellington Bay, the capital city and the North Island's most southerly point. It greeted me, sparkling on the South Pacific waters, colourful houses and waterfront promenade. There was only one thing for it: time to knock this hangover into shape and get our road trip started!

'I need a latte!' I shouted through the open window to the working harbour below. Followed by, 'Hello, New Zealand!'

CHAPTER THREE

Middle-Earth

GRAHAM

As I look west out of my window at home, down onto the long sandy foreshore of Petone (or Pito-one as it was originally called), it's hard to imagine that the now-urban landscape of houses, shops, cafés, light industrial warehouses and an oil depot were once a giant expanse of thick forest and vegetation that filled the land as far as the eye could see. Woven through with streams and a long, wide river, this was what greeted those early settlers. And, if I look out of my kitchen window to the east, I can still see impenetrable bush stretching like a green wall, which is what those first arrivals in New Zealand would have seen surrounding the harbour.

Let's take a trip down the lane of recent history. We are not talking 500 years, or even 300. It was the 19th century when that historical meeting between those brave European ocean-goers and a people who had lived in seclusion for nearly half a millennium took place.

It took someone who had never set eyes on this land to come up with a plan to make it habitable, for it was Edward Wakefield who first saw the real potential of New Zealand for settlement. Son of Edward Wakefield Senior and the extravagantly named Susanna Crash, young Edward was an undisciplined, impulsive character who succeeded in being expelled from every school he attended. Any restraint imposed by his first wife ended when she died. He then decided that it would be a good idea to kidnap a 15-year-old schoolgirl, Ellen Turner, heiress to a fortune, in the hope of forcing her father to help him enter politics.

Married in Scotland, he was arrested in Calais before the marriage was consummated and spent the next three years in prison.

It was here that he saw first-hand what poverty was doing to people in Britain. This was a time when only men with land could vote, and if you fell on hard times, there was no welfare state to help break your fall. Coupled with the Poor Law, which brought the threat of the dreaded workhouse, and the Chartist riots that were being ruthlessly suppressed by the state, Wakefield saw a population in need of an opportunity. While in prison, he published an article: 'Cure and prevention of pauperism by means of systematic colonization'. On his release, this charismatic force of nature formed the 'National Colonization Society'. Without the help of the government, but with the aid of some venture capitalists who knew a good investment when they saw one, he went on to create the New Zealand Land Company. [Sam: Catchy name.] The company, based in London, persuaded those with a useful trade to forsake Britain and travel to a place where they were promised a piece of land, an opportunity and a world free of deprivation.

Let's pause for a moment to fully imagine what the collision of these two worlds would have been like. You have spent roughly 110 days floating in appalling conditions, having left a world of economic misery at home, leaving behind few prospects other than the workhouse or starvation, and you finally wash up in Wellington harbour. All around you is thick, impenetrable forest stretching down to the shore and you are greeted by scantily clad people whose faces are covered in elaborate tattoos, carrying clubs and spears, who do not understand anything you say. *[Sam: Sounds like Glasgow on a Saturday night.]*

Quite understandably, the local tribespeople for their part would have stared in a mixture of horror and disbelief at this giant floating vessel, something that dwarfed anything they had ever seen, a barque of 550 tons carrying 58 men and 90 women dressed in tailored garments, pale of face, looking like ghosts, stepping onto YOUR land. It is a testimony to BOTH sides that any progress was made at all!

Wakefield's capitalist proposal was for the land to be divided. A tenth was assigned to the Te Āti Awa *iwi* (or tribe), which might have seemed fair at the time (the local Māori chiefs seemed to think so as they agreed to sign the document in good faith). However, it soon became apparent that both sides had very different notions of the deal and what ownership of land looked like. Like their Highlander counterparts, the Māori didn't feel 'ownership', they felt 'belonging', so it was instantly going to cause confusion when the British assumed an understanding of land purchase that simply didn't exist in the Māori mind. It was the Māori version of *dualchas*, the Gaelic word for 'culture' or 'tradition'.

Meanwhile, it is worth noting that the local Māori population saw the arrival of the Europeans in many ways as a guaranteed protection from the depredations of other tribes who had swept down from Hawke's Bay in the north during the appalling Musket Wars (more on that later), which had laid waste to other local tribes, forcing them out of their homes. The local chief, Te Puni, welcomed the arrival of the Europeans. With their enemy closing in, Te Puni and others engaged in crucial debates about the sale of the land. There was, however, considerable opposition. A year after the deal was struck, Te Puni admitted the land had not been his to sell, but that he had been unable to resist the offer of blankets and guns. Even when he tried to backtrack on a deal that he admitted he didn't understand, he continued to be a friend and ally of the settlers.

Was he duped by the cunning Europeans? Did he betray his own people? Or did he do his best in the circumstances? I will let you decide. When he died in 1870, he was given the equivalent of a state funeral, with the Bishop of Wellington conducting the funeral service, the Superintendent of Wellington and the Minister for Native Affairs among the pallbearers, and three volleys fired over his grave by the local Rifle Volunteer Corps.

As for the Europeans, when they arrived, it was to a landscape they were totally unprepared for. Where were the flat sections of land suitable for farming? Instead, they literally had to hack and carve their way through that dense bush to even get a foothold.

The local Māori people helped them ashore, presumably flabbergasted by the detritus floating in the water – pianos, sewing tables, bicycles, prefabricated housing and any amount of unusable trash that bobbed on the shoreline, abandoned by their owners as they hauled their lives onto dry land.

One thing the various tribal groups would have had in common was the utter shock and horror felt when they first encountered Europeans. Picture for a moment a group of local tribespeople out fishing, maybe gathering sea urchins (or *kina*) for supper, when a giant British sailing ship hove into view, perhaps bristling with cannons, and packed to the gunwales with Jocks. Remember that they had lived in splendid isolation for hundreds of years, only indulging in local tribal disputes (massacres). One minute you're weaving flax and singing songs, the next you're being forced to welcome ship loads of Glaswegians. I imagine they would've uttered the Māori equivalent of 'What the actual fuck!?' The word used to describe Europeans, *Pākehā*, which now essentially refers to any non-Māori, literally meant 'pale, imaginary beings resembling men'. No. Not the Welsh. *[Sam: Brave man!]* As in many other languages, a word was used to set one group against another as being 'not from round here'.

And for the Europeans, after many brutal months spent at sea, they were greeted by a bunch of heavily tattooed people armed to the teeth performing a terrifying dance (*haka*) that definitely did not bode well for their continued good health.

On both sides, such a situation was a recipe for conflict.

And yet, in spite of misgivings and distrust of the newcomers, the Māori helped the Europeans build housing. As Te Puni declared: 'We want to live in peace and have white people come amongst us. We want our children to have protectors in Europeans . . . we will sell our land and harbour and live with white men.'

However, after an initial period of acceptance, so began the miscommunication, confusion and sense of betrayal that was to mark the growing settlement of New Zealand as a whole. Instead of the 'nine or ten *Pākehā*' that one chief believed would be coming, he was faced with 200 or more with the arrival of every ship.

'How many of these buggers are there?' he undoubtedly asked. Eventually, many of the settlers, dismayed by the swampy land, earthquakes and flooding, struck out across the harbour to create Wellington itself. It wasn't for another thirty years that there was even a rail link between Wellington and Petone, leaving those who remained in Petone to make their own way amid an increasingly hostile native population. As you will discover . . .

But let us talk about the capital city itself, Windy Wellington. Thus known for, well, its windy nature. But there is more! Wellington has earthquakes. On any given day it experiences one. Some are so small that you don't even notice them, others so big that your house feels like a giant's hand is shaking it around like a snow globe. The biggest one I ever experienced was in 2014. I was in bed, enjoying a blissful sleep (it was early on in my friendship with Sam so at that point I wasn't subjected to the screaming nightmares that now regularly invade my slumber).

Then it STRUCK.

It's funny how earthquakes often decide to say hello in the middle of the night. Like a particularly awful wake-up alarm. *[Sam: I've heard rumbling emanating from the camper van at night; I put it down to McTavish's bubbly constitution.]* It took me a moment to register what was happening. Earthquakes are so strange; they completely alter your perception of reality. How can my house be shaking and shuddering? Why am I swaying and walking into walls? Our friend and sometime co-star, Duncan Lacroix, no stranger to a big night, is an expert in that feeling and thus well-prepared for seismic activity!

My ex-wife flew out of bed and began screaming. (It was the earthquake – not something I said!) She ran downstairs, screaming at the children: 'OUT!!!! OUT!!!! GET OUT!!!!'

Then the children started screaming. Hope was two years old; Honor was seven. There was A LOT of screaming. *[Sam: We all know who was screaming the loudest, McT.]*

I, meanwhile, was calmly trying to reassure them as I gently ambled down the stairs. I was tempted to stop for a quick coffee on the way outside. It was only then I remembered I was completely naked!

The house continued to dance around like Duncan Lacroix on a Friday night while I searched in vain for something to put on. For some reason I settled on my ex-wife's coat, which was, sadly, three sizes too small, and then I left the house to join my screaming family in the garden with me resembling a man wearing stolen children's clothing. I think the arms might've reached my elbows while the length left nothing to the imagination. While I, looking like the kind of guy who exposes himself to passers-by, continued to try and calm my hysterical family, I looked up to see my neighbours in the garden next door looking on appalled. Come to think of it, maybe it wasn't the earthquake that was causing my family to scream in terror . . .?

Welcome to Wellington! *[Sam: I will never be able to shake that gruesome image from my mind.]*

The biggest recorded earthquake in Wellington was in 1855. It was so big that it caused the land to rise by 2m (6.5ft). One of the wealthier residents at the time was one Baron von Alzdorf, who was so terrified of earthquakes that he'd decided to build a massive, solid, earthquake-proof house. And so it came to pass that, on the day in question in 1855, he was sheltering inside his massive stone house when it collapsed, killing him instantly, thus making him the only casualty of the 1855 quake.

***

New Zealand wouldn't exist in its present form without the Wakefield brothers, Edward (who I mentioned earlier) and William. Two British colonial administrators and entrepreneurs, who not only established and organized the large-scale British settlement of New Zealand but also had key roles in the settlement of Canada and South Australia.

William became the Principal Agent for the newly formed New Zealand Company. To say that this company indulged in a spot of false advertising is like saying that Sam Heughan occasionally talks about his whisky brand. They said that Wellington offered acres and acres of flat, fertile land suitable for farming and would provide an arcadian idyll for prospective purchasers. And purchase they did! The only snag was that the 'flat, fertile acres' turned out to be either impenetrable jungle or a muddy swamp. One person who was definitely not happy was Isaac Featherston, who happened to be editor of the local newspaper in Wellington. Dear old Willy Wakefield interpreted the subsequent editorial attack on the New Zealand Company as a barely disguised accusation of thievery. In those days, the solution to having your honour impugned was to challenge the offending party to a duel, sometimes with swords, but often with pistols. Not so much a case of 'You'll be hearing from my lawyer,' more a case of 'You'll be hearing from my .65 calibre smooth-bore flintlock pistol fired at a distance of thirty feet!'

William and Isaac found themselves both staring down the business end of one of these weapons. Featherston fired first and missed. One can only imagine the stomach-turning moment as Featherston realized he'd have to stand still and let a very angry man fire a massive piece of lead at his chest. To do otherwise, such as flee, move or duck, would have been the mark of a coward.

Even as I write this, I can hear the mental gears of Heughan devising how to incorporate duelling into our next *Men in Kilts* season. *[Sam: Noted, thank you.]* William Wakefield took his duelling pistol and fired into the air, uttering the immortal line, 'I would not shoot a man who has seven daughters.' (Which was curious from a man who liked to kidnap them.) So, Featherston lived another day, probably retiring from the field in haste to attend to his underpants.

DAY TWO, 7.22am

SAM

McTavish was grumbling, or at least that's where I think it was coming from. An internal rumble, like the movements or tremors deep within the earth's core before a volcano erupts. I can sense seismic activity within the bearded one, perhaps owing to us spending so much time together. And I can always tell when he's about to blow. Or perhaps it actually *was* an earthquake. 'Drop, cover, hold,' I mumbled. Having googled the facts with oodles of free time during my incarceration, I had learned there had been only around a hundred major quakes since 1815 (McTavish's year of birth) with very few fatalities. 'No need to panic,' I thought to myself.

I soon realized the rumbling definitely *was* coming from McTavish.

And I knew exactly why . . . we had been called *early* for hair and make-up! Not in a glamorous trailer or movie-star dressing room like McTavish was used to, but crammed into a small hotel room, the costumes, props and camera equipment piled high, leaving only the bed and bathroom free. I felt sorry for the crew member who had agreed to sleep here. 'Half a bloody hour too early!' McTavish growled, spraying crumbs of his mega-bun-breakfast across the room. I forget the name they give to this local delicacy, similar to the Scottish Scooby Snack, a soft roll filled with everything available to the sleep-deprived but creative chef: crispy bacon, fried eggs, grilled tomatoes, fried mushrooms, black pudding and perhaps a sausage or two. McTavish's bountiful bun – which he didn't finish – was only the start of his breakfast. Then he dug ferociously into a granola and Greek yoghurt pot as a 'snack', like a man who hadn't eaten for days. He even pocketed my breakfast pot. 'For later, in case I get hungry,' he explained.

I sipped on a second extra-strong large black coffee which the runner had rustled up. 'Scotty' was a mountain of a man, super lean with a wide smile and polite manner, sporting a bandage on his elbow, no doubt from doing too many bicep curls or punching a wall. He had told us he'd be our runner and driver (when needed) and 'could supply anything you fellas need, just name it'.

[Graham: Ah, Scotty! A heart of oak if ever there was one. I had first worked with this legend of a man on The Hobbit. *He was the stunt double for William Kircher, who played Bifur – or maybe it was Bofur, or Bimbong, or whatever he was called. I can never remember. Scotty comes from a long tradition of Kiwi men who can be described by that favourite New Zealand word, 'staunch'. Staunch means reliable, uncomplaining and ready for anything. The kind of man you could drop behind enemy lines and know that by the end of the week he'd be back having survived untold dangers, natural disasters and starvation. In other words, the exact opposite of me. What he'd done to deserve looking after Sam and me is anyone's guess. He's probably writing his own book right now entitled,* Driving Around New Zealand with a Right Pair of Twats.*]*

By this point, McT had finished his elevenses and was relaxing on the sofa bed next to me. 'It really is ridiculous,' he grumbled. 'I just don't need to be here.' Now I admit, I need a little 'tickle' (actors' terminology for man-grooming) to get my hair out of my face in the morning, perhaps some concealer to hide the late night in Wellington, but McLavish doesn't actually need much. *[Graham: So says the Scottish Kim Kardashian. His make-up and hair take so long they have to tag team in shifts, so that one groomer can catch up on sleep while the other soldiers on. I won't say that Sam has to immediately begin applying his next day's make-up as soon as we finish for the day, but it's close.]* I mean, he doesn't have much to work with. The groomer brushed the crumbs from his beard and applied a little colour to his nose and then he was done.

Just then, Squeezy, our *Men in Kilts* production team safety officer, popped her head round the door. 'Ah, good, you're ready for the safety meeting? I'll see you outside.'

[Graham: Squeezy is one of those Americans who smiles far too much. Now I understand the need to show off the expensive dental work as

often as possible, but there is something vaguely disconcerting about someone who is constantly smiling or laughing. They begin to look a little unhinged. Now, I'm not saying Squeezy is unhinged, just that this level of grinning can sometimes be associated with sociopaths. Talking of sociopaths, over to you, Sam . . .]

She disappeared before McTavish could toss the remains of his breakfast at her. 'I'm not going to any bloody safety talk! Jesus, do they think I'm a child? What is the world coming to? Perhaps they'll tell me to make sure my laces are tied or check I haven't forgotten my packed lunch.' And with that, he skulked off to find yet more caffeine.

[Graham: Indeed. This should be added to my giant list of grievances. The endless obsession with health and safety. Every time I film, the cast and crew are gathered together to be told the mind-bogglingly obvious. They practically tell you to remember not to jam your fingers in electrical sockets or pour petrol over yourself, just IN CASE you don't realize it could be a bad idea. It's either that or be careful that you chew your food properly and remember to flush the toilet. It is worth noting that the 'Health and Safety Briefing' was conspicuously absent when we did the Rere Rockslide, but we'll get to that. If this bizarre obsession had been around in the Second World War, the servicemen would've died of old age waiting for the safety briefing to be over.]

Being the responsible executive producer that I am *[Graham: cough]*, I followed Squeezy outside and stood alongside the rest of the crew in the car park. We had a busy day ahead of us, starting with a trip to Wētā Workshop, the spiritual home of all things special-effects and props. It's the main workshop and production centre in Wellington for film and TV, and responsible for creating and building the props and prosthetics for multiple feature-film franchises such as: *The Lord of the Rings, Tomb Raider, Stranger Things, Gremlins, The Witcher* and, of course, *The Hobbit.*

But back to the morning's safety meeting . . .

We stood in a circle, two metres apart, everyone staring awkwardly at one another. Squeezy spoke, muffled slightly by her mask. 'Please remember to wear sensible footwear, sunscreen and hydrate when you can. Thank you.'

'That's it?' I thought. The bearded one was right. For once. *[Graham: I rest my case!]* Safety meeting over, it was time to hit the road and that's when the perfectly timed McTavish appeared, a fresh latte in hand and a spring in his Birkenstock-clad step.

'Right, let's get going! I need to be done by five, I've got a dinner booked. Where's the van?' he asked. Almost on cue, there was a loud roar, accompanied by a clunking of gears, and our trusty ride rolled into view, surrounded by a thick black cloud of smoke. Scotty stopped the camper van next to us and jumped out. 'Here you go, fellas, she's a treat!' he said as he tossed me the keys. Our chariot, our home from home, stood blazing white in the hot January sun, with blue detailing and silver rims. She was a beauty and I was in love.

'What a heap of junk! Jesus – couldn't you come up with something a bit more . . . cool?' Graham sighed. 'Or just something a little more practical and, well, reliable. Look at it, it's ready to fall apart!' He kicked the rims and a wheel cover fell off, revealing a rather worn and rusted interior.

'She's got character!' I said defensively. *[Graham: So did Benito Mussolini! Just not one you'd want to rely on.]* I pulled at the side door, hoping to reveal my surprise inside. I pulled, then pulled again, but the door didn't budge.

'Here, allow me. I've been doing press-ups with my children balancing on my back.' Graham pushed me aside and started to tug at the stubborn door.

'Might help if you unlock it first,' Scotty sniggered. 'Day one getting off to a great start!' I clicked the dated key fob and the door swung open, with Graham still holding on.

'Whoooooa! Christ, careful! I don't want an injury before we've even started, Heughan! No crazy business!' I smiled to myself, thinking, 'Little do you know, there'll be plenty of opportunities for that, I assure you, my bewhiskered friend.' I ushered him up the steps and revealed the glory of our mobile home within.

'I'm . . . speechless . . .' Graham gawped. 'What a . . . uh . . . "nice" surprise. Decorated it yourself, eh?' The camper van was filled with useful (and useless) nick-nacks that I had either bought at a local charity store or smuggled into the country in my suitcase.

'I wanted you to feel at home!' I replied. I'd brought some trinkets from Scotland and small accessories from our Scottish camper van in Season One. It was important to keep McT comfortable (and sedated) with such reminders of home as stuffed Highland cows, maps, folding chairs, trinkets, fluffy dice, tartan throws and even a cute Scottish bagpiper that played a jaunty and welcoming tune, 'Scotland the Brave', every time you passed it.

Duh duh dee dee dee dee dee duh duh dee dee dee dee dee . . .

'SHUT that damn thing up!' McTavish pressed the butt of the Highlander piper, hoping to silence the musical treasure, but instead he started it off again!

Duh duh dee dee dee dee dee duh duh dee dee dee dee dee . . .

'NO! STOP, you bloody thing!'

Duh duh dee dee dee dee dee duh duh dee dee dee dee dee . . .

'WILL *duh* YOU *dee* SHUT dee THAT BLOODY THINGORIWILL . . .!' And with that he tore it off the wall and threw it into the toilet, its muffled bagpipe tune lamenting as it went down. 'Right, lovely job. Now, let's get going!' he bristled and slumped into the passenger chair. 'You do know how to drive this thing?' He turned back as I hid the emergency bottle of local single malt whisky under the bed.

'Yeah, of course, same as in the UK, right?' I answered, hoping he'd not call my bluff.

'Right,' he confirmed and turned back to explore the contents of the glove compartment, perhaps smelling the stash of Scottish shortbread I'd also concealed from view. With his exemplary nose, he could sniff out a biscuit at a hundred yards.

'Same as the UK, only the opposite,' I said as I slid into the driver's seat and turned the van key over, hoping she'd start the first time.

KABANG!

The white whale with wheels exploded into life, shaking all our treasures from the dashboard and a framed picture of the Highlands of Scotland onto the floor. 'Well, here we go! We are on the road again!' I joyfully shouted above the din of the ancient carburettor. 'Next stop, Wētā.' I slammed my foot on the accelerator. *BEEEEEEEEEP!* A loud danger sound rose above the cacophony of the engine, the bouncing interior design elements and Graham's incessant complaining. 'You imbecile, the handbrake, the RUDDY HANDBRAKE!' he exclaimed.

'Ohhhh yeah. It's been a while.' I released the brake and the beeping stopped.

[Graham: Was this deliberate, I hear you ask? Isn't this what happened in our original trip in the Fiat Fiasco? The answer to both those questions is surely a resounding 'Yes!']

A knock at the window and Scotty poked his angular head inside. 'All right, boys, follow me, not too close. We should make Wētā by nightfall at this rate,' he said, with an ironic smile.

'No, we need to be done by five. I've got a dinner . . .' said McT in a kerfuffle.

BEEEEEEEEEEP! I pulled the handbrake again. 'Sorry!' I shouted, and with that we rolled out of the car park, onto the main route out of Wellington.

Our road trip had begun.

GRAHAM

The van was indeed a formidable opponent throughout our journey. I'm not sure of the make but it was probably created by an obscure Kazakhstani car manufacturer, much in the same way that Frankenstein created his monster.

If a van could stare at you with contempt, this one did so. As we approached it, its wheel arches noticeably slumped as if in a giant sulk. The design of the passenger side made it almost impossible to get inside without rupturing something or crashing your head against the frame. Once sat down, the seat felt like a piece of cloth sewn around a pile of rocks. *[Sam: That's your fault for not wearing underwear.]* Sam likes to imply that his constant wrestling with the handbrake was part of some quaint humorous ritual he liked to indulge in. In fact, the van simply hated him, and me, and was trying its best to stop us driving. The laughably named 'toilet' resembled something designed by a satanic midget; you practically had to have your torso and legs sitting OUTSIDE while your ass hung precariously on the seat in order to drop the kids off at the pool. *[Sam: What a sight!]* I think parts of the van may have been made of Lego. *[Sam: I loved that van.]*

It was in this desperate vehicle, masquerading as something two grown men could sleep in, that we drove the windy, hilly streets of Wellington to our first port of call on this epic Aotearoan perambulation. As Heughan parked the Kiwi Kalamitous at the Wētā Workshop in the Miramar suburb of Wellington, I felt a wave of excitement wash over me. It was one of the days I had been looking forward to the most because, as we have established, I am a giant nerd. But I knew (like all of us) that Samwise's 'nerd' lay just beneath the surface, too. I mean, he likes to present this rugged, outdoorsy exterior, aided and abetted by countless outdoor sponsorship deals that decorate him head to toe in waxed fabric, wool and Gore-Tex, but deep down, I knew he wanted nothing more than to be in the sandpit with me playing with the toys.

SAM

Absolutely! I would add to this, my family's tenuous connections to *The Lord of the Rings* (my brother being named after an elf, Cirdan) and my teenage obsession with Warhammer fantasy board games. As a youngster, my High Elf army was a sight to behold; I spent hours into the night (when perhaps I should have been studying) painting the miniature figurines and arranging them into their majestic, noble battalions, ready to face my best friend's fearsome army of the Undead. I loved *The Lord of the Rings* movies and was thrilled when I worked on the *Bloodshot* movie, as Wētā designed and built the exoskeleton for my character, Jimmy Dalton. As an ex-Navy Seal, he had been in a horrific IED (Improvised Explosive Device) explosion while in combat and had lost his legs (and part of his humanity). I saw Dalton as part frog, part dinosaur, like the Navy Seal Bonefrog symbol. (In the Vietnam era, Navy Seals were known as frogmen.) His brain had also been affected, by the nefarious surgical procedures conducted by RST – a fictional secret military project that enhanced soldiers with cutting-edge technology.

I spent a few thrilling months in Cape Town, South Africa, filming the movie. Dalton was a dick (I imagined him as a mouth-breather) and I loved playing him. He lived on impulse with his multiple injuries, both physical and mental, affecting his judgement. The character was so popular that we had many discussions with the studio about creating an origin or prequel TV show about the character based on the comic book series. Aside from hanging out in a tepid swimming pool with Vin Diesel or dropping from the ceiling attached to wires like some futuristic Cirque du Soleil performer, one of the most fun aspects of the job was hanging with Aussie Rob and Kiwi Dave from Wētā. Together, we drank Hansa beers, talked crap about each other and had a thoroughly good time. They were both technical geniuses, self-professed geeks and had worked on a number of Wētā films around the world. They told me about the incredible, intricate work they did, such as building functional weapons or sculpting ogres' gruesome heads. I was fascinated and my inner geek was fully revealed. They didn't mention Graham's oversized nose or discuss the girth of his prosthetic wrists, needed on a certain film, perhaps burying those traumatic memories to the dark recesses of their warped genius minds.

GRAHAM

The extraordinary Wētā Workshop was founded in 1987 by Richard Taylor and Tania Rodger, who met as teenagers. I think Richard first proposed to Tania at seventeen. After a couple of attempts he eventually wore her down and they have been married ever since. Sort of like the Claire and Jamie of New Zealand without all the eye-popping violence, time travel, and moody expressions. I have seldom met a happier couple than Richard and Tania, who have two wonderful children, a globally respected and hugely successful business, as well as fistfuls of Oscars and countless honours that fill cabinets at their offices in Miramar. To enter the world of these two is to feel a profound sense of one's own underachievement. I sometimes think Richard Taylor has cloned himself (if anyone can, he can) because he accomplishes SO MUCH! They really landed on the world stage with *The Lord of the Rings*, which showcased the extraordinary talent of not only Richard and Tania but also the colossal gifts of the Wētā family they work with.

[Sam: There is something about Richard. I suspect he may be from another world – an alien intelligence, perhaps – working to give insight to us human beings, expanding our minds and making fantasy a reality.]

I had the pleasure of working with him on *The Hobbit* and I shall never forget our first day on the production, part of which was a tour conducted by Richard himself. (I have since been on that tour perhaps ten times and it's always inspiring.) Having previously criticized the overuse of the word 'awesome', I can attest that on this occasion the use of that word is justified. As I, along with the rest of the dwarf band plus Martin Freeman (who played Bilbo Baggins), were led around the workshop, our jaws literally dropped.

The American actor, Elijah Wood, who played Frodo Baggins in the film said, 'It's Willy Wonka's Chocolate Factory without the candy.' I can think of no more apt description. By the time you leave, you have been rendered speechless by the talent and dedication of those who work there. Richard has since become a good friend and I treasure my visits to his farm outside of Wellington with my kids, and just catching up with his brain-exploding tales. There are few people you meet in life that you can describe as truly special. Richard is one.

An example of how he thinks differently was when I did what they call a 'show and tell' on *The Hobbit*. This is when you get into full costume and make-up, plus weapons, to show the director, producers and Richard what you look like with everything in place. I was standing there in my full Dwalin gear. *[Sam: No doubt complaining about the weight or lack of frothy coffees.]* Peter Jackson, Fran Walsh and Philippa Boyens (the director, writers and producers) were sitting making notes with Richard off to one side, sketchpad in hand. After various questions about Dwalin, I said that I thought my character would name his axes. I proceeded to tell the story of Emily Brontë's hounds, Grasper and Keeper, and how they had always stuck in my memory. I said that I felt those would be good names for Dwalin's axes. I honestly meant it as a character note, something only he would know. However, the next day, Richard presented me with my axes with the names Grasper and Keeper engraved in dwarvish runes. I still have them at home in my 'Hall of Him.'

[Sam: CAUTION! I do not advise entering McTavish's dungeon. A fearful place. A massive cave in a grim thicket marks the entrance to his dungeon. Beyond the murky cave lies a narrow, worn room. It's covered in small bones, roots and broken stones. A torch sheds light on skeletal remains, frayed and mutilated by time itself. At the far end of the room, a large metal door blocks the path. Messages in strange languages are all over it, somehow untouched by time and the elements. This must be the home of some fearsome ogre! Then, suddenly, a terrifying yell echoes from the depths, as if from hell itself: and . . . 'Where's my bloody latte?!']

So it came to pass that over ten years later Sam and I arrived in our camper to meet Richard. I was delighted to observe Sam's face as he was dazzled by every aspect of the workshop, before we visited one of the make-up rooms, one of my particular favourites. This is a room filled with face casts taken from people throughout history, collected over time by Sir Richard Taylor. Peter Jackson also has a similar room, even larger, of course. Among the faces are those of actors such as Errol Flynn, Sean Connery, Johnny Depp, Cate Blanchett, Scarlett Johansson, as well as people like Abraham Lincoln and even Napoleon. And, there among them, looking down, is little ol' me.

Now, I'm not sure if any of you have had your face cast in plaster but it's not for the claustrophobic. The result shows you how you truly look. No expression, just a warts-and-all you. It's a humbling experience, except for annoying people like Errol Flynn and Tom Cruise with their perfect symmetry. However, 99 per cent of us look as if we are either having a stroke, or our faces are melting!

I felt strangely proud to have Sam standing where my journey on *The Hobbit* had begun, like a beaming uncle showing his young muscular apprentice where the grown-ups worked. *The Hobbit* was such a singularly significant part of my career, a watershed moment, and to share its origin story with Samwise himself was a special moment. And yes, I was rubbing his nose in it.

In preparation for our visit, Richard had chosen to display my prosthetic from the trilogy. *[Sam: Yes, it appeared there were a great MANY effigies, all in the form of the Bearded One, dotted around the walls, like a temple to McT.]* For those unfamiliar with all things prosthetic, the process involves taking the claustrophobia-triggering 'cast' of your head (or whatever you want to use for prosthetic purposes . . . ahem) where they literally cover your head in thick gloop leaving just your nostrils uncovered so that you can breathe. Then they cover it in a quick-setting bandage-like material and, after about 20 to 30 minutes, cut you out of it. What's left is a perfect 'negative' of your face, which they fill with silicone and make whatever they want, to exactly, and uniquely, fit your face.

The prosthetic mask was sitting atop the life cast of my good self like some strange misshapen helmet mounted on a severed head. It's a strange feeling indeed to look down at your own head sitting on a table, something I sometimes think Sam longs to do with me.

The gingery one seemed to truly enjoy it. I've never seen him 'ooh' and 'aah' so much, except when he's talking about his own whisky.

Richard had also brought along my prosthetic arms. These were quite wonderful and were designed to give Dwalin his Popeye-like forearms. I've always felt a bit of disdain for my own forearms. My father had Dwalin forearms, honed from years as an apprentice printer, with thick wrists that strained against any watch strap, whereas mine have taken after my mother, giving any watch I wear the look of a dangling bracelet.

The prosthetic arms weighed two and a half pounds each (that's five pounds in total, Sam), and were pulled on and off more times than Jamie Fraser's kilt. The young woman tasked with putting them on and pulling them off was called Natalie. By filling the prosthetic appendages with talcum powder, she was able to put them on with minimal grunting and straining. *[Sam: Too much information.]* Again, the comparisons with Jamie Fraser's undressing seem alarmingly apt! When it came to their removal – invariably after sweat-inducing bouts of fighting on set – she had to haul on them like a docker until they finally flew off, showering the unfortunate girl's face with a mixture of the talc and my sweat. This came to be affectionately known as . . . 'Dwalin milk'.

Much as I would've loved to demonstrate this ritual on Sam's own face, I had to settle for him holding the arms. He was quaintly squeamish about handling them. *[Sam: Yes, I felt distinctly uncomfortable handling his flaccid forearms, knowing he'd sweated and grunted inside them.]* I realized that in their limp state they resembled a pair of large snakes. *[Sam: Hmmmm.]* It was then I made the connection: Sam Heughan is afraid of snakes. It was at that moment when I knew that, one day, however far in the future, I would use that nugget of information and contrive to bring snakes (preferably at least a dozen) and Sam Heughan into confined proximity with one another.

[Sam: At your own peril, McT. At your own peril.]

Then it was time for us to 'go under', the phrase used to describe the process of having prosthetics applied to your face. Sam would be turned into a dwarf. I nearly wept with joy. Having been subjected to dwarven make-up roughly 300 times, it almost made all of those occasions worth my while knowing that Sam was about to do the same. And it was decided that I would be made into an elf.

We couldn't see each other's progress. When I heard them say to Sam, 'It's time to apply the moustache,' I may have shed a tear. Having prosthetic make-up applied is a strange process. For a start you're literally having something glued to your face, which is not normal. Couple that with the fact that what is being glued is turning you into something resembling Quasimodo, and it becomes an altogether disconcerting experience, like having your identity replaced by some alien being. Talking of alien beings, I could hear Sam chortling away on the other side of the mirror. We decided to name our characters. When I was making *The Hobbit*, all the dwarves had similar names depending on their family groupings: hence Ori, Nori, Dori, and Bifur, Bofur, Bombur. My brother was called Balin, and we suspected we had a third brother called Stalin who was weirdly never invited on any quests. Sam chose to be the third brother of Oin and Gloin by naming himself Groin, while I settled on being Legolas's older bearded elven brother, Legless. [*Sam: My idea, thank you!*]

Finally, it was time for his Groin to be revealed (sorry, I couldn't resist). Sam stepped from behind the mirror to reveal a bearded, hairy, bulbous-nosed apparition dressed in Sam's usual sleeveless top. He looked like a drunken biker who liked to work out.

It was brilliant. I laughed so much I may have wet myself. And the voice! During the transformation, Sam's voice had dropped two octaves and he was now completely unrecognizable. Like Jamie Fraser after a particularly challenging winter on Fraser's Ridge having decided to form a really shit motorcycle gang.

[*Sam: Yes, the transformation was incredible. The nose (so suspiciously similar to McT's that I wondered if he did actually wear one in the movie or used his own) started the transformation into the foul-mouthed dwarf; the wig and ears completed it. Finally, Groin was ready! YES! Ahhh, you're all a bunch of ***ts! (For some reason my dwarf had a very gravelly voice and extensive knowledge of expletives!)*]

I, on the other hand, had long flowing black hair, pointy ears and an incongruous grey beard and looked like a particularly bizarre version of Ozzy Osbourne.

[*Sam: It really made Groin feel uncomfortable and he kept his distance, hurling obscenities at this freakish elf.*]

Our final stop on this odyssey through Wētā involved meeting the legendary Peter Lyon. [*Sam: We were still dressed as two ex-Death Metal band members from Middle-earth.*] Peter is a master swordsmith and has created some of the most memorable swords ever to grace our screens, including those in *The Lord of the Rings* and *The Hobbit*. Such is his skill that he creates his masterpieces and tempers them to perfection by eye alone. Some time ago I had decided that what was missing from my life was an actual basket-hilted broadsword and dirk. I'm not sure why I needed this but perhaps it was my lizard brain anticipating future time spent with Sam. When we met to discuss the sword-and-dirk combo, Peter asked if I wanted them to be sharp. I hesitated . . . wondering how 'Yes! The sharper the better!' might sound. Instead, I quietly nodded and said, 'Hmmm, yes?' To which Peter Lyon uttered the immortal line, 'Good. What's the point of a sword if it isn't sharp?' It's at this point I should mention that Peter closely resembles the actor in *Manhunter* who plays the psychopathic killer, Francis Dolarhyde, aka the 'Red Dragon', played by the superb Tom Noonan. Needless to say, it was an uncomfortable moment. Now it was time for Peter to present me with my pair of very sharp weapons under the watchful eye of Heughan. They were superb. Words cannot describe their fearful beauty. It was amazing to hold something that was exactly what those men had grasped in their hands on the field at Culloden. *[Sam: I can't tell you how jealous Groin was! He salivated over the precious things and was desperate to caress the expertly forged weapons of legend. 'Oooh, look how they shine, Legless. They're ****ing beautiful!']*

I had looked forward to it for nearly two years, Peter working on them in between Wētā projects as a favour to me. I'd just never imagined I'd be receiving them looking like Ozzy Osbourne, standing next to Sam with the following written on his arm . . .

Groin 4 EVA!!

CHAPTER FOUR

Graham's Favourite Massacres

GRAHAM

It is important to note that the Māori people, prior to the arrival of Europeans, didn't have a notion of nationhood. In fact, even being 'Māori' was not an idea that the dozens of *iwi* (tribes) would have understood. Their loyalties and identities were tied to their *iwi*. In the same way that Highland Clans didn't walk around talking about being Scottish: they were MacGregors, MacDonalds, Campbells, McTavishes, etc. And, like those tartan-clad Highlanders, Māori disputes were with those neighbouring *iwi* (or clans) that had something THEY wanted.

This local loyalty and kinship was reflected in the language. Just as 'clan' translates to 'children of', and 'Mac' is 'son of', the Māori often named their *iwi* in similar ways: Ngāti Porou (of the East Cape region), Ngāti Kahungunu (off the East Coast), Ngāti Tūwharetoa (of the Central North Island) and Ngāti Maniapoto of the Waikato region. Ngāti translates as 'offspring of', and *iwi* is the Māori word for 'bone'. These *iwi* or clans were the literal bones of their people. They were bound to them, and they would fight to preserve them.

Intertribal conflict had always existed. It was an integral part of their political system (like the Highlanders) and was a legitimate cultural response to crimes or offences of any kind. They fought hand to hand using weapons made of wood or greenstone. In other words, the body count was relatively low. Little consolation to those that died, but at least there was still an *iwi* left when the dust settled!

With the arrival of the Europeans, suddenly the Māori wanted those miraculous objects they carried with them to settle those disputes: muskets. And, between 1818 and the early 1830s, Māori traded their goods for muskets, embarking on a campaign of war with each other that stretched the length and breadth of New Zealand. At that time a musket could be bought for the equivalent of 150 baskets of potatoes, or ten pigs. When you have spent the last 400 years settling disputes or seizing land using only wooden clubs and spears, the idea of a weapon that could kill at such a long range and could put an end to your rivals for good was too much of a temptation. Like the Highlanders, it turns out that people living in a harsh environment on marginalized land like hurting each other. Quite a lot. And, like their Highland counterparts, this approach to inter-clan rivalry always seems to bring out the best, or worst, in a family.

It is hard to place ourselves in their time, with our own modern understanding or supposed morality, but in terms of their own personal history of warfare, for the Māori, this was the equivalent of discovering nuclear weapons. The Ngāpuhi in the North were the first to really see the terrifying potential in muskets; they purchased 300 of these deadly modern weapons and wreaked havoc across the North Island. Their victims faced slavery, death or exile. Gradually, more tribes realized the potential of these alien weapons and so began a series of conflicts that resulted in, at minimum, the decimation of some tribes, and at worst, their complete extermination. It's estimated that, by the time the 'Musket

Wars' ended in the late 1830s, more Māori had died than the total number of New Zealanders – 18,000 – who died in the First World War. And this was at a time when the entire Māori population only numbered roughly 100,000. It was a slaughter. By the end of the 1830s, the strain of maintaining these wars and the impact of European disease gave way to economic rivalry. Some tribes chose to ally with the growing numbers of Europeans against their rivals, while some resisted the creeping spread of European occupation.

Which brings us to one of the other notable features of New Zealand history in the last 200 years: massacres. *[Sam: Graham's favourite subject.]* Given that New Zealand is a small country (well, certainly a country with a small population), it has had more than its fair share of massacres in its short history, including the genocide of 2,500 of the Moriori on the Chatham Islands by the local Māori invaders. It often seemed to start with an 'accident' or 'misunderstanding' on the part of the British (e.g., the Boyd Massacre and the Wairua Affray, which we'll come on to). These 'misunderstandings' led to *utu* (revenge) on the part of the local Māori, which inevitably led to escalating reprisals by the British, and yet more bloodletting by the Māori.

For those who have read *Clanlands* and *The Clanlands Almanac*, you can see a depressingly familiar pattern here. *[Sam: And Graham's persistent fascination with all things stabby.]* Basically, New Zealand in the mid-19th century was Scotland in the 18th century, with the added irony that the local natives here were busy exchanging murderous blows with those of Highland descent.

MASSACRE BAY

The first encounter between Māori and Europeans took place in December 1642 at what is now called Golden Bay. The bay is at the north-eastern tip of South Island and is a short hop in a plane from North Island or, if you are us, a three-hour ferry crossing and a bladder-bursting drive in the Kiwi CrampMyStyle on a winding, hilly road reminiscent of the Highlands of Scotland. It was named 'Golden' not because of its gloriously sunny weather but because of the gold discovered there in the nineteenth century.

Originally, however, it went by the charming name of Massacre
Bay. Well, actually before that it was Murderers Bay but the name
was changed – presumably in case people mistakenly believed it
was a bay populated by psychotic serial murderers. Changing it to
Massacre Bay cleared up the confusion!

I have a map with it marked Massacre Bay.

'Going away anywhere nice for summer?'

'Yeah, taking the wife and kids to Massacre Bay next weekend.'

'Fun times.'

Unlike some of the other mass slaughters (but by no means all),
this particular battle was really all a bit of a misunderstanding.

It would be like arriving at the wrong house for dinner, insisting
on coming in anyway while the owners try to guide you away to
another location, until, finally, they decide to butcher you on the
doorstep.

Abel Tasman, a Dutchman of considerable navigational skill,
was on a quest for the 'South Land', the fabled southern continent.
He had already found an island off Australia and in a moment of
breathtaking egotism named it after himself – Tasmania. Then it
was on to New Zealand . . .

For Abel, 16 December 1642 was not a good day. In fact, nor was
17, 18 or 19 December. The Dutch ships arrived at night and were
followed stealthily by Māori warriors in numerous *waka* (Māori
watercraft like canoes), curious to know who these pale men in
tall ships were.

What followed over the next few days can, at best, be described
as a cultural misunderstanding, at worst, a gigantic Dutch cock-up.
The *waka* went out to greet them. The Māori blew on some kind of
instrument, presumably a conch shell. The ship's captain instructed
the sailors to respond. The hornpipe, perhaps? Whatever it was, the
Dutch weren't taking the hint. Now this blowing through a shell
was almost certainly designed as a warning rather than a musical
greeting. To the Māori, these pale strangers seemed suspiciously
like *patupaiarehe*, fair-skinned fairy folk or ghosts, who were feared
because they stole women and children. Given the fact that they

suspected these weirdos to be some child-kidnapping gang, blowing on a shell seems pretty tame.

Imagine their surprise when they not only responded to the challenge but then fired a cannon in the air as a sort of salute! Now remember the Māori people had never seen firearms. They knew nothing of gunpowder, so just imagine how they felt when they heard a cannon?

Added to this, Tasman had arrived smack in the middle of *kumara* (sweet potato) growing season. *Kumara* were a vital source of food to the Māori and were fiercely protected. To top it off, they had anchored near the cave of the *taniwha* (a supernatural being) Ngarara Huarau. The Māori were naturally concerned that these strange uninvited visitors might awaken the dreaded sleeping monster.

There were also a lot of *waka* there, way more than usual, which suggests Tasman rocked up in the middle of either a funeral or a very important tribal meeting. All of this making the perfect backdrop for a good old-fashioned massacre:

1. A sleeping, NOT TO BE DISTURBED, supernatural cave dweller
2. Massive local gathering of warriors
3. *Kumara* season
4. Possible child abductors

After the shell-blowing failed to warn the Dutch off, the Māori regrouped on shore.

'They're still here, chief!'

'I know! It's strange, the conch-blowing almost always does the trick.'

'What shall we do?'

'Gather the lads, it's time to do the *haka* for these *kumara*-stealing child kidnappers!'

The *wakas* rowed out to the ships and treated the still blissfully ignorant Dutch to a verbal *haka*. Nowadays, we are witness to the small, relatively benign *haka* of the New Zealand rugby team. Imagine the Dutch sailors watching boatloads of tattooed, angry warriors screaming at them with blood-curdling passion. Tongues protruding, beating arms and chests in unison. The message seems pretty clear: 'Do NOT mess with US!! F#@k OFF!!'

The Dutch, however, saw this as an invitation for them to wave linen at the Māori from onboard ship, no doubt oohing and aahing over the simply tremendous dancing that was going on. 'Look, Captain, all the warriors are sticking their tongues out AT THE SAME TIME!'

'Yes, think of how much practice they've had to do. This really is a great honour. Tremendous choreography!'

It was literally like a group of men shouting, 'We're going to cut your heads off and drink your blood,' to which the Dutch responded, 'Kettle's on! Fancy a cuppa?'

The Māori, having delivered their most terrifying *haka*, returned to shore no doubt slapping each other on the back saying, 'That should do it!! They'll be gone by morning.'

Imagine their surprise when, instead of leaving, the Dutch moved their ships closer, believing that the *haka* proved that 'these people apparently sought our friendship'.

Yes, I know! I know what you're thinking. Abel Tasman might have been a whizz with the navigational instruments, never got seasick, and probably could deliver a superb sea shanty but . . . well . . . WHAT AN IDIOT!

The Māori would've been despairing at this point: 'Chief! The conch didn't work. The *haka* . . .?'

'Yes, I KNOW!'

'So, what's the plan??'

'Time for some killin''

So they sent out some warriors in more *wakas*. Abel Tasman compounded his idiocy by sending a small boat of men to greet them. 'Look, Captain, the natives still want to be friends!'

'Super! Send a boat of volunteers to meet them.'

'Should we be worried that the natives are armed to the teeth with clubs, tomahawks and spears?'

'Probably just gifts. So sweet.'

The heavily armed Māori delivered the 'gifts' by killing most of the people on the pilot boat, leaving a couple to swim back in desperation, and dragging one of the bodies back to shore. To do what? Well, put it this way, I doubt they were planning on giving him a Christian burial.

Finally – FINALLY! – Abel Tasman got the message.

'So, definitely no gifts? You're sure?'

'No, Captain, just dismembered corpses.'

'Oh well . . . perhaps they don't want us here?'

He duly left without actually setting foot on New Zealand, writing in his journal that the meeting 'must teach us to treat the inhabitants as enemies'. No shit, Sherlock!

It would be over 120 years before another European set foot on this land – when Captain James Cook's ship the *Endeavour* first made landfall in 1769 at present-day Gisborne, later anchoring at Ship Cove, Queen Charlotte Sound on 16 January 1770.

THE WAIRAU AFFRAY (MASSACRE)

Another contretemps worth mentioning was the quaintly named 'Wairau Affray', which happened in 1843 just across the water from the capital Wellington, at the top of the South Island, at Tuamarina, Wairau. Today it is a beautiful holiday destination, but not so back then. The word 'affray' has much more benign connotations than 'massacre' – an affray sounds like things got a bit out of hand, some harsh words were exchanged, perhaps a drunken scuffle? In other words, a Friday night in Glasgow with Duncan Lacroix. A massacre definitely conjures up buckets of blood, lots of screaming, perhaps the odd head on a stick and DEFINITELY significant numbers. Which is what this was.

Affray is definitely misleading. I don't think those that were summarily executed in Wairau were thinking, 'Hey, at least this isn't a massacre!' It represented the first armed conflict between the Māori and their new *Pākehā* friends. Firstly, the Ngāti Toa tribe led by Te Rauparaha decided that they liked the look of an area near Wellington (then Port Nicholson) called the Kapiti

Coast. This guy was affectionately known as the 'Napoleon of the South', mainly for his fondness of launching campaigns against the South Island in his hunt for greenstone. At one point he hired a British ship, hiding 100 of his most terrifying warriors on board and launched a surprise attack on one of those Southern tribes. He captured the local chief, his wife and daughter and several other tribe members. The South Island chief then strangled his own daughter rather than subject her to the abuse that awaited her back at Te Rauparaha's pad.

Te Rauparaha wasn't too pleased when he discovered the strangled body of the daughter and proceeded to kill everyone, but not before torturing the chief strangler himself. I'm not sure Napoleon would've approved. So now Kapiti was in the hands of Te Rauparaha and his musket-wielding warriors.

Meanwhile, the Māori had largely been rubbing along well enough with Europeans until they started moving in in their thousands. Upon discovering they'd been sold a lie in Wellington, with its steep hillsides and swamps, a party of European migrants, led by Captain Arthur Wakefield (how many bloody Wakefield brothers were there, I hear you ask?) pushed further and moved to the fertile land of the Wairau Plains, which were guarded by Te Rauparaha. Captain Wakefield and his merry band of settlers decided to send in a survey party in the hope that the local Māori would just have to accept them.

The conversation probably went something like this:

'What are you doing here?' asked the chief.

'Ah, we're moving in,' responded the Europeans.

'But that wasn't in our agreement.'

'Technically, that's true, but we're here now, so . . .'

'Wait there, while me and my men get our muskets and tomahawks.'

The Europeans then tried to cross the Wairau River, against these reasonable objections by the Māori, tried to handcuff the chief (bad idea), and then in the confusion that followed, accidentally shot and injured the wife of the chief's brother.

Oooops.

Several Europeans were instantly killed. The rest were surrounded and captured. Nine of the Europeans, including Wakefield, were then executed on the spot in revenge for the injury done to the wife. In the subsequent furore, the European-appointed governor, Robert Fitzroy, resisted calls for vengeance, instead taking the pragmatic view that any such action would result in more deaths, and more conflict. This clemency probably saved many lives.

So, in dealing with the locals, it is always best to remember NOT to point your musket at the chief's sister-in-law, unless you want to end up in an affray.

***

And now for something completely different . . .!

FIVE THINGS YOU DIDN'T KNOW ABOUT GRAHAM MCTAVISH
By Sam Heughan

1. He first started wearing a fake beard while playing an angry dwarf and loved it so much he made it his signature look. He actually has ginger hair, hence the constant anti-ginger comments to deflect from the truth, but hides it under a bald cap.
2. Graham is dairy intolerant. His constant intake of caffè lattes upset his second stomach (he has two) and this causes him much discomfort, which explains his grumpy demeanour.
3. His 'fear of heights' is actually completely untrue. He doesn't really mind them. He has a real fear, Arachibutyrophobia – fear of peanut butter sticking to the top of his mouth.
4. He started his career in amateur wrestling tournaments. A casting director spotted him while being choked out during a Dagestan freestyle tournament by Vladimir 'Max' Voltage.
5. The Grey Dog is a firm believer in polyamory, flat-earth theory and the single currency. He holds shares in lunar property and only ever wears underwear one size too small.

FIVE THINGS YOU DIDN'T KNOW ABOUT SAM HEUGHAN

By Graham McTavish

1. He is a passionate water-colourist and has had numerous exhibitions in the village where he grew up.
2. He didn't speak until he was nearly four years old but can now speak five languages: French (fluent), Norwegian (passable), Sinhalese (fluent), Gaelic (passable) and English.
3. He completed his schooling in Sri Lanka.
4. He has an irrational fear of squirrels after a particularly unpleasant childhood incident.
5. He once competed in the European pétanque championship, coming fifth.
6. His farts smell of lavender.

(Okay, that's six!)
Two of these are true.

CHAPTER FIVE

Animal Antics

DAY THREE, MORNING

<u>Location: Akaroa, on the Banks Peninsula, south-east of Christchurch, New Zealand</u>

Named after botanist Joseph Banks, who sailed with Captain Cook on the *Endeavour*, the Banks Peninsula was originally an island formed by two volcanoes, the craters forming Lyttelton and Akaroa Harbour, where the Hector's dolphins swim. Local *iwi*: Ngāi Tahu.

SAM
Let's play a game. Think of an animal that best describes you. Picture it.

This was a regular exercise at drama school; we would have to pick an animal, visit the local zoo, study the movement, attitude and characteristics and then represent the creature back in class. Like a bizarre menagerie, or open zoo, our hour-long sessions would have lions attacking parrots and chimps scratching their asses in front of the tutors. One time I was even called upon to portray a piece of fur on a tiger's back . . . peculiar. But I digress. I would describe myself as perhaps a horse (flighty, wild), giraffe (tall, elegant) or perhaps a bull. I am a Taurean – stubborn, determined, slow to anger and big . . . I would never have called myself a dog. However, I think Mr Dolittle McTavish (what an apt name) has previously described me as a golden retriever. *[Graham: It was actually a springer spaniel, known among the rest of the dog world for their annoying bounciness. In fact, all of these animal comparisons are predicated on the animal in question – horse, giraffe, mongoose – struggling with its already diminished mental acuity.]* I'm not sure I should take offence; I like them – friendly, happy dogs that can be amused for hours by a ball . . . okay, he's kind of right.

However, the animal most closely related to McT is something we met in New Zealand. Not a grumpy sea lion, vicious bird, nor a comedic penguin, but actually a shaggy four-legged terrier named Gordon. (Oh, and a kiwi bird, which we'll get to later on . . .) Despite his dour looks, sagging moustache and tufty bits (not describing Graham here but the dog!), Gordon was a superstar and a champion dolphin-spotter.

The previous day, we had flown from Wellington to the South Island. Rather tired and a little rusty behind the wheel from the excitement of being somewhere new, plus the previous night's festivities, Graham and I had driven to . . . um, where? *[Graham: Akaroa! Were you literally driving blindly, hoping for the best? Or just until you ran out of road?]* Anyway, we were standing on the dock in Akaroa, looking out at an angry ocean. Dressed in seafaring clothes – think less pirate, more marine biologist – we awaited to board our vessel alongside two new canine friends. These two dogs were skilled and were going to seek and show us the elusive Hector's dolphin, the smallest and rarest marine dolphin in the world.

The trained maritime mongrels could hear the dolphins' sonar calls and signal to the captain of the boat the best place to spot the small aquatic mammals. It was all very exciting and our tails were wagging in anticipation. But unlike our four-legged friends, moments before boarding the boat, McTavish had refused to get off the sofa to put his collar on, so our poor make-up artist had to apply his sunscreen and lipstick while he lay on the couch, munching on his treats. 'Walkies!' I tried to coerce him into leaving his basket and join me outside in the rain. McTavish wasn't moving. 'Come on! Come see some cute dolphins named Hector.' I tried again, only managing to tempt him outside with the promise of a cookie and fresh caffè latte. As we boarded the boat, an eager black-and-white spaniel named Alfie jumped aboard and went straight to the bow of the boat, its paws leaning over the edge. Back on the pier, Gordon, the scruffy terrier, looked on dubiously. 'Come on, Gordon!' I called. 'If McTavish can do it, you can.' Both the terrier and McT were sporting bright-orange lifesavers, and at the same time they gingerly climbed aboard HMS Dolphin-spotter. Gordon scampered up the steps and disappeared into the captain's cabin, never to be seen again, instantly finding the safest, driest and most comfortable spot on the boat. McTavish wasn't far behind him. I made my way to the bow to join Alfie and we set off to spy some dolphins.

'Bloody hell! I can barely stand, let alone see ruddy dolphins!' Graham barked, suddenly next to me. He wasn't standing but half-kneeling, holding onto the railing and rolling from side to side, despite us barely having left the harbour. 'I can't see anything; this rain is terrible!' he barked again. 'Wooooooo – fuck, I think I'm going blind!' I stood next to him, barely feeling the roll of the boat, and wondered if he'd been at the secret stash of whisky or maybe had found access to the captain's barrel of grog.

'Haven't seen any dolphins yet!' I called out above the wind and ever-increasing rain. 'Alfie would let us know, I'm sure.' I looked down at my furry friend as he jumped up and scuttled across to the far deck. Alfie was all a-quiver, up on his haunches, paws up on the side, his wet nose twitching. The professional dolphin-spotter stared into the choppy blue waters and wagged his tail. 'There!'

I screamed, 'Hector is here! Hundreds of Hectors!' To be fair, it was more like four, but riding the waves like a gang of billabong pro-surfers was a group of small, agile wee dolphins, leaping and gliding on the waves. They made our surfing attempt in 2021, while shooting the first season of *Men in Kilts*, in the Hebrides off the Isle of Lewis, look pitiful. McTavish had sunk more than swum and I had barely managed to stand, let alone nail the cutback.

'Bitchin' waves, bro!' I'm sure the dolphins said to Alfie as they passed, our doggie friend wagging his tail faster. He looked ready to leap onto the pocket of the wave, should the opportunity arise. 'Well done, Alfie.' I patted his drenched, shaggy head. 'Aren't they incredible? There's only around 7,000 left on the planet and we are lucky to see a whole bunch of the wee guys . . .!' Alfie and I looked back to Graham, but there was no sign of my landlubber companion. He'd staggered back to the captain's quarters to join Gordon on the couch, no doubt both finishing what was left of the ship's rations.

GRAHAM

Ah yes, the dolphins. I've always loved dolphins. I mean, who doesn't love dolphins? You'd have to be a monster to wish ill on these delightful mammals whom I've often suspected of being way smarter than us humans. Well, some humans more than others, naming no Sams. *[Sam: Insert dolphin laughing noise.]* When you see a dolphin in the ocean you just know he's looking at you with undisguised pity. Hence the number of rescues performed by dolphins on hapless Homo sapiens. I'm sure they all gather in their pods at the end of a long day frolicking in the ocean and compare notes on their latest encounter with the two-legged imbeciles named us. Have you ever seen a video of dolphins? They are always having the BEST time. Leaping, sometimes alone, sometimes in groups. They even LOOK like they're smiling – as if they are enjoying the most fabulous party that you know, deep down, you'll never be invited to.

So it came to pass that a boatload of walking embarrassments climbed aboard a boat, festooned in waterproof clothing, life jackets, equipped with a pair of alleged 'dolphin-spotting dogs' to set off to look at some animals having way more fun than we were.

The dogs in question claimed to be able to find these Hector's dolphins. Well, of course, THEY didn't claim this, their owners did. The dogs remained strangely silent when I asked them about their ability to find these Delphinidae.

Sam claims they had names, 'Gordon' and 'Alfie'. I've seriously always been puzzled that humans believe dogs respond to names. As if one neighbourhood dog looks at another and thinks, 'Ahhhh, there goes Trixie'. They respond to sounds, so if in fact you called out, 'Adolf, Goebbels! Walkies!' guess who would've been bounding aboard wagging their tails? *[Sam: 'Here McTavish, here boy, walkies!']*

[Graham: The joke is that our wee four-legged companions can't speak English, whereas last time I checked I just about still could . . .]

We had been lucky with the weather up to this point, but today New Zealand decided to park a gigantic weather bomb over our heads, solely dedicated to giving us endless rain and wind. As for my bouncy friend Samwise's account of the experience, I often wonder if he was there at the same time as me. Did he notice anything that actually happened or has his frontal lobe deteriorated so much that he has to resort to endless fiction in order to fill these pages? *[Sam: You struggled to remember the dogs' NAMES!]* Was he conducting an experiment on himself using hallucinogens? In fact, the more I think about it, this would explain so much about that day, the whole trip, perhaps indeed his entire life up to this point. Perhaps he was so irrevocably damaged by his on-set experience at the hands of Tobias Menzies in episodes 15 and 16 of Season One of *Outlander* that he has lost whatever tenuous grasp on reality he may once have had. All this is by way of trying to understand why Sam's description of the day veers so far from the actual truth.

I spent an equal amount of time on deck as he. *[Sam: Total fabrication. You were snoozing and drinking tea. Perhaps dementia has finally consumed what was left of your fragile grasp of reality, Doris?]* Admittedly, some of that time was spent on my hands and knees shuffling desperately as I clung to anything that might stop me pitching into the ocean. I think the nautical term is pitching and rolling. When the horizon is constantly going up and down while you skitter sideways as the boat conspires to catapult you into the deep. *[Sam: It wasn't that bad!]* One of the crew did start vomiting. A lot! I think he then spent the rest of the trip locked in the 'head' (you see I DO know my nautical terms). Either that or he was thrown overboard by Sam. I'm not proud of my fear of boats but if there's one thing I've become used to feeling whenever I'm near Heughan . . . it is FEAR.

Our doughty cameraman, Simon Weekes, a lean, weathered Englishman with startling blue eyes and a rakish grin, was leaning half off the boat, his assistant holding him by the belt, while he skilfully wrestled with the camera to get the perfect shot. (He lives in Cornwall, which practically makes him a pirate, so I don't feel quite so bad.) All this while I basically crawled across the deck like a discombobulated crab. Why am I always surrounded by such devil-may-care individuals? Simon and the second cameraman, Alan, were always risking life and limb. Crammed into the back of a go-kart hurtling downhill backwards, hanging 300ft off a cliff edge, zip-lining while filming, I could go on but this is a small hint of what's to come in this adventure. They probably rode on the backs of the dolphins just to get an interesting POV. I was surrounded by adrenaline junkies. Even Goebbels the dog was hanging over the side.

Which brings me to the dogs and Sam's assertion that they could 'find' dolphins.

The dogs were clearly frauds; grifters who knew a cushy gig when they found one.

Adolf spent the whole trip lounging below wearing a GoPro, while Goebbels just lay on deck looking baffled at the water hoping that nobody would notice. The dolphins themselves were magnificent though. Gliding easily through the waves, criss-crossing our bow while my knuckles whitened around the railing. Finally, I stood up to give a brief impression of confidence aboard ship while the boat continued to try and disgorge us into the ocean like so much vomitous flotsam. As I watched the dolphins surge ahead and out of view – and while Adolf and Goebbels continued to fool everyone but me about their actual abilities – I could swear I heard Hector's namesakes utter a collective sigh of contempt, leaving us inferior mammals in our ludicrous outfits bobbing far behind.

***

DAY THREE, EVENING

Location: Oamaru, North Otago, South Island

The largest town in North Otago, with Victorian impressive architecture, a steampunk village and penguins! Local *iwi*: Ngāi Tahu.

SAM
Once we had dried off, peeled off our wet clothing and McTavish had stocked up on doggy treats, it was time for the drive to our destination for the night . . . a mere 300km (186 miles) south, near the town of Oamaru. Our faithful old camper van rose to the occasion, and after four hours of driving in rather damp (dare I say Scottish 'dreich' conditions – I thought it was summer down here?) we arrived at the five-star boutique Bates Motel, I mean . . . Hotel. We parked the camper in the small car park at the back and looked up at the imposing wooden building. It towered over us, like some ancient Victorian manor, with what looked like classic old-fashioned gaslights, which eerily lit the entrance in the gloom as we wearily climbed the wet steps to the door. A heavy velvet curtain twitched and, out the corner of my eye, I thought I spotted a pair of eyes peeking from behind it, lit by red candlelight. 'I'm so tired, I think I'm seeing things. That drive was looong.' I rubbed my eyes and looked again towards the darkened windows, but the apparition had vanished.

'Yes, I'm bloody famished, hard work doing nothing,' Graham agreed and pulled the long doorbell chain.

'DONG . . . DONG!'

A heavy bell rang out. And no sooner had the ringing stopped than the ancient wooden door slowly creaked open. 'After you . . .'

I said, motioning Mr Hangry inside. I wanted to head straight to bed, still feeling discombobulated after the past few weeks of incarceration, travel and recent activities but, of course, McTavish insisted: 'First, there is dinner, not a quick bite either!' He smiled, rubbing his stomach and stepped inside. Apparently, he expected a lavish McTavish three-course affair as the hotel had been recommended by the Grey Dog in the first place. Because, of course, Bates Hotel was one of Graham's favourites – a place he'd come to relax after one of his fabled (imaginary) epic bike rides.

***

Evening Menu for Graham and Sam

To Start

A Jus of Canterbury High-country Salmon cured with Soy and Makrut Lime, Baby Artichokes, Baby Gherkins, Marinated Garden Vegetables and a Blue Cheese Mash

Main Course

Otago Merino Lamb Striploin with Wild Plum Sauce, Purple Plum Purée, Oamaru Plum Potatoes, sautéed Baby Carrots, Broad Beans and Chinese Plum Sauce

Dessert

Marlborough Fig Tart with Fruity Frangipane and a Figgy Sauce Coffee, Tea and Gaviscon served in the drawing room

'Well, that sounds delightful,' said Graham, sitting opposite me and smacking his lips. 'Now, what are we drinking?' The dining room was like something out of Black Jack Randall's fantasy, with more thick velvet curtains, chunky wooden flooring and mediaeval furniture. I started to sweat and took a large gulp of the ice-cold wine Graham had ordered – Waitaki Valley, Two

Brothers Chardonnay, the most expensive on the list. *[Graham: This may be true.]*

I peered down in the gloomy light at the menu again, my eyes watering, perhaps due to the candle smoke. I'm sure it read: 'Stripped down to the loins with wild plums, a Duke of Sandringham Tart, Tiny Fragipan Hole and an ice-cold nugget.' Was I seeing things? I needed to escape, and fast. The combination of the pre-dinner drinks, whisky/wine and a large Manhattan cocktail, plus the enormous, empty Jack Randallesque lodgings, creaking floorboards and ominous ticking grandfather clock, left me feeling as though I had entered an alternate reality. The owners, two very charming yet uncannily similar gentlemen (it was hard to tell them apart) would appear suddenly, bearing yet more delicacies and strong liquor for us to sample, then vanish through a side door hidden in the wooden panelling. It was very unnerving. 'I think I need some air,' I gasped, perhaps suffocating from the heat of the open fire. Graham looked up, previously ensconced in some old leather-bound book, no doubt recounting the history of the hotel. (He always brings a leather-bound book to dinner, perhaps to avoid speaking to yours truly.) There was no sign of other occupants. 'Mmmm, well hurry up, dinner will be ready soon and then we need to go see the penguins.' The bearded history buff leaned back in his chair and poured himself another glass of wine, his slippers hanging onto his bare toes as he turned a dusty page.

'Right,' I stammered. 'The penguins, can't miss them.' I pushed back the ancient wooden chair and stumbled towards the large wooden door, the frosted glass distorting the outside world and stopping the daylight from entering the vast hallway. 'Remember, they only appear after dark,' Graham's voice bellowed from the depths. I twisted the brass door handle and took one look back at my epicurean companion happily reading his book and hoped that he'd be there on my return and not have simply vanished into the woodwork. 'Going far, Mr Sam?' I nearly jumped out of my skin. One of the two gentlemen, I couldn't tell which, had appeared next to me, wearing an apron that read, 'Please Kiss the Chef.'

'I've basted the sirloin and now it's resting; don't want to waste the juices.' He pointed a pair of antique tongs at me, adding, 'Don't be long, Sam.' I nodded and made my excuses, pushing the door open into the grey light outside. I set off as fast as I could, without breaking into a full gallop. A thick fog hung around the house and lush gardens. I looked on my mobile app, trying to determine the quickest way to the ocean, but its GPS seemed frazzled and just spun around as I tried to navigate. 'Must be downhill,' I thought and followed an empty road down into a nameless suburb. I passed house after house, each the same as the one before. Turning left, then right, then retracing my steps, but I was lost. I paused to regain my breath and tried to get my bearings, the featureless homes staring back at me. A solitary, unusually large tabby cat hissed as I passed by and disappeared into the shrubbery of a garden. I decided to run. I needed to get to the ocean, so I lengthened my stride and was enveloped by a thick cloud of fog; everything went quiet.

I could hear just the muffled sounds of my steps, which slowed, then stopped. My heart thundered in my ears . . . and then I heard it. A bell, low and soulful. It rang out through the fog and breaking waves. I surged forward through the mist and arrived on the main promenade looking out at a dusky sea. Old rusted-red rail tracks criss-crossed the crumbling concrete promenade, and a rotten footbridge led across the disused tracks to the beach beyond. A lonely seal shuffled from the grey sand and dived into the hazy water, disturbing a group of seabirds as they dispersed and escaped into the blanket of gloom.

Following the tracks along the promenade, I came across what looked like an old steam locomotive, captured in full motion, bursting through the cement, as if driven from the earth's core at breakneck speed, or escaping the devil by rail. As I stared in wonder, I felt a cold, damp presence behind me, as if someone had placed a wet rag on my shoulder. I turned slowly, fearing the worst. There, in the dense mist, a figure was revealed with thin, skeletal legs; it smelt of iron and steel and towered above me, its red eyes glowing in the dim light. The clouds swirled and a strong breeze blew the cold sweat on my neck, causing me to tremble. The figure didn't move, standing sentry, a large graphite spear in its robotic hand, guarding the way ahead. I took a step back, my eyes focused on this terrible terminator, then another step, easing my way backwards until the guard was hidden by mist. I hurried off in the opposite direction, hoping to find some signs of civilization. I passed an ancient rusted tractor, more broken railway carriages and a derelict building that read: 'McGrath Warehousing, Stock and Station Agents and Auctioneers' in worn, partially removed signage. Some graffiti on the window read: 'Really, really good things are in here!' I didn't stop to look inside.

Then, further into the town, a boarded-up doorway caught my attention. 'The Oamaru, whisky shop'. Finally! I'd heard about this single malt whisky from the South Island and was desperate for a taste. Peering through the windows, I spied a disused bar with chairs slung in disarray, scattering the floor or perched on tables. 'No chance of a dram tonight,' I thought . . .

I turned and screamed. 'Gahhhhhhhhwhatareyoudoinghere Jesus CHRIST!' Assistant Squeezy stood staring at me, then raised her clipboard and wrote a note. 'Just checking,' she said, ticking a box then, turning away, she said: 'You don't want to be late. The penguins never are.' With that, she disappeared into the mist.

I ran. Faster than Graham being chased by a Highland cow. I hoofed it back up the road, past the houses, angry cat and back to the creepy wooden Bates Hotel, bursting through the door and into the dining room. 'Graham, this place is crazy. It's SO weird! You'll never guess what I saw . . .?' I panted, collapsing into the sturdy dining room armchair.

'Yes, I know, it's a steampunk village – Victorian steam-powered sci-fi at its best. Pretty cool, eh?' he said, mid-chomp on a mini vegetable, fork and knife in hand. 'Guess I'll have to share the rest of this whisky with you, then; it's good. The local one.' He poured me a glass of amber gold and I knocked it back, grateful to finally taste this fabled dram and revive my spirits. 'Mmmm, delicious!' So, I had stumbled into a steampunk village, not something that would immediately spring to mind and impossible to discern in the gloom, but at least I knew I wasn't hallucinating. 'Just wanted to work up an appetite . . .' I said, attempting to explain myself. No sooner had I uttered the words than one of the gentlemen hosts appeared, sporting a different coloured apron than before, and slid a sumptuous, steaming plate of deliciousness before me. 'Better eat up,' he said with a smile. 'It's almost dark, and the penguins are certainly about.'

GRAHAM

As Sam correctly says, I was already familiar with the Bates Hotel, having cycled there with my writer friend Paul Kavanagh three years earlier. We had cycled 560km (350 miles) from Mount Cook and this was our end-of-journey treat. *[Sam: I assume it took you three years to cycle?]* And what a treat it was! While Sam went on his evening hallucinogenic stumbles around Oamaru, I availed myself of the wine collection.

I had no idea that Squeezy shared Sam's love of nocturnal wanderings around the back streets of strange towns but my ginger friend is certainly correct about the uncanny likeness between our hosts. As one left the room, the other appeared through another door as if by magic looking all the while like he who had just departed. As a result of this somewhat disconcerting atmosphere and, after a magnificent tasting menu with matching wines, and local whisky, I may have indeed barricaded myself in my room, but then when you're on a road trip with Sam Heughan, this is always a sound policy.

SAM

Oamaru holds some very strange traditions, most notably the steampunk memorabilia and vintage industrial buildings I had discovered on my evening wanderings. And it recently became the world's capital for steampunk, making it into the *Guinness Book of Records* for the largest gathering of steampunks in one area. The Wētā Workshop donated a container load of strange artwork and statues, which are now dotted around this peculiar town. A Victorian fete is held each year on Waterfront Road and I believe McT would fit in well, perhaps competing in the pipe-smoking competition, teapot-racing or penny-farthing race.

And so to the penguins that everyone was so eager for us to see! They are known by the Māori name kororā, or more commonly as 'little blue penguins' owing to their slate-blue plumage, which helps camouflage them in the ocean to protect them from predators. Busloads of tourists travel to Oamaru each year to watch their peculiar nesting habits, and one day some 'clever bird' decided to build an amphitheatre to watch this activity. And so, slightly sozzled, that particular evening Graham and I found ourselves sitting in a wooden spectators' grandstand, like an ancient Roman amphitheatre, quietly waiting for the action to begin. To further compound the whole surreal experience, Graham had insisted we polish off a second bottle of expensive wine, so we were feeling, well, really rather jovial and slightly dazed by the whole affair. The cute penguins, unaware of our inebriation, were still gathered safely out at sea, forming battalions – which McTavish will no doubt liken to the D-Day landings. As the sun sets each day, these 'rafts' of brave birds return home after feeding far out in the Pacific Ocean. It's believed they travel up to 50km (31 miles) a day, collecting food to then bring back to their awaiting young, safely hidden in underground burrows.

One by one, the groups or 'rafts' of penguins caught the surf and returned to shore, beaching themselves on dry land with varying degrees of success. One would assume the birds knew the most direct route to the safety of their burrows, but alas, there were one or two stragglers or hapless chaps that got lost along the way. The chubby sea lions watched in bored amusement as a few scouts led the way – up the beach, jumping from rocky outcroppings to the steep grassy slopes of the colosseum, a mad flapping 100-m (109-yd) sprint, like some feathered version of *Squid Game*, the contestants diving through various holes in the wall surrounding the protected bird community. Then it was a further breathless scramble to locate their burrows. Apparently, birds mate for life. However, we were reliably informed that there was the occasional 'chancer', a promiscuous individual that would invite himself into another couple's cave. Invariably, this unwelcome guest would be ejected in a flurry of feathers, but you may find a 'throuple' in the more salacious parts of town. The world's smallest penguins are open-minded as well as cute as hell! We enjoyed the show, toasted the returning heroes with a nip of Kiwi whisky from a discreet hip flask, and made our escape into the night before we were propositioned by a waddle or two.

GRAHAM

My main observation about these tiny penguins was that they were clearly not blessed with a lot of brain power. Perhaps all their energy was diverted into their swinger parties as they waddled between each other's burrows to see if the penguin next door was interested in a wee bit of houghmagandy. Given the fact that their routine is PRECISELY the same each day you would have thought that they'd remember a few key facts. A cursory glance at Wikipedia informs us that the main eater of penguins is none other than the massive lazing hulks that are dotted around the shore of their base, namely, sea lions. Nevertheless, they race ashore every night and make a point of literally waddling past their principal predator as they make their awkward way towards their tiny Hugh Hefner-like burrows.

It would be like me deciding to build my beach cabana in a spot that required me to swim through a shiver of sharks. And yet the sea lions never seem to bother them. As we watched, they barely looked up. Either they had already eaten so many penguins the day before that they would have been sick if they'd eaten another, or they were drunk, blind, and/or stupid. And so, the penguins made their way successfully to their teeny-weeny Playboy mansions without incident after a very convincing re-enactment of the opening of *Saving Private Ryan*. Meanwhile, the sea lions yawned and Sam and I reached for another bottle of delicious Pinot Noir.

Inside 'The Beast' that was driven at breathtaking speed. The photo was taken by our pre-pubescent driver for the day.

A rare photo of me smiling as I relish Sam's discomfort inside a helicopter.

Two men, who know nothing, about to subject hundreds of cows to our udder ineptitude.

Close encounters with a Tuatara. This reptile, endemic in New Zealand, is part of the Rhynchocephalian family dating back 250 million years to the Triassic period. Tuatara are the only surviving species. Basically, a dinosaur.

A photo that sums up so much.

Sam in a kayak in Milford Sound as I head back to land and a latte at full speed.

Alfie, one of the imposters that pretended they could find Hector's dolphins, on his way for a lie down complete with pointless GoPro.

Sam looking impossibly handsome and windswept while I am weighed down by the largest sporran known to man.

A right pair in the back of a van.

My Moko.

Inside Moko 101. I have no words.

Enjoying a moment of not having my amygdala
assaulted. Note the empty wine glasses...

A rare photo of some of our crew. Alan, our second cameraman, and to the
right of picture is Simon Wilkes our famous Director of Photography/part-
time pirate/adrenaline junkie/co-conspirator in my pain.

Climbing into our prophylactics preparing to luge!

A photograph of an early settler from the Otago Settlers Museum. This was one of the friendlier pictures.

Sam pointing at what appears to be a tiny ladder that people have signed at Fleur's restaurant.

Not exactly 'A River Runs Through It'. Our sad attempts at trout fishing.

Waiting my turn as Sam descends into a shark cage. Words I never thought I would write.

Part of our wonderful day at the Marae, learning about Māori culture.

Nevis Swing. The keen observer can see
our legs are ABOVE our heads as we
seemingly plummet to certain death.

An unusual photo showing the exact moment when
two sphincters tighten simultaneously.

CHAPTER SIX

Celtic Connections

DAY FOUR, MORNING

<u>Location: Dunedin, Otago, South Island</u>

Dunedin – from the Scottish Gaelic name for Edinburgh, Dùn Èideann – is the second-largest city in South Island (after Christchurch), and the principal city of the Otago region.

GRAHAM

After a delicious breakfast under the watchful eye of the American twins, it was time to clamber back into the awful camper and motor (if chugging along in that thing can be called that) 120km (75 miles) south to visit one of my favourite cities in all of New Zealand: Dunedin.

After the usual wrestling with the handbrake and the stashing

of whisky flasks into every part of the van, we said farewell to the
gastronomic delights of Oamaru and headed south.

No place epitomizes the Scottish influence on New Zealand
more than the pretty city of Dunedin. In fact, no place says
Edinburgh more like Dunedin, mainly because Dunedin is the
Celtic name for . . . you guessed it . . . Edinburgh. *[Sam: A Dun is
Gaelic for a fort. Hence Dundee, the fort on the River Dee.]* The street
layout and street names are modelled on the New Town area of
Edinburgh, complete with names of posh Scottish aristocrats and
German royalty, like Dundas Street, Hanover Street, Frederick
Street. *[Sam: No McTavish street, surprisingly.]* So when walking
around the city you could be forgiven for believing you were in
fact *in* the Scottish capital, as Dunedin is nearly indistinguishable
from it, other than the fact it was established in the 1840s, has palm
trees, and Edinburgh was founded 700 years earlier.

Our first port of call in the heart of the city was Toitū Otago
Settlers Museum and I was really looking forward to it. It's a great
place filled with just the kind of thing I love (history) and entirely
free from the kind of thing Sam loves (precipitous drops, ridiculous
levels of speed, brushes with death, exploding amygdalae). *[Sam:
And Sassenach products!]*

Our guide, David, was a descendant of one of the first settlers.
Probably related to one of those fire-and-brimstone Free Church
of Scotland madmen, who came over with Donald and Norman
the Fervent, whose idea of 'free' is precisely the opposite. Basically,
paid-up members of the joy police. Which perhaps is why our new
friend seemed to view us with some suspicion, understandable in
Sam's case – he was probably dressed in an overly tight tank top
with his biceps bristling at the edges, his shaven chest peeking
over the top like a pair of angry molehills, plus a pair of denim
hot pants. I'm not sure Sam has ever ACTUALLY worn denim
hot pants, but I would not be at all surprised. *[Sam: Do sequin skin-
tight flares count?]*

David took us through the story of Dunedin. In fairness he
was probably a little nervous. Some people are born to be guides,
enthusiasm bubbling over, the urgent desire to make you hungry for

history, more history, with an extra portion of history – these people are wonderful. This man was not one of those. There's no doubt he knew his stuff, but he was as dry as an oatcake, like a black hole of tedium, sucking all enthusiasm from the atmosphere, leaving Sam and I reaching for the nearest weapons to mercifully club each other to death. Dull, with a capital 'D'. A lovely man, I'm sure. Beloved by his friends and family, kind to animals, but – if his performance that day was typical of his usual demeanour – he should never be allowed to try and kindle interest in anything other than in him leaving the room forthwith. So, we distracted ourselves with the immense number of portraits in the room in which we found ourselves. As Sam forced a rictus grin on his face, my eyes roamed around the extraordinary portraits, many of the subjects related to the man in front of us, which I found slightly alarming for some reason.

Not a lot of smiling going on in those pictures. At the very least they looked as if the artist had chosen a freshly buried corpse to be his inspiration; at most, they looked like they were about to leap out of the frame and berate you for allowing a smile to creep into your eyes.

One in particular caught Sam's attention. He insisted it looked like me. Apart from the fact it was of a man (but maybe not?) and had a beard, it looked as much like me as Lady Gaga. I don't actually know what she looks like but I don't think she's bald with a beard. *[Sam: The similarity was undeniable – bearded, sour expression, bald noggin and I'm certain, if you listened closely enough, you could hear this lifelike painting complaining about the lack of caffeinated refreshments.]* Sam became increasingly agitated as he insisted it was a portrait of some 19th-century doppelgänger. 'Look mate! It's YOU!'

'No, Sam, it isn't.'

'Stand next to it, you'll see!'

'No.'

'It's amazing.'

'It's not.'

And so it went on while our dusty friend manfully tried to continue with his tedious tirade.

Eventually, even Kevin-the-director knew it was time to call it a day (perhaps only to stave off any suicidal fantasies). Our friend was thanked and led away, while Sam continued to bounce around shouting. 'He could be your BROTHER!'

***

A brief word about our director Kevin. In the first season he wore a yellow beanie hat EVERY day. He cultivates a sort of East Coast (he's from New York) middle-aged slacker look. He sported one of those fashionable haircuts (I admit I have hair envy, by the way) *[Sam: FINALLY – he admits it!]* that is popularly known as 'the fash', not because of its fashion credentials but because of its resemblance to the hairstyle of choice taken by none other than Adolf Hitler. I'm not saying Kevin is like Hitler but I just wish to note the hairstyle choice.

I left him and Sam and went for a solo wander to find out more about Dunedin. The year 1848 saw the first arrivals to this city drift into the harbour aboard the wonderfully named ships the *John Wickliffe* and the *Philip Laing*. I suspect it's only a matter of time before Sam has a ship named after him. I would opt for the *Steaming Ginger*, and probably another called HMS *Lavender*. Sadly, the few people already in Dunedin didn't learn until the last minute that these ships were arriving, so there was literally nothing for the new arrivals to shelter in.

'What are those on the horizon, Dad?'

'They look like ships.'

'Where are they going?'

'Erm . . . here!'

'Oh dear, better start building some hovels, Dad!'

Our friend Wakefield (if you remember), that all-round dodgy real-estate agent, had advocated for a class settlement in Wellington and its surrounding areas. One that reflected the range of people back home, from peasant to capitalist. This prompted a Scotsman, George Rennie *[Sam: Was he the arch enemy of Mr Gaviscon?]*, to advocate a Scottish settlement in the south of New Zealand: 'We shall find a new Edinburgh at the Antipodes that shall one day rival the old.'

The Free Church organizer was a Captain Cargill who had fought Napoleon in the Peninsular War (definitely not a picnic, so sailing to the other side of the world probably felt like a Four Seasons-style vacation), and his eager accomplice was Rev Thomas Burns, nephew of dear old Rabbie (national poet of Scotland, Robert Burns). Given the content of much of Burns's poetry, I can't imagine it was quoted freely by those early Presbyterian settlers, but there is now a statue to the Scottish bard looking majestic in central Dunedin.

Now, as we know, New Zealand was chosen to be one of those places that Scots fled to in the 'hungry Forties' (1840s) to escape the greedy depredation of their land by the unscrupulous gentry. The South Island deal struck was that 144,600 acres were to be divided into 2,400 plots, at a cost of two pounds an acre. One lucky fella was sent to find a suitable place and, after sailing around the South Island ruling out Lyttelton, he finally decided upon the bay he dropped anchor in: Dunedin. Thus, by a seemingly random act of chance, the settlement was born, and history was made. Thus, by such seemingly random acts of chance, Dunedin was born, and history was made.

Wakefield came down from Wellington and handed out wads of cash to the local Māori. It probably seemed like a good idea at the time to both parties but the whole thing is really quite extraordinary looking back. A group of financiers investing in a place they've probably never seen, persuading people of all backgrounds to sail the most difficult passage to the other side of the world.

The second ship, the *Philip Laing* (named after one of the family who built it in Greenock), set off from Scotland on 27 November 1847. On board was a perfect cross section of Scottish society: shepherds, farmers, butchers, weavers, cabinetmakers, engineers, bakers, masons and bricklayers. In short, everything you needed to start a community with the blessed exception of politicians. It's also worth noting that no actors were on board. *[Sam: That's where they went wrong. Imagine the below-deck entertainment they could have contributed to!]* Among them were men who had up to seven family members with them like Thomas Burn, or James Brown (presumably not the great rock and roll singer), whose wife gave birth to a son while on board ship. Along with them were the usual suspects of Highland clan life: MacGregors, MacLeans (I bet THEY didn't get on, as they continue to feud, even disputing where the famous Rob Roy MacGregor is buried!). Other clans included MacDonalds, MacDiarmids, a Ross, a few Stevensons, MacKays and, of course, a Wallace!

[Sam: No Heughans?]

[Graham: Surprisingly no. I think that was probably more the sound they made as they were chucking up their breakfast over the side.]

Imagine the scene. It would've been cold, with wind coming in off the Atlantic to the port of Greenock. It was a small ship, carrying 247 passengers. The nerves, excitement, children, infants, all types of men and women converging around this single purpose: to establish a new life leaving everything they had ever known far behind. What were their thoughts as their homeland slipped from view over the horizon, leaving behind tearful friends and relatives? What must have motivated them to undertake such a journey into the unknown? This wasn't like today, where travel can take us anywhere in a day, and crucially can take us back a day later if we so wish. This trip was probably forever. And it took 117 days without sighting land ONCE, finally arriving in Dunedin on 15 April 1848.

What would they have thought of their new home? Their soon-to-be New Edinburgh in the southern seas, like a distant planet in a far-off galaxy. Here they were.

On arrival, things had to be built. However, in the meantime, people slept in the bush. One man remarked: 'If I had been in Scotland, I would have been dead. I lived several nights in the bush, but found no ill effects from it.' Needless to say, he probably existed on a diet of nails and sawdust back home. Barracks were eventually built (probably with their bare hands, while singing hymns), one for the Scottish settlers, one for the English, with the unmarried and married kept strictly apart. Shortly after their arrival, Captain Cargill, that veteran of the Peninsular War, addressed the gathered settlers: 'My friends, it is a fact that the eyes of the British Empire, and I may say of Europe and America, are upon us. The rulers of our great country have struck out a system of colonization on liberal and enlightened principles. And small as we now are, we are the precursors of the first settlement which is to put that settlement to the test. And keep your bloody hands off the unmarried women.' (Maybe not that last bit . . . but then again?)

Whatever our views on colonial expansion may be, and it is difficult to view history through a modern lens, and inadvisable to apply moral and ethical value judgements to a time we will never truly understand, it cannot be denied that those who set off on this perilous adventure into the unknown were definitely not short on courage. For not only did they settle, but they flourished. What remarkable people they must've been. *[Sam: Did they also bring that famous Edinburgh condiment, chippy sauce? Served in all good chip shops.]* And it must be acknowledged that our dour guide at the Otago Settlers Museum was directly descended from these early pioneers.

***

DAY FOUR, AFTERNOON

Location: Larnach Castle, on the ridge of the Otago Peninsula, Dunedin, South Island

Larnach Castle is New Zealand's only castle, built by entrepreneur and politician William Larnach. Privately owned by the Barker family since 1967, it is now a tourist attraction.

BEEKEEPING

GRAHAM
In the grounds of Larnach Castle, there be bees. Where would we be without bees? Bee-yond help? (I'm sorry I couldn't resist.) *[Sam: Buzz off.]*

Bees really are one of nature's most remarkable creations. I have never been stung by a bee. (Wasps, yes. Hornets, indeed! But bees? No. I've always looked bee-nignly upon them.) Bees are my friends.

Well, actually, they are friends to all of us, truth bee told. (Okay, sorry, enough bloody bee puns.)

[Sam: I have bee-n stung actually. Once in South Africa, a bee got stuck under my eyelid, the poor thing, and proceeded to empty the contents of its stingy bowels into my face. For several years afterwards, randomly, the old sting would flare up on occasion.]

[Graham: Holy Mother of God! How on earth did it get stuck UNDER your eye?!]

Anyway, we arrived at Larnach Castle, the only castle in New Zealand, which is unsurprising given no one who would have fancied building one had actually turned up in New Zealand until the 19th century. We parked up the 'White Elephant', otherwise known as our camper van, and along with our doughty crew, made our latest selection in a long list of ludicrous outfits. This afternoon it was the turn of the beekeeper outfit. You've probably seen them, an all-encompassing white onesie with a giant white hood and a see-through net visor. Coupled with gloves and booties, all duct taped firmly to our wrists and ankles. Sam requested a sleeveless version but fortunately common sense prevailed.

After clambering into our very hot and unattractive outfits in the camper van (definitely not designed for such a purpose, like doing star jumps in a sauna) we rounded a corner outside the castle into a buzzing welcoming committee. Squadrons of bees zipping about in alarm at the sight of what appeared to be two giant babies walking towards them. Standing next to the hive was our beekeeper. 'The duct tape seems a bit excessive,' I said to break the ice.

'Bees like to get into the gaps,' muttered our resident beekeeper darkly. Our guide for all things bee-like was, er, let's call him Dave. After a few moments, I suspected he was closely related to our guide at the Dunedin museum. Any attempts at livening things up by us was met with withering bafflement. The most searching of questions was responded to in monosyllables. The equivalent of conversational tennis in which the other person doesn't even possess a tennis racket. The bees were chattier. *[Sam: They were delightful. And Italian. Ciao!]*

But all our frustrations with the conversation, the sartorial catastrophes that we were wearing, even the drive here (the usual buttock-clenching race against time), faded into the background at the sight of our tiny winged friends. I've always loved bees. In the insect world they are just, well, bee-loved (another pun that I couldn't help).

If you see a bee, your instinct is not to kill it. If it's struggling, you want to help it. If it's trapped indoors, you gently try and help it escape. They bring out the best in our insect husbandry skills. The opposite of flies, basically, whom you never get tired of pulverizing on a window pane or choking with noxious spray. Or mosquitoes! What is more satisfying than crushing a tiny mosquito against your leg like an angry sadistic giant? This last example is something Sam of course is mightily familiar with. His hands are never far from smashing himself in the face whenever there's a midge about! [Sam: That's true.]

Our friend removed the top of the hive and what lay inside made both Sam and I gasp.

No, not a pair of Duncan Lacroix's underpants, but a writhing sea of bees atop a vast factory of golden honey. We all know how important bees are: 90 per cent of wild plants and 75 per cent of crops depend on animal pollination. A third of every mouthful of food you eat relies on little fellas like the bee. They are amazing creatures: with a brain the size of a poppy seed they are able to distinguish between the concepts of same/different and above/below. Almost like an actor. They've even been trained to score goals in 'bee football' with the reward of sugar.

They don't exactly have long lives. Females last about six to seven weeks, and the male drones for 55 days (which means they could only manage one episode a day of *Outlander* for the first four seasons before they popped their little bee clogs!).

And, of course, the males have the added treat that, after mating, well . . . they promptly die, basically during the finale of Season Four.

I wonder if they know they're going to die in advance. I guess not. After all, there are no males to warn them, and the females aren't going to whisper during tiny bee coitus, 'This is going to kill you by the way.'

Perhaps the male bees are just a tiny bit suspicious?

'Anyone see what happened to Barry?'

'Yeah, he's not around, is he? Saw him yesterday.'

'What was he doing?'

'Looked like he was about to do, you know, that mating thing.'

'Funny. I didn't see Benjamin either after he did that mating thing . . .'

'Yeah! Probably just a coincidence. Ooooooh, hey, phwoar! Look at the thorax on her!'

Bees also die after stinging you. Again, is this something that they are briefed on in advance? *[Sam: Yeah, the one that was enamoured with my face I think died, perhaps trying to sabotage my career, on a kamikaze mission.]*

'If you detect danger to the hive, you know what to do!'

'Sting them, sir!'

'Correct!'

'Do we report back to you after we've stung someone, sir?'

'No need, you'll be dead.'

'Excellent, sir.'

They really are selfless creatures. The epitome of putting the collective first, with absolutely no room for individuality. The sort of Chinese Communist Party of the insect world. As they buzzed around us, Sam and I were firing questions thick and fast. These creatures were simply astonishing. We learned that bees need to fly 88,500km (55,000 miles) to produce just one pound of honey, and in its lifetime a single bee produces about half a teaspoon. They fly at an astonishing 24km/h (15mph) for distances of up to 13.5km (8.4 miles). Relative to its size, that would be like Sam driving the camper van at around 2,400km/h (1,500mph) for the entire length of Britain. *[Sam: Oh, like the* Speed *movie? But with a sticky twist. I'm up for the challenge!]*

We took turns holding the tray of honey, which was surprisingly heavy. I think Sam may have started doing bench presses with the hives but I was too busy marvelling at these brilliant, tiny guardians of our ecosystem flying in circles around me. What were they thinking? Did we look like giant white flowers? Probably not, just giant annoyances disturbing the equilibrium of their joyous sole purpose: making honey for their queen. Some of them settled on my arm (probably for a rest), others continued patrolling around my head, no doubt looking for a way in. Others just stayed with the honey. It became clear that they all knew their roles. It's not called a hive-mind for nothing.

Eventually, our beekeeper appeared to fall into some kind of coma (or perhaps he'd just exhausted his monosyllabic vocabulary), and we took it as our cue to thank him and leave.

As we shook hands with our giant plastic mittens, out of the corner of my eye I spotted Simon (our supremely resourceful cameraman) briefly unzip his bee suit to reach for something important (he was a very keen vaper). As he did so, I saw one of our tiny friends, probably only halfway through Season Two of *Outlander* in a bee lifespan, scoot inside to get to know Simon better.

As I walked away, through the muffled environment of our beekeeping headgear, I heard one single, sharp, solitary cry:

'OW!'

[Sam: Poor bee.]

CHAPTER SEVEN

The Eighth Wonder of the World

DAY FIVE, MORNING

Location: Milford Sound/Piopiotahi, a fjord in an inlet of the Tasman Sea, in south-western South Island

Milford Sound is within Fiordland National Park, Piopiotahi Marine Reserve, and the Te Wahipounamu World Heritage site. It is New Zealand's most visited tourist destination.

SAM

I was flying, rising above snow-capped mountains, jagged peaks and rushing waterfalls. Soaring like a bird (not a flightless one) but free, the wind my master, gliding above the air pockets, propelled by a fresh breeze. Diving into a jaw-dropping valley and limitless fjord, I marvelled at the landscape. 'YES! I can fly! I'm freeeeeee!'

I screamed, my words carried by the wind. Then, perhaps my time had finally come, or I had flown too close to the sun, but my luck finally ran out. Too many times I'd pushed Lady Luck and Lady McTavish into yet another extreme adrenaline-fuelled sport. My wings crumpled, feathers fell from my body and I stalled mid-flight. Suddenly, the ground rushed towards me. I imagined my body and brains smashed against the pristine white snow. Blood and guts spread over New Zealand's mountainous landscape. 'Arrrrgh noooooooo!' I fell, dropping thousands of feet a second, the wind an angry storm in my ears, whistling to a furious crescendo, moments before impact. 'ARGH!'

My eyes shot open and I hit my head on the bunk bed above me. 'Not again!' I yelled and sank back onto the single sheet and makeshift pillow inside our trusty camper van. I breathed a sigh of relief – I was alive! Not scattered over the side of a mountain but in my lovely camper van on solid Kiwi ground, albeit down under.

'Will you please shut up!' McTavish's booming voice echoed off the cheap Perspex walls. 'I'm trying to get some rest. And don't make that cretinous noise in the helicopter,' he grumbled.

'Helicopter? We are going in a helicopter?' I repeated, more to myself than my sleep-deprived companion. 'I don't trust them,' I replied, pulling my sheet up to my eyes. 'Do you know how many people have been killed in helicopters? Fallen to their death. It's essentially a human blender, a coffin with blades! It can't glide. If anything goes wrong, we are Scottish sushi – little bits of human flesh, finely cut up for a giant's feast. I'm not going. This is a BAD idea.' The sweat rolled down the small of my back. 'Anything else but that. I just don't trust them. And I'm sorry but I don't trust YOU!' I jabbed a finger into the base of the top bunk and into McTavish's reclining back.

'Oh, put a sock in it. You'll be fine,' he said. 'Just have a whisky before we go. You usually do,' added my uncompassionate friend.

'Whisky?' I shot up again, my head not even acknowledging the second bump against Graham's bunk. 'Whisky cures everything.' And with that thought, I got up and poured myself a measure of Oamaruvian single malt I'd stashed for moments of survival like this one and took a large gulp. 'Okay, I'm ready. Let me just get my kilt on; if I die, I want to die commando!'

'Naturally,' McTavish replied and turned over, clutching his Kiwi teddy bear and leather-bound book. *[Graham: Sam Heughan, a man forever trapped in a fantasy of his own making.]*

After a quick breakfast of porridge and black coffee and a long wait – make that a very, very, very, very long and tedious wait while a crew member drove 80km (50 miles) to source Graham's latte – we were finally ready to start the day. And my first ever ride in a helicopter over the Milford Sound, described by poet Rudyard Kipling as the Eighth Wonder of the World. *[Graham: I think I told YOU that, Sam.]* Or am I confusing him with the guy who made exceedingly good cakes?

I pushed my fears aside and we swaggered across the tarmac in Glenorchy, our kilts swinging in unison. The sun glinted off my sunglasses – we looked every bit *Top Gun*, rather than two men walking to their doom. Our pilot, a remarkably dry and seasoned fellow, with twenty years' aviation experience, assured us it would all be all right. 'If we die, you won't know about it. It'll happen too quickly,' he said without a smile. *[Graham: I may have stolen a glance at Heughan at this moment just to witness his face turn pale, while I smiled inwardly.]* I wondered if, after twenty years of ferrying actors and tourists around, this was the day he'd finally had enough? Perhaps secretly thinking mountain suicide might be the better option.

'Roger that,' I replied. 'Chocs away, spin the main frame and put the dinner on.' Trying to sound as hardened and confident as I could, the pre-flight whisky was working its magic, giving me all kinds of Kiwi-courage. *[Graham: Fortunately, our pilot had his headphones on and had put Sam's microphone on mute.]* Now don't get me wrong, I'm game for virtually anything, but I have to be in control, and if it's not me in control, then certainly NOT McTavish. It's my safety blanket. I admit that seeing Graham quiver or go deathly silent with his beard drooping gives me a kind of courage, a silent confidence, a reassuring happiness, a smug relief that my companion is suffering terribly and may, hopefully, even soil himself. It's elating, almost transcending exhilaration, and it gives me pure joy! *[Graham: And there we have it, ladies and gentlemen, Exhibit A in the impending lawsuit.]*

However, when he's smug and happy, like when he beat me at the Highland Games on our first *MIK* trip together, his whole body vibrates and his beard stands on end; even his bushy eyebrows can't hide his happiness and dance around like two hairy caterpillars on MDMA. But today, McTavish was cool. Cool as a cucumber. (If they have those down under? Suspiciously, I hadn't seen one on the entire trip.) Because McT was used to flying around hobbit country, dressed as an angry dwarf with oversized thumbs.

The blades of the helicopter spun and we started to lift off the ground. I kept my eyes fixed firmly on the ageing pilot, watching for any sudden movement or terminal desire. And, if he had a heart attack, I wanted to be there to jump over to the controls and perhaps wrestle us back to terra firma?!

'We have lift off!' the pilot mumbled through the headpiece and I wondered if he had twenty years' experience as a rocket pilot. I looked back at our faithful crew, safe on the ground, waving us off. They looked sad, perhaps one or two even wept, knowing this would be the last they ever saw of us, or perhaps it was just the few hours' respite they'd get from McTavish's constant coffee and snack demands that made them emotional. Only one stepped forward, the safety producer, Miss Squeezy, and she mouthed the words, 'Don't crash!'

[Graham: I think I may have shouted back, 'Stop smiling!']

The small four-seater copter shot straight up – well, actually more to the side, kind of diagonally and then it lurched forward, running low over the treetops. Finally, our pilot, perhaps deciding to live for another day, pulled back on the joystick. (*Joystick*. Hmm. Just think about that for a second.) We climbed into the sky even faster than McTavish downing a latte. 'Wow,' I gasped. 'Just wow.'

[Graham: It's funny how the actual words he uttered – 'Shit. Shit! Oh, SHIT!!' – sounded so different in his own head.]

The view that greeted us was from a fantasy drawing, a painting, a CGI landscape which needed only dinosaurs or a spaceship to complete this otherworldly terrain. 'More wow!' Graham replied. Despite having filmed all over these mountains for *The Hobbit*, he couldn't hide the wonder and awe at what our eyes were seeing. The water, in a deep basin below us, was a vast, pristine sea loch like its smaller Scottish brothers Ness or Lomond. Surrounded by jungle, green and dense, the epic mountains rose out of the ground, as if powerful giants had pushed them from the centre of the earth, creating a dramatic and broken landscape. Jagged peaks and icy blue glaciers spread towards the sky.

And we were flying directly towards them.

DIRECTLY towards them.

A sheer cliff face of grey, solid, impenetrable, face-altering, body-breaking granite loomed larger and larger in the windscreen until it completely filled our view. We were hurtling towards the mountainside, my nightmares finally coming true. 'This is it, dear friend! It was nice knowing you!' I bellowed over the comms, a tear-filled eye trying to catch Graham's for one final moment before we plummeted into the rockface and our bodies were never seen again, obliterated by the immovable ridge.

'Why? Where are you goinggggggggg . . . ahhhhh!?' Graham's arms flew out to brace himself as 'Maverdick' the helicopter pilot made a sudden lunge on the joystick and the helicopter did a wee hop in the air, narrowly avoiding the summit of the peak and we cleared the top by a McTavish baw-hair.

'You chaps enjoying it?' Captain Copter said as he turned back, a wry smile creeping across his face, but I guessed his eyes were black and cold beneath his aviator sunglasses. This pilot was the real deal. A real big deal. A big ****hole. And I loved him. 'Hahahaha YES! AGAIN!' I yelled. *[Graham: At this point Sam is referring to the sick bags he keeps filling to the brim with his own breakfast.]* And he did just that. We climbed and darted through the clouds, admiring the epic landscape and untouched beauty. It was enough to make a grown man cry. 'Haha, yeeeeesssss! Again!' Then, one final plunge, some expert navigation and we circled back and, before we knew it, we had landed.

On a glacier, 2,100m (7,000ft) high! It was summer and we

were standing on a frozen glacier in glorious sunshine and . . . silence – except for Graham's stomach. Epic wilderness and vast mountains all around. The engines fell quiet and we took in the view. It was so impossibly beautiful, my mind couldn't process the epic panoramas.

'Thank you, buddy,' I said, removing the last of the emergency booze from my sporran and cracking it open. 'Here's to you and sharing this epic journey with you. A day of firsts. My first helicopter ride. You actually broke my helicopter cherry!' Graham was silent. 'Perhaps we are also the first to ever be here? Intrepid explorers! The first men in kilts on a glacier?' Graham looked at me, considering, perhaps, trying to break it to me softly, or maybe just eyeing up the flask, hoping I'd left him a dribble.

'Um, err, no. Not the first,' he said, hand on exposed knee, his tartan skirt flapping in the breeze.

'Well then,' I said, 'maybe the first people in commando, on a glacier.' He sighed and put out his hand, gesturing for the flask.

'Yes, fine, the first in commando. Now give me that.' *[Graham: And pass the sick bag.]*

GRAHAM

There are few places on earth that exceed the hype. There are a handful of places that truly defy description, where language seems lacking. I have only truly experienced this three times in my life: seeing the aurora borealis, visiting the Grand Canyon in the early 1980s, and Milford Sound. This is the opposite of Cumbernauld, where *Outlander* has its studios – a place whose town motto is 'What's it called? Cumbernauld!', and for which the words 'bland' and 'sprawling' were invented. It was a long drive on a particularly curving road and I struggled to keep Sam's attention on the tarmac as he 'ooohed' and 'aaahed' at every turn. 'Eyes forward!' I barked but it was no wonder Sam was like a kid on e-numbers, such sublime beauty is beyond all comprehension.

When you see Milford Sound for the first time, you'd believe dinosaurs still roam the earth, such is the grandeur of the primordial, untouched wilderness, which has remained largely unchanged for millennia. In Māori it is called Piopiotahi, after an extinct native bird, the piopio (sort of like the sound you made as a kid when you pretended to shoot someone). It was called Milford Sound by the fabulously named John Grono who named it after his native home town of Milford in Wales. Sadly, the resemblance to the Welsh Milford Haven ends with the name; its only claim to geographical distinction is the giant oil refinery rising out from its environs.

Formed by glaciation over millions of years, the Sound itself is a fjord, created when the sea flooded a glacial valley. It is dotted with fabulous peaks that rise like some CGI designer's dream from the 300m- (985ft-) deep fjord. One is called the Elephant's Head, another the Lion's Head and, of course, there is the iconic star of every photo ever taken of this place – Mitre Peak. It is truly jaw-dropping. When the first people discovered it, the local Māori tribe, they must've felt they had reached the gates of paradise.

To say it rains here is to put it mildly. At 635cm (250in) a year (even more than Sam Heughan's monthly consumption of whisky), and as much as 25cm (10in) PER DAY, it is by far the wettest place in New Zealand and one of the wettest in the world. So much water falls that it results in tree avalanches on the surrounding cliffs. Mercifully, on the day we went, there wasn't a cloud in the sky. To crest one of the mountains and see it for the first time was as if it had been conjured from the imagination of Gandalf himself. In fact, we shot a great many location scenes in the area for *The Hobbit*. Despite being a playground for local Māori, who had acquired knowledge of tidal patterns and fish-feeding over many generations, it was not until 1812 that the Europeans first ventured between those forbidding cliffs.

We arrived at our helicopter on this cloudless day to be piloted by one of the legends of the chopper world. His name was Alf. He has done it all: *The Lord of the Rings*, *The Hobbit*, *Mission Impossible*, *The Chronicles of Narnia*, et cetera. *[Sam: Didn't seem to remember you, though; perhaps had something against oversized dwarves?]* You'd expect such a man to have the weathered face of a maverick, chomping a cigar, a worn baseball cap set at a jaunty angle, perhaps even scars on his handsome, lined face with a pair of piercing blue eyes. But no. He looked like a semi-retired schoolteacher: short, balding, quiet and with a sense of humour as dry as Duncan Lacroix's throat in the morning. Sam was unusually quiet, almost as if he'd taken a sedative (oh how I wish!). And then I discovered the truth.

Heughan was scared.

Of helicopters.

I may have wept with joy.

I almost certainly laughed like a hyena on drugs.

There is a God!

[Sam: I wouldn't say scared. Mistrusting. I hate not being in control or in a flying vessel that cannot glide. A plane with no engine will at least glide a little. A helicopter with no engine equals a human blender plummeting to earth.]

[Graham: Or just, you know . . . scared?]

I first flew in a helicopter on *The Hobbit* when we were filming on the Rock and Pillar range in the South Island. (This was where we see the ruined city of Dale in the second film.) I never imagined that, on my first experience in a helicopter, I would be covered in prosthetic make-up, a false beard, and a muscle suit but . . . hey . . . you never know what's around the corner.

But what was round the corner for Sam was too delicious to contemplate. An hour of payback. It was my turn to look at his face growing pale as we wobbled into the air. To see his hands sweat as we swooped over a mountainside, feeling the thermals buffet the blades of our tiny chopper. To see him mouthing a prayer as we flew within feet of a 300-m (985-ft) waterfall. Finally, he knew fear! *[Sam: Sorry, no. I was probably mouthing obscenities at you.]*

While I knew only joy at his ginger expense, it was glorious to see the icy grip of anxiety coil around him, to hear his quiet pleading with the pilot to 'be careful'. In contrast, I wanted him to pretty much fly upside down with the doors open! *[Sam: Ummmm, I think the altitude may have affected your memory somewhat?]*

We eventually landed on the Franz Josef glacier and enjoyed this most bizarre of experiences: walking around in thick snow and ice on a summer's day. We toasted our journey so far. Sam came out with some nonsense about being the first men in kilts on the glacier. There'd probably been a dozen already that day alone! *[Sam: Are you telling me there are multiple helicopters, filled with men 'going commando', flying around New Zealand's highest peaks?]*

It was soon time to climb back on board the helicopter and fly home to where our camper van awaited in Queenstown.

And that's when our pilot decided to fly through Skippers Canyon and the iconic Shotover River: 22km (13 miles) long with winding, narrow cliffs, it has been the scene of many movies. To say we flew through it is not to do justice to our intrepid helmsman. I mean, we were flying about 9m (30ft) above the river, cutting through the canyon. At one point we were close enough to see the smile on a man's face as we zoomed over his head. Such a smile was absent from my companion's face; instead, a rictus expression gripped his features. I may have shouted 'FASTER!' or 'LOWER!', I can't remember in all the excitement, but what I can remember is that by the time Sam had finished being put through this ass-cramping flyby, it wasn't so much the Shotover River as the Shatover River . . .!

What a day!

But there was no time for reflection over lunch or to put our feet up because upon our return to solid ground I was immediately informed it was time to drive to the water itself (apparently arranged by Heughan as a little 'extra'). We rendezvoused with the rest of the gang and trundled along to meet with 'those' people who were going to take us out into the deep waters of Milford Sound. For some baffling reason they brought along two massive kayaks for company and yet another startlingly awful outfit. These garments, waterproof moo-moos complete with a giant rubber skirt and rubber booties, combined to place this in the top three worst outfits I've ever worn. (And believe me there's some stiff competition.)

I don't like kayaks!

***

DAY FIVE, AFTERNOON

SAM

'If you don't stop moving, they can't get you!' I yelled, walking in circles and occasionally slapping myself, shaking my head. Graham just stared. The sandflies didn't seem to bother him. Perhaps descendants of the Scottish midge, these persistent airborne blighters were larger and more determined to land on your face or commit suicide by tangling themselves in your hair. But, as with Scottish midges, McTavish didn't attract them. Or perhaps it was Graham's lack of a barnet?

Dressed in French style, as maybe a loving nod to his soon-to-be-wife, he donned purple-and-black-striped, skin-tight pantaloons, waterproof slippers, a neon-yellow spray jacket, a bright-orange lifesaver and what can only be described as a plastic girdle or oversized, all-purpose mini skirt. It was in fact a 'spray-deck', used for sea kayaking to keep the intrepid adventurer dry (or at least protect his purple leggings) but looking back, the ensemble was quite remarkable. *[Graham: I think both of us often wondered whether our costume designer was on a mission to make us look as ridiculous as possible. She succeeded.]*

GRAHAM

A word about the wardrobe. We had our fittings in Wellington prior to starting the trip. Our costume designer (different from our original designer on our Scottish escapade) had previously visited me at my home and carted away suitcases full of my clothes as options for the show. So when I arrived for the fitting, it was in the confident belief that I would at least like what I would be wearing because, after all, they were my own clothes.

So it was with a creeping sense of dread that it dawned on me that the clothes I would be wearing were outfits that Kevin and our designer thought worked best as opposed to what I would actually choose to wear in any version of reality. I quickly understood that 'worked best' generally meant me looking like I'd stepped out of a Victorian gentlemen's club (all that was missing was the pipe), while Sam's look was surfer dude/gym rat portrayed in an extensive collection of clothing rejects from *Magic Mike 4*. At one point it was suggested I should wear knickerbockers (not sure when this was for, possibly at one of the several moments when my nerves were being shredded to the max by yet another assault on my fragile sanity). I politely declined. As for the luge outfits (still to come), well, put it this way, I'm glad I've already had kids.

SAM

We looked like a pair of silent movie actors – Graham resembling a French Keystone Cops villain! Our rubber waterproof slippers squelched as we ambled over the cobbled shore to the awaiting kayaks. 'See! Keep moving and those little buggers won't get yooo . . . uuugh!' I choked on a fly that dive-bombed my mouth and spent its final moments lodged in my throat.

'Is this get-up REALLY necessary?' Graham sighed, more concerned about his appearance than the plague of winged beasties.

'Yes, gah! Safety first.' I coughed up another ant and bent down to pick up one end of the seaworthy kayaks. 'Don't worry, it'll be fun!'

Graham eyed me suspiciously. 'And when have you EVER been concerned about safety?' he barked, nursing his back as he helped lift the kayaks towards the water. I pretended not to hear him and busied myself with checking the shallows for any trace of sharks or man-eating crocodiles, occasionally slapping myself when attacked by a bloodsucking flying ant. 'Looks safe enough, come on, I'll go first,' I said, hoping to lead by example but secretly unsure if that was a good idea. Moments earlier a local fisherman had thrown some unused bait into the water from the nearby pier. I watched in horror as a number of Galapagos sharks, smooth, dark shapes below the water, fought and tore at the flesh in a feeding frenzy. My only comfort was that I hoped our outfits might scare away the aquatic predators, as they notoriously hated French mime artists, especially bald Marcel Marceau impersonators! Perhaps they'd go for McTavish first, his splashing and monotonous complaining similar to the noises of a drowning baby elephant. 'Shark bait!' I thought, only to have my reverie interrupted by his dulcet tones.

'May I remind you, I almost drowned ALREADY this week! I'm totally justified to say no!' Graham had made up some fantasy story – perhaps he'd read it in one of his classic novellas or borrowed the narrative from a silent movie he'd watched late at night. According to him, earlier in the week, he and his whole family capsized in a boat far out at sea. The boat sank, disappearing to the bottom of the ocean, never to be seen again but luckily, our brave hero rescued everyone, pulled them ashore to safety and probably nursed an abandoned puppy back to health at the same time.

GRAHAM

In fact, Garance, Hope, Honor and I, and our skipper, almost drowned after our boat capsized in the north of New Zealand. We were on vacation, waiting for Sam to emerge from his Club 18–30 MIQ experience. We had gone fishing for snapper, enjoyed a picnic on a beautiful remote beach and were on our way back when a freak wave lifted the boat end over end, resulting in some of us being trapped under the overturned hull. The locals said they'd not seen a wave like that in that area for over 25 years. It was definitely the kind of experience to make you think twice before climbing into a kayak in Milford Sound next to a notorious lunatic.

SAM

Okay – it did sound very terrifying and, in fact, I was surprised McTavish had agreed to this part of the adventure. Especially after his reaction when I'd tried to convince him to join me kayaking on our last *Clanlands* adventure around Scotland. Instead of accompanying me on a beautiful sunset paddle around Loch Awe, my heroic friend decided to retire to the hotel bar to drink chilled white wine and sample the tasting menu.

'This time will be different,' I smiled and pushed out into the pristine blue water. We were to kayak across Milford Sound, while admiring the unique landscape and looking as butch as possible (in our striped pyjamas). I paddled hard; droplets of cold, crystal-clear water ran down the oar and splashed in my face. It was exhilarating. The jagged peaks reflected in the clear water, like a perfect mirror or a gigantic landscape painting, capturing the vast blue sky. The sun shone brightly; the silence and sheer majesty of the setting overcame me. All memory of the bugs had gone and I had forgotten about the sharks, forgotten about the silly outfit . . . and . . . had I forgotten something else? Someone?

'Graham!'

I spun the craft around, looking back to shore. I had paddled far into the great sea lake and was surrounded by deep water. I spied a neon-orange speck on the shoreline waving an oar at me. 'Not commmming!' his voice echoed, causing small ripples across the water. 'See you at luuuuuunch.' The purple-and-black-striped legs disappeared and I was alone again, floating on the water, with a severe case of déjà vu.

CHAPTER EIGHT

Scotland on Steroids

DAY SIX, MORNING

Location: Queenstown/Tāhuna, Otago, in the south-west of South Island

Queenstown is a resort town built around the Queenstown Bay inlet on Lake Wakatipu. It has an urban population of 15,800 (June 2022). The nearest cities are Dunedin and Invercargill. Local *iwi*: Ngāi Tahu.

SAM
Halfway down the long, thin, Z-shaped Lake Wakatipu in the region of Otago, just to the north-east of Milford Sound, is an inlet called Queenstown Bay where the settlement of Queenstown or Tāhuna is. The lake was shaped by glaciers millions of years

ago and along it are views of mountain peaks and ranges such as the Remarkables, Cecil Peak, Walter Peak and just above the town, Ben Lomond and Queenstown Hill. Originally, this was the setting of New Zealand's short gold rush, when gold was discovered on the Shotover River in November 1862. But after a few years, the gold fever waned and the town went into decline – until more recently (and this is the bit that really interests me) when it gained a resurgence to become the adrenaline capital of, not only New Zealand, but the WORLD!

YAZZZ!

After a late-night arrival, I awoke under a fresh sheet in a spacious, comfortable and well-lit hotel room, in the centre of Queenstown. No grotty camper van or sounds of McT's snoring; a welcome night off from our four-wheeled travelling home-from-home. I leaped out of bed feeling bright and energized, opened the sliding doors and stood on the balcony, taking a deep breath, my lungs welcoming the fresh air that blew across Lake Wakatipu. The dramatic Southern Alps – the aptly named Remarkables, and they really are – outlined the horizon. Their sheer slopes were covered in magnificent trees that reached up to the sky, hiding the adrenaline-fuelled activities beneath their foliage. This welcoming small resort town of south-west Otago is a pilgrimage destination for adrenaline junkies and thrill-seekers.

On the large lake, speedboats, kayaks, yachts and jet skis drew patterns across its blue waters and, in the mountains to the north and the east, zip lines, bungees, go-karts and mountain biking were only a handful of the activities available in the natural playground. I could almost hear the joyful screams of the adventurous daredevils as they threw themselves off a cliff or out of a plane, high above the glorious mountaintops.

'Aaaargh!' No, I really could hear them. At least I thought it was them. 'Yeeeeaaaahhhh!' Another blood-curdling yell shook the whole balcony; its epicentre: the bedroom next to mine. 'Ah, the early morning call of the Lesser-spotted McToovish bird,' I thought. Flightless, fearful and decidedly not nocturnal, it was a rare creature, seldom seen in this perilous activity terrain.

'Yeeeeaaaahhhh! Oh my God!' The scream came again as I silently smiled to myself. McTavish was getting out of bed with his usual gusto, aching body parts causing him to moan in complaint. And well he should complain. Yesterday, to lure my fearful companion to this Mecca of madness, I cheerfully told him we would be doing some 'minor activities but nothing to get the blood up, old boy'. I hadn't mentioned the luge – hurtling down a mountain on four wheels with no parachute or bungee cord in sight. 'Besides, with my injury, we'd better be careful,' I added, as I strapped on a Velcro brace to my left knee to protect my torn MCL. 'Let's keep it very tame,' I said to my anxious companion.

All activity was out, by order of my orthopaedic surgeon. But given the opportunity to torment McTavish . . . NOTHING would hold me back, torn medial ligament or not.

[Graham: It is now that we can all witness the full extent of Heughan's lunacy. It actually sounds like a REAL medical complaint. 'I'm terribly sorry, madam, but you are suffering from a rare case of "Heughan's lunacy", there's nothing I can do.' This is a man who would actually risk permanent serious injury JUST to annoy me, and/or watch me suffer.]

To ease my adventure-shy companion into a false sense of security, I had planned some far-from-fearsome activities. Dodging all the scary stuff, I took McScaredy on a charming gondola ride (450m (1,476ft) high up over Bob's Peak – I wonder if Bob knew?) to admire the exceptional panorama below. Despite the height, Graham enjoyed his little ride out, commenting on the 'marvellous view and equally marvellous snacks available in the mountaintop café'. I assured him the descent would also be marvellous and surprisingly gentle.

After, clad in full motorbike safety gear (albeit 1970s retro) we tore down the mountain in primitive go-karts. Graham was less than impressed but I assured him that the ride was designed for children – really not that scary. However, a couple of local boys, no more than maybe nine years old, looked disparagingly as McTavish edged his way down the slope, remaining at pensioner-pace. 'You wanna race, old man?' they jeered, staring us down as best they could, given their diminutive stature and oversized lollipops.

McTavish shunted his kart forward and flicked a rude gesture in their direction. 'Bloody kids, should read more,' he grumbled.

McSpeed actually compared the luge to a Formula 1 race! And, I admit, I couldn't resist the urge to go as fast as I could in this oversized box with wheels . . . only to capsize and crash into the end barriers, tipping my kart and twisting my already damaged knee.

'You really should be more careful,' Graham puffed as he finally caught up with me. 'Don't want to do anything too crazy.'

'No, you're right,' I lied. 'Let's play it safe,' I said as I limped towards the exit, my plan formulating as the net slowly closed around my unsuspecting companion.

Prior to Graham 'luging it' – geddit? – I had arranged a visit to Queenstown Kiwi Park, a mini local zoo for endangered species, full of fluffy, harmless birds and various four-legged lizard creatures. Graham was in his element, quoting facts and figures and stroking fluffy things – like the flightless kiwi bird, with its long snout and little wings, mere stumps hidden by feathers. The poor bird was so embarrassed, it tried to hide away in its burrow underground. 'Ah, isn't he cute, like a sort of bird-dwarf? Didn't you play one once?' I asked. 'Totally harmless,' I said, as the keeper held it firmly in his arms. Graham looked on in silence; little did he know that the very same warbler had recently ruptured a previous employee's spleen by slashing them with its long, sharp talons! Ha-ha! Graham seemed fascinated by the wee fella. However, things did get a little awkward when the shameless kiwi suddenly upended itself – with the help of the handler – spreading its legs and revealing its 'cloaca' in all its feathered glory!

[Graham: I feel the need to defend the kiwi's dignity. Far from upending ITSELF, it was grabbed and exposed to us. The poor creature turned its head away in embarrassment while its genitalia were offered up for close inspection.]

We gasped in silence, then moved onto the next exhibit quickly, hoping not to offend the shameless stomach-ripper. 'Charming,' Graham mumbled through his beard. 'Perhaps we should do some more activities, these birds are crazy.' *[Graham: Me saying this would be akin to a boxer putting on a blindfold and asking his opponent to repeatedly smash him in the face, i.e., IT WOULD NEVER HAPPEN!]*

GRAHAM

And, if you thought that birds in New Zealand didn't get stranger than the baffling kiwi, it's time to introduce – the moa. These were big birds. I mean, really, really big.

The female stood at over 2m (6ft 6in) tall and weighed about 250kg (550lb). They are related to other 'ratites', an unfortunate name for their species of animal. I mean, who wants to say they are part of the ratite family? Not to be confused with the elephant bird of Madagascar or the 'Duck of Doom' of the Miocene era in Australia, which were as tall, but bulkier and heavier.

Until the arrival of the Māori in roughly the 14th century, these birds had had a very comfortable life. Their only predator was the equally gigantic Haast's eagle, which makes a bald eagle look like a sparrow. But other than this pterodactyl-like killer, the moa were free to wander around New Zealand with their very tiny heads (only 23cm (9in) long) and nibble at tree branches and generally feel pretty good about their moa-ness.

Unfortunately, it wasn't to last. The Māori arrived from Polynesia and immediately realized what a truly excellent food source the moa was. In a land with no domesticated animals (they came with the Europeans), or any mammals (apart from a bat), the source of protein that the moa provided was invaluable. Being flightless birds (who needs wings when you can do everything on the ground?), they were embarrassingly easy to kill. One can imagine a group of moa (what is the collective noun for moas? A 'complacency', perhaps?) standing around looking very tall and feathery, glancing with disdain at all the smaller flightless birds. The kiwi probably developed quite an inferiority complex during this time, forever humbled by its massive cousin.

'What's that?' asked Millie the moa.

'There's a lot of them and they're all on two legs,' said her friend, Merv the moa.

'Maybe they want to be friends with us because we're feathery, big and generally awesome.'

'Hold on! They're throwing pointy sticks at us!'

'And now they're clubbing Malcolm the moa to death!'

'But . . .'

And then they were extinct. Yup. They were hunted to extinction. For meat, bones and feathers. By the time there was only one left, he/she was probably praying for death from sheer loneliness. And so around 500 years ago the last moa was killed and eaten. It wasn't until the 1830s that Europeans discovered their remains. For a while, New Zealand became known as 'the land of the moa', until people realized it should actually be called 'the land of the oh-there-aren't-any-left-because-they've-all-been-murdered moa'. From then on, the title transferred to those little cousins who had been spared apocalyptic extinction and New Zealand has, ever since, been the 'land of the kiwi'.

SAM

As we left the zoo, I casually mentioned I'd got a 'little something for tomorrow, nothing much, just a little thing.'

'Tomorrow?' Graham looked up from a half-eaten granola bar, his beard divining danger, like a wildebeest smelling lion. 'What's on tomorrow?' he enquired.

JUDGEMENT DAY! I wanted to scream at the top of my lungs, the echo bouncing off the distant peaks, stopping local hillwalkers in their tracks and even making a kiwi bird blush. Instead, I just shrugged. 'You'll see, it's really easy.' I smiled and handed him another coffee. McTavish stared at me and then took a large gulp of tepid milky caffeine.

'GOT HIM!' I thought. McTavish was trapped.

GRAHAM

I know Sam likes to think that I knew nothing of his plans. However, I have spent enough time around he-of-the-proud-pecs to know that, when he uses the terms 'gentle' and 'easy', I should expect the opposite and understand that what he actually means is 'harrowing' and 'excruciating' with a sprinkling of 'nerve-shredding torture'.

After our encounter with the spleen-bursting kiwi, that little vicious flightless bird with thighs like pistons and a tiny cloaca, it was time to luge. The Queenstown luge (like so many things in Queenstown) appears to have been invented by someone either drunk or on hallucinogenic mushrooms. Perhaps Duncan Lacroix? *[Sam: My hero.]*

It is a concrete racetrack for midget-sized go-karts descending fast down a mountain, overlooking Lake Wakatipu. It would be an amazing view if it weren't for the fact that you spend your entire time avoiding either smashing into small children or catapulting over the side of this twisting track of death.

To get to the luge you have to ascend in a gondola. Now, unlike my previous experience at Glencoe, this was not operated by a prepubescent child and his Shrek-like father and nor was it exposed to the open air.

Warm, cosy and enclosed, you glide up the mountain enjoying the amazing landscape around you. It is only when you get to the top that the fun (or lack of it) begins. To get to the start of the precipitous luge, you have to be taken by chairlift.

Once more I was trapped next to Heughan with a tiny metal bar being all that stopped us falling to our deaths while he laughed himself silly trying to persuade me that the chair we were in was dangerously unstable. Let's talk for a moment about getting on the chairlift. Why are they on a non-stop loop? Every time it's my turn to get on one, I stand waiting in silent dread as it circles towards me like a malevolent park bench, ready to slam into the back of my legs. It's even worse with skis – not that I would even consider such an insane idea.

[Sam: I love skiing and I love chairlifts. It is the most serene and beautiful way to take in the scenery, only ruined by Graham's constant grumbling. He did once burst into song during the shooting of Season One of Men in Kilts, *when we took a ski chairlift up Glencoe, reciting* The Hobbit's 'Misty Mountains' *theme tune. At which point I really did want to get off.]*

Anyway, back to New Zealand. I was standing next to Sam, both of us wearing helmets that had been fully checked for safety but still managed to look far too small for us, making us look both absurd and hopelessly unprotected all at the same time and, bang on cue, the chair slammed into my legs! I fell backwards, while Sam pulled the protective bar down just fast enough to ensure it would crack the top of my head in the process.

After a relatively short ascent, during which Heughan probably tried his best to dismantle the chair with his bare hands just for giggles, it was time to get off. As with the start of this chairlift trip up the mountain, the end also seemed designed to cause maximum anxiety because the wretched contraption has to keep going round and round like some demented drunkard. As you approached the top you had to lift the protective safety bar and prepare to leap from the chair and scamper to safety.

If you got off too early you would fall backwards down the very hill you'd come up; too late and you risked either swerving to the right and heading downhill desperately holding on to the chair or being smashed in the spine by the pursuing metal sofa!

[Sam: It's really not that complicated.]

Annoyingly, Heughan stepped off and sauntered to safety while I flung myself forward and then launched myself left with my head down, desperate to avoid the relentless mechanical advance of the steel bench that was hot on my heels. I don't think I once looked anything other than terrified while Sam managed to appear cool and serene just to spite me. *[Sam: It's a ride for kids.]*

We were then herded into a tiny storage cupboard to change into our 'outfits'. I vaguely remembered these from our costume fitting a few weeks earlier in which I seemed to be constantly put into ever-more-ludicrous garments, while Sam paraded in a bewildering collection of sleeveless tops. *[Sam: Ah . . . now we get to it.]*

However, the full horror of our outfits was only apparent once we'd put them on and realized we would be wearing them in public. Apparently, they were vintage motorcycle all-in-one outfits. On us (because they were one size too small), we looked as if we'd been squeezed into a pair of giant leather condoms. And so it was that, looking like this, we finally ventured outside, quite literally bursting from the closet. It is worth pointing out here that while we had closed the track for filming, the public were allowed to use the track in between takes. In other words, the top of the mountain was crammed with families staring in horror at these two grown men walking out in a pair of S&M onesies. I think some mothers may have covered the eyes of their children.

It was time to luge. The go-karts were tiny. I mean, absurdly small. Climbing into them like two leather-clad stick insects, we looked as if we had stolen them from a kids' playground. We were given basic instructions on how to go forward, how to stop, how to turn – simple stuff, you may say. Kevin thought it was an excellent idea to pump dry ice across the track as we ran to get into our kiddie cars, like a grotesque parody of Le Mans. This merely resulted in heaping further embarrassment on us both, while the crowd impatiently looked on, secretly hoping that we would crash.

Heughan seemed strangely immune to this public ridicule. He kept jumping up and down and slapping his leather outfit, grinning maniacally. He had even painted two lines of black under his eyes to make him look 'dangerous'. Obviously, we all know by now that he needs no such adornment to warn of his unhinged personality. *[Sam: Go-faster stripes which helped to block out the glare of the sun.]*

I looked across at the throng of families and noticed several children shaking their heads in sympathy. One particularly worrying boy looked at me and drew his thumb across his throat. Clearly, he knew something I didn't.

Then we were OFF . . .

Heughan was ahead. He had, of course, decided to make this a competition, creeping forward hunched like some monstrous orange beetle. I crawled after him at first but then picked up speed. My policy, when descending at speed down a solid concrete track with hairpin bends, tunnels and gravity-defying humps in the road, is to exercise caution. I have ludicrous ideas, like slowing down for bends, for instance. Sam, in contrast, seemed to treat this as a challenge to see how out of control he could be. I would catch the sound of him howling in front of me like a demented farmyard animal while I concentrated on not painting the walls with my face. Sometimes I would catch up. He even let me pass him and, for a brief moment, I thought, 'Actually, he's not so bad' – only to discover that it was so that he could ram me from behind in an effort to throw me out of the kart and actually run me over with his miniature coffin on wheels!

Finally, he, of course, surged past. *[Sam: Easy – like taking candy from a kid. But not the thumb-gesturing kid at the top, he was mean.]* I approached the end of the Track of Damnation only to see him sprawled across the concrete close to the finish line. I may have paused for a microsecond to see if he was still breathing but in true Tortoise-and-Hare fashion, I coasted across the finish line smiling inside my giant lurid contraceptive. I can't deny it. It felt good! *[Sam: I won though.]*

It was then that I was told we had to do it another five times! For different camera angles. So it began all over again, like some Dante-esque circle of hell. Waiting with dread for the remorseless chairlift to take me back to the top.

To do it all over again. *[Sam: I won again.]*

And again.

And again.

And . . . Sweet Jesus, AGAIN! *[Sam: You guessed it, I won every time.]*

***

DAY SEVEN: JUDGEMENT DAY!

SAM

I was up extra early with Kevin as we prepared for a veritable Adrenaline Sandwich for Graham to endure . . . I mean enjoy! We bundled the Grey One, still mid-breakfast, into the van and sped off with him, like a kidnapping from a care home. Before Graham had even finished his latte he was wailing: 'I don't want to go down a cliff!' Because first up was a spot of Monster Off-Roading at

Oxbow Adventure Park, to the east of Wakatipu Lake, 30 minutes from Queenstown.

'I don't want to go down a CLIFF!' he repeated. The crew on the other side of the glen could hear his protestations even over the roar of the vicious, supercharged V8 engine. 'We ARE going down a cliff!' he yelled again as the one-of-a-kind four-wheel-drive off-roading monster growled again, then thundered across the valley, silencing our pathetic screams as we drove at almost 90 degrees straight down a rocky cliff. At the bottom, we were alive, somehow; it seemed impossible what this vehicle could do, defying gravity and physics. As the vehicle lined up down a straight desert track through the New Zealand brush, a moment of respite. McShouty pulled down his dust guard to scream at anyone listening, 'Make it stop, please, shoot the driver!' In answer to his relentless pleas, the nameless madman at the wheel, spurred on by my cackling, gunned the monster truck on steroids and we shot off.

'Killllllllllthedriverrrrrrrrrrr!'

Graham's voice disappeared into the mountain pass. What felt like seconds later, at breakneck speed, we appeared over the ridge and hurtled back towards the awaiting crew. After a dramatic handbrake turn, we pulled up next to a quiet pond and the driver slammed on the brakes. The rush of blood that had shot into our heads – from being almost upside down and then slammed into our seats as the vehicle accelerated – had stunned us both. Just the sound of heavy breathing and the occasional whimper from McTavish emanated from the vehicle's hulking chassis. 'Is it . . . is it over??' Graham gasped through his clenched teeth.

'Not yeeeeeeeeeetttttt!!!' I screamed in amusement, as the joyrider hurtled the vehicle into an extended doughnut, spinning the vehicle and the content of our stomachs round and round, as if caught in a tumble drier. Eventually, the vehicle stopped and we clambered out, ducking under the roll bars and safety cage, stumbling dizzily in a line towards what looked like refuge.

GRAHAM

The day began like any other day. As I got dressed, my amygdala had no idea what horrors lay ahead . . .

It was at an institute for the criminally insane masquerading as 'an adventure park'. Akin to describing a boxing ring as a playpen. The track was designed to test the very limits of the squat off-roading monster we climbed into. I'd never actually heard an engine make a noise like this before. This went beyond growling and approached something reminiscent of Lacroix after a particularly bracing Indian curry. With descents and turns that defied physics, at one point we were driving at 90 degrees to the ground with our faces painted in choking dust, my screams drowned out by the malevolent roar of the gigantic engine. On their promotional website they say the following: 'Note to Guests: the only barrier between you and the full force of gravity is your harness'. Comforting? NOT!

I feel that it's important to talk about the driver. The kind of people who do this for a living are, in my humble opinion, a menace to society. Their eyes always seem to be staring at some far distant point on the horizon (certain death?) and they are always smiling in that way that suggests they know something you don't. Something that usually involves prolonged screaming. They also look like they haven't started shaving. Our driver ticked all these boxes. Come to think of it, this sounds remarkably like someone I know.

SAM

A few hours later, next on the agenda at Oxbow Adventure 'Paradise' were jet sprint boats! The pond was still and the silence, after the vehicle's mighty roar, was welcoming. Comfortable beanbags and chairs were set up along its shoreline. 'Oh, thank God. Perhaps a little calm paddling, perhaps some boating?' Graham's teeth chattered. 'A punt, perhaps, or a harmless row boat?'

'I know how you hate kayaks and the like,' I replied, 'so this is a little more . . . safe.'

'No, I don't hate them, it's you I hate; being in a precarious situation on water with a madman at the helm,' he grumbled, fingering the safety helmet, unable to release the safety mechanism.

'Well, you'll be pleased, I'm not in charge this time but there is someone I want you to meet . . . Sam! Meet Graham.'

At that moment, a blond boy appeared, similar in height and build to me, perhaps younger (more like 15 and barely past puberty) with a huge shit-eating grin (as my American friends charmingly describe it! Ha-ha). My double shook Graham's already trembling hand firmly. 'Wait, WHAT?! He's a Kiwi version of you?! And he's called SAM?!' Graham stared in disbelief. How had he been duped into this day from hell only to find himself confronted with not one but two adrenaline junkie madmen named after an annoying hobbit?

'Yeah, hi, you ready to go?!' Sam #2 smiled, his teeth taking up half his face, as if he was in a constant state of excitement (or terror).

'Sure, Sam, how bad can it be?' I smiled back, trying to calm McTavish, who had gone suspiciously quiet.

'Pretty bad, Sam,' he replied and coaxed us under the safety cage and into the tight confines of a small motorboat (with a VERY large engine). 0–100km/h (0–62mph) in 2.5 seconds, these jet sprint boats didn't mess around. Luckily, McTavish had no time to object; the whole day he had blindly got on with it, as if shell-shocked. The adrenaline had affected his ability to think straight and he'd followed me into each activity like a demure and complacent New Zealand sheep. At this moment, I didn't feel bad – I knew there was worse to come. But I did question if the old fella's brain might not be able to take this adrenal overload. No one had ever pushed McTavish this far; we were way beyond his limits. Abseiling in Scotland had pushed him (literally) over the edge and I just didn't know how he would react, flying across a pond at 200km/h (124mph)!

His clammy hand clutched mine. [Graham: I DID NOT HOLD YOUR HAND!] He braced his head back into the tight seat and I wondered if his eyes were closed under the dark sunglasses; I suspected they were. 'All right boys, ready, hold on tight!' Sam #2 lined the little boat up on the short pond and, as I wondered what would happen when he hit the far end, suddenly, we were there!

The boat had leaped across the water; spray and wind caught in my throat as I screamed:

'Fuuuuuuuuuuuuuuuuuuuuuuuuuuuuuuuuuuuuu . . . . . .'

A sharp turn – impossible to comprehend how we didn't just shoot off across the beach and into the mountainside – and the boat shot back across the water to the pier and launchpad we had just left. We spun and slalomed across the pond, the boat zigzagging and cutting in different directions. I screamed, laughed and shouted for more, but my zombie friend remained completely silent. It wasn't until Sam #2 cut the engines and we glided back into the harbour that Graham moved to speak.

'Where . . . where did you learn to do that? I mean, you're not old enough; you're a child!' he stammered slowly, as if revived from some deep slumber, pond water and dirt dripping from his soggy beard.

'Yeah, you're right, I just turned 18, but I played a lot of computer games,' Sam#2 super-smiled back. *[Graham: Once again, I rest my case.]*

Firmly on dry ground and once able to walk straight, I made sure Graham had plenty of food (and some more coffee, just to keep his heart going and the adrenaline up). This next activity would be a real challenge and one I wasn't sure we would both survive . . .

***

DAY SEVEN, AFTERNOON

Location: Paradise, Glenorchy, northern end of Lake Wakatipu, Otago, South Island

SAM

In 1987, when Kiwi A J Hackett threw himself off the Eiffel Tower with nothing but a thick elastic rope around his ankle, he announced to the world that his homeland was ready for action. The following year, the world's first commercial bungee jump opened at the Kawarau Bridge, a few miles east of Queenstown. Mercifully for Graham, he would not be partaking in the 43-m (141-ft) jump at Kawarau today. However, he was still going to be high up, far, far above the ground because, drum roll . . . it was time to present Graham with his meaty main course (and I'd been really, really looking forward to this moment . . .).

We were going ZIP-LINING!

We headed north in our trusty van, the crew in convoy, to Glenorchy, at the top of Lake Wakatipu – a picturesque mountainside town with a strong and whisky-sounding Scottish name. The original Glen Orchy in Scotland is actually just a wee glen in Argyll and Bute with no settlement, only a few tumbledown buildings. It was home to the infamous Clan MacGregor until they were outlawed in 1603 by King James VI and the Bridge at Glen Orchy is depicted in the 1995 film *Rob Roy* (the eponymous lead played by Liam Neeson) as the place of the attempted lynching of Rob Roy MacGregor for rustling cattle.

Thankfully, Graham wasn't going to be lynched today and he'd also been cured of his vertigo after completing an abseil in our first instalment of *Men in Kilts* on the Isle of Skye. I felt proud of my contribution to helping the Grey One, who'd overcome so much since we met. *[Graham: I hadn't been cured. Crucified off a cliff, more like, my fears compounded.]* So, zip-lining in Glenorchy was going to be a walk in the park for Our Graham. Well, almost. Imagine dangling 30m (100ft) up, whizzing extremely fast through paradise – a walk in the park. Ha-ha. Weeeee! He was going to LOVE it.

We parked up at the Paradise Lines location and the crew began to unload the vans and to set up. Consisting of eight zip lines totalling a 1-km (0.62-mile) distance, my co-conspirator, Kevin-the-director, and I exchanged glances. We had successfully lured McTavish to this final adrenaline location simply by telling him the name: Glenorchy.

'Ah yes, I know Glen Orchy in Scotland, I'm very fond of the place. They have a great hotel there . . . an amazing menu.' My companion perked up at the thought of a tasting menu. But as he got out of the camper, he wasn't looking so perky. However, because he felt zip lines were in his comfort zone – because he'd 'done it when the kids were younger' (probably at a playground and only a foot off the ground!), he was putting on a good show.

Kevin-the-director took me to one side, barely stifling his sniggers. He pointed up into the forest canopy. 'He-he, how about we get him up there?! You keep him occupied, strap him in and then we record him going over the edge!' A New Yorker, high-energy and creative, Kevin could belong on stage in a dive comedy bar in downtown Manhattan. *[Graham: Minus the comedy part.]* With a sharp wit and an evil genius mind, we had schemed together throughout the morning to lure McTavish to his doom (while creating Starz TV gold!).

'You just need to wear some safety equipment, Graham,' I said. 'You know how Miss Squeezy is with health and safety.' And before McTavish could argue, Squeezy appeared with a harness, helmet and large pair of gloves for each of us and quickly manhandled Graham into his zip-line gear with her surprisingly strong forearms and wrench-like grip. Kevin gave me the me the thumbs up behind his back. Perhaps the prior activities had helped to deaden Graham's reflexes and self-preservation mechanism, because he didn't even put up a fight.

'It's a bit of a walk to the top,' said Kevin. 'I mean the view . . . ya gonna schvitzin!' And with that he scuttled off up the steep climb through the forest to the hidden clifftop drop.

'Director? More like a dictator! You sure about this, mate, not sure I trust the snivelling bugger?' Graham paused on the rocky path.

'Yeah, it'll be fine, bud, better keep going, don't want to miss the view,' I replied. 'Besides, Squeezy was eyeing up your harness – she probably wants to tighten it!'

Graham instinctively reached down between his legs and adjusted himself. 'Christ! It's the only part of me that *doesn't* hurt! Save yourself,' he whispered over his shoulder and hurriedly shuffled up the forest path, disappearing into the trees. Fifteen minutes later we reached the top and were panting hard. Graham suggested a 'break'. I agreed, knowing to go gently with the old goat. I looked around me and couldn't fully take in the beauty of the aptly named

Paradise Lines. I looked over at Graham, who was still panting, the grandeur temporarily lost on him as he hotly anticipated what was to come.

I spied Kevin a little way off, standing close to the cliff edge. He was bent over, hand on his mouth, trying to stifle a scream, or perhaps trying not to throw up. Either the cliff was terrifyingly high or the short hike had dislodged the grime in his NYC lungs and he was coughing up black soot. Either way, I knew the plan must go ahead. We had led Graham this far and the payoff was about to happen.

'So, zip-lining, feeling good about it, mate?' I casually asked, throwing a pine cone into the forest, hoping to distract him from the actual question. His verbal agreement was all I needed; after that, any repercussions were on him. Callous, I know, but I knew I wouldn't hear the end of it and needed a firm alibi should he or his wife Garance decide to berate me afterwards for throwing my bearded friend off yet another cliff.

'Oh, I've done it before with the kids, I was fine. It was just a little one, a couple of feet off the ground, which went slowly. They loved it,' he happily reminisced.

'Mmn, good. Well, this'll be easy. Let's get you going so we can get back to the hotel in time for dinner,' I baited my hapless, hungry victim. 'Each zip line is named after a *Lord of the Rings* character and, guess what? Our instructor, Dougie, is from Scotland!' I called after him as Graham was led down a small ravine towards an invisible precipice.

Dougie said, 'Hi' and Graham visibly relaxed knowing there was a Caledonian connection. 'Oh, you're from Scotland,' he said. 'What brought you heeeerrrrrrrrrrrrr . . .' Graham went very pale and totally silent. Not because of the beautiful views of Mount Aspiring or Paradise but owing to the perilous 200-m (656-ft) canyon, with a sheer drop to the rushing Oxburn river and deadly rocks below.

'You're doing fine, mate!' The words stuck in my mouth and I turned to Kevin who had also grown quiet, his city skin more ashen than usual. He signalled to me with the universal sign language for 'stop' or 'end it', his hand performing a slicing action under his neck. Another interpretation would be: 'He's dead meat.' I gave Kev the thumbs up as Dougie, the-jolly-Scotsman-down-under, quickly strapped Graham onto the line and pushed him towards the edge.

'No! No . . . wait . . . am I? Where do I put my hands? What do I doooo . . .?' Graham jabbered.

'Just hold on and don't look down,' Dougie replied cheerily and with that, he gave Graham an almighty push!

Now, I could tell you Graham did not survive. Or that he lost the contents of his bowels some 200m (656ft) up over beautiful Glenorchy. But what actually happened was that he hurtled backwards to the other end of the zip line screaming, somehow managing not to pass out or have a heart attack, because Graham's natural instinct – much like the kiwi bird – is to hurl expletives while aggressively beating his chest.

'HEUUUGHAN!!!! I HATE HIM!!!!'

And . . .

'WHY??? HEUGHAN, WHYYYYYY??!'

On the other side, his feet firmly on terra firma, he half stood, half hung onto the camera crew, still screaming obscenities at me as I flew towards him across the valley, trying to capture the steep drop and terrific views on my GoPro camera. Once I reached the other side, our hero had calmed his fit of Tourette's and greeted me with a large bear hug. Or perhaps it was an attempt to strangle me, I'm unsure, the blood and adrenaline of the experience had taken over his whole frame. I'd liken him to an Orc, from the aforementioned *Lord of the Rings* (*The Hobbit*, he will no doubt counterargue), growling, drooling, sweating and squinting hard, perhaps the sunlight turning him from good guy to evil ground-dwelling monster. It was a fitting comparison as the next zip line was named 'Orc's Chasm'; it raced through a tree tunnel and a slot canyon before passing over a waterfall only metres above the river.

'Well done, mate! So proud of you,' I said, just out of striking distance. 'You did it!'

Graham, doubled over, his hands on knees, pleaded breathlessly: 'Thank you, but please can we go home now?'

'Sure, we're done. But the only way back is down the valley. Only seven lines to go!' Graham stood tall and looked me in the eye. 'If I can do that jet boat and the off-road buggy thing, off a ruddy cliff and not eat lunch and survive without caffeine, then I can damn well do anything . . .!'

'Anything?' I repeated. 'I'm sure you can . . .' I smiled from under my safety helmet, adjusted my harness and gave Kevin the director a thumbs up from behind my back. Little did Graham know we would push him further than even I could imagine. That is if he survived the next few days . . .

GRAHAM

I have actually always enjoyed zip-lining. It's a regular feature of my holidays with my kids. After having had my central nervous system torn into little pieces and scattered to the wind during our monster truck/jet boat assault at the hands of pubescent thrill-seekers, I was looking forward to the relative calm of gently gliding through the air from the safety of a steel cable strung between two points. I was on safe ground (even if it was in mid-air).

So I approached this particular day with a sunny, positive outlook. I remember turning to Sam as we set off on the hour-long drive to the location away from the jet boat lake where I had screamed myself hoarse, saying: 'I think I'm going to enjoy this. I love a zip line! It should be fun.' Looking back with the benefit of traumatized hindsight, I should've found Sam's reaction deeply suspicious.

For a start he said nothing. Already, this is unheard of. Where was the witty response? The enthusiastic agreement? Where was the 'Absolutely, mate! Can't wait'? Instead, there was only the ghost of a smile playing on his lips as he plunged the gear stick into first. My lizard brain was trying to warn me . . . *[Sam: Muahahahaha!]* 'Open the door now!' instructed my thoughts. 'It doesn't matter that the van is moving at 25mph, just throw yourself at the mercy of the asphalt!'

But no, I ignored my brain, probably reached for a Kit-Kat and settled back to enjoy the drive. If my senses hadn't been on alert in the van, they definitely began to wake up when we arrived. For a start, it was deserted. Our resident sadist, Kevin-the-director, and his grinning companion, Squeezy, were already there. Simon 'Balls of Steel' was there assembling his 'kit'. He smiled knowingly at me – but 'knowing' what, exactly, I thought.

Kevin looked distracted. His whole attitude was exaggeratedly jolly, while Squeezy kept giggling and wrestling with her fanny pack. *[Sam: A nervous twitch.]* All of this was beginning to add up to alarm bells.

Then we were introduced to our guides. For a start, one of them had that 'I've never needed to shave because I'm so impossibly young' look (you see what I mean about a pattern?). The other was . . . Scottish. The type of Scot that is a certain breed. The breed that created the abseiling instructor, or the Glencoe chairlift operator. You can see the expectation in their eyes that you, Graham, are just going to be another spineless coward that they have to look after.

How right they were.

We were given a safety briefing and took part in a demo, which involved hooking and unhooking ourselves and our ball-chafing harnesses to a static line suspended between two poles. For some reason I found even this alarming. I'd never had to do this before. Then I looked around for the first zip line. Where was it? That's when I became aware that Simon 'if-it-isn't-terrifying-I'm-not-going' and the rest of the crew were beginning to hike. Uphill. Sam slapped me on the back with a hearty, 'Let's go, mate!'

In my experience, this invariably warrants the response, 'Let's not.'

The climb went on and on. A steep, zigzagging path with no sign of an ending. Our harnesses and carabiners jingled like a pair of carthorses. It was only when I saw the crew stop and start to unload that I knew we'd arrived. Kevin went forward to scout ahead. Sam trotted along to join. I didn't.

Then I heard Sam utter the immortal words 'Oh shit,' accompanied by a burst of laughter. That should've been my cue to dump my harness and select reverse. Instead, I found myself walking forwards, towards the source of 'Oh shit'. My legs seemed to be more curious than the rest of me because my brain was definitely thinking, 'This is not good.' But my legs just couldn't wait to see what awaited the rest of me.

Then I saw it. It was as if the forest had just given up growing at a certain point. There were no more trees. That was because the land had also given up growing.

It was a chasm.

Not a gap.

Not a divide.

A chasm with maximum yawning attached.

An aching void with only the glint of the sun bouncing from the endless steel cable that stretched away from me into the distance. I should add that what constituted 'the distance' was probably in another time zone. Perhaps even a different season of the year, such was its mind-bending dimension. The zip line (for that is what it was) disappeared into the treeline of a faraway zip code, with a vanishing point which made it impossible to know if it was in fact attached to anything at all, apart from a few hopes and prayers.

I couldn't speak.

'Are you all right, mate?' said Sam. Which in Sam-speak actually means, 'I know you're shitting it; all of my dreams have come true.'

[Sam: True, true.]

I thought of the abseiling on Kilt Rock on Skye. It was like *Groundhog Day*, even down to the dour Scot placed in charge of my safety. Kevin asked who wanted to go first. I still couldn't speak. So Sam came to my rescue. 'Graham will go first.'

I could feel the eyes of the crew upon me. I think I heard our Scottish guide mutter something like, 'Don't worry, you'll be fine.' But he could have equally said, 'You're fu#*ed.' He ran through a series of instructions which just sounded like white noise. Kevin was barking encouragement. 'You've got this. Go, Graham.'

Go where? To my death? A familiar feeling was beginning to rise within me. A mixture of nausea, disbelief and rage. He'd done it again! Again!!! The ghost of a smile should've warned me. He knew. He knew it would terrify me. He'd probably scouted the location for this exact reaction. At the very least, he'd probably googled, 'Where can I make Graham McTavish shit himself on a zip line?' I'd always loved zip lines. I'd never been fearful of them. *[Sam: You fool.]* But that was before I'd encountered a zip line fashioned by Satan.

I was instructed to sit into the harness and hold on to the carabiner clip to stop myself twisting in the wind (yes, just like a hanging corpse). The guide said he'd count to three and then push.

It was at this point I genuinely felt like I couldn't do it. I was hyperventilating, my hands were gripping the carabiner clip like a crazed chimp, and I said: 'Wait! Wait! I'm not sure I can do this!'

In fairness, no one insisted I go. No one dismissed my fear, because this was real fear. (Hello darkness, my old friend.) I genuinely felt like I couldn't do it. And then my mind settled (or perhaps the ego had landed) and I gave voice to the thought that was bubbling in my mind and I said: 'Let's go.'

And then . . . I did.

CHAPTER NINE

There Be Sharks

DAY EIGHT, MORNING

<u>Location: Invercargill, southern tip, South Island</u>

SAM

The day started at dawn. Graham was even more difficult to rouse than usual, his adrenaline levels having crashed after yesterday. We gave him latte after latte in an attempt to jump-start the old banger and finally, we were on the road again, Graham groaning, as we drove south in the Kiwi Kramper to Invercargill, the southernmost and westernmost city in New Zealand.

We met the crew at the marina. Graham blanched on arrival, suddenly remembering what was in store: CAGE SHARK DIVING. He walked sombrely down the jetty to our boat, which we climbed aboard. *[Graham: The boat was the exact replica of the boat from JAWS!!!]*

I looked down at the emaciated buoy (why do Americans pronounce it 'booo-eeee'?) and considered the enormous ocean-dwelling creature that could have decimated this large plastic safety device. 'We. Are. Gonna. Need. A. Bigger. Boat,' Graham breathed in my ear, the first of his many *Jaws* quotes.

The buoy was cut into many pieces, as if a whole family of sharks had used it to sharpen their teeth, hundreds of bite marks covering its surface. Noticing our stares and procrastination, the captain, a swarthy, bearded fellow who I suspected had an anchor tattoo on his chest, hoisted the broken device from the floor and tossed it overboard. 'Argh, that's no shark, just gets cut up when we hit the sides of the dock,' he said in a growl, and wandered off, hiding a large bloodstained machete in a bin. I gulped and looked at my bearded companion. 'Perhaps I've gone too far?' I wondered. I sort of like the old bugger.

As we headed out across the blue, we inhaled the sea air and took a moment to catch our breath. The schedule of this trip was gruelling, even for me. The plan today was to drop anchor off Stewart Island (New Zealand's third-largest island) in the Foveaux Strait, located 30km (18 miles) south of South Island. To the rear of this questionable ocean-going vessel, a large cage was attached. The size of a small bus, it looked big enough to keep any marauding mammals out, or in fact, keep us locked in, with one small weakness . . . 'It has bloody great holes in it!' Mr McBreathy squealed, his waterproof fishing gear possibly hiding the excrement dripping down his leg. 'Keep all body parts inside the cage', the safety sign commanded. The cage, despite its robust frame, had viewing holes all around, which even I could see a nosey great white could easily jam its mouth through and use our body parts as toothpicks.

'Oh great, so this is how it all ends? I've survived being thrown off a cliff, driven at breakneck speed by a moron and oh, yes, sleeping next to you each night in that crusty camper van; even the questionable handbrake has survived to see another day but this? This! This is how I'm going to die . . .?' McTavish muttered to himself as the shark-diving boat powered out into the blue yonder, in search of some hungry fish.

We stood shivering on deck. Graham was staring at something, as if he'd seen a ghost. He pointed slowly, looking down, 'What . . . the hell . . . is that?' I looked, hoping I wouldn't see a member of the Jaws family sucking on my leg, but he was actually pointing at my swimming trunks. 'Oh, these? They're budgie-smugglers,' I admitted. 'And they have pineapples on, and sharks hate citrus, and pineapple on pizza, I imagine, so I thought it'd put them on to put them off, so to speak!'

'Firstly,' said Graham gravely, 'sharks don't eat pizza. Secondly, you'll be wearing a wetsuit, so they won't see your pineapples, you tit!' Graham barked the last word, which meant he was beginning to really freak out. We were now far out in the Foveaux Strait, miles from land; Graham had no way of escaping his fate. The safety video, moments earlier, had reinforced the realization that he most likely wouldn't survive this adventure. The video had told us of the multiple ways we could be injured: drowning, crushed by the cage, trapped in the winch, slipping on the wet deck, falling down the stairs, hit by moving equipment, or bored to death by Graham's geological facts! But it had failed to mention the obvious: EATEN by a bloody gigantic great white . . .

'SHAAAARRRRKRKKK!'

Graham bellowed, his voice scaring off the seagulls feeding on the chum floating on the water. A splash behind me and the brief visitor was gone. 'What did you see?' I asked excitedly.

'A bloody shark thing! Well, I think it was a shark – tail, head, big black eyes . . . whiskers . . .' He stopped.

'A seal,' I smiled and patted him on the shoulder. His beard drooped. 'You saw a seal; now let's get those wetsuits on, sharks wait for no man . . . pineapples or not.'

'GGGGGgggaahhhh . . . puff puff puff . . . . . . arrrrrrg hhhhyoubloodyOHMYGODddddd!!' Graham groaned, similar to the sounds he made in the bathroom each morning, although this time it was in public.

The wetsuits were tight. In all the wrong places. We had to dislocate an arm and a hip to pull them on. My pineapples hidden from view, finally encased in rubber, we stood on the side of the submerged cage, ready to descend into the cold water below. Graham looked like an extra in a 1940s aquatic war movie, his moustache poking out of the face mask like our seal-friend's whiskers.

'You first,' I offered kindly. 'You've come this far . . . AND did I mention how proud I am of you?' I added, trying to coax him down the steps into the awaiting death trap.

'Nope. No. Not me. You. You go. Not I. Noooo way.' He stood, arms folded defiantly. So I pulled down my mask, turned on the GoPro and slid into the water, hoping to lead by example, like a Scottish synchronized swimming display team – without the skill, or music.

Once under water, it was a different world. I took a second to get my bearings. Looking out of the really rather large viewing holes, I could see maybe 3–6m (10–20ft) away. The water was murky and swirled around the boat, smashing the cage against its hull. A small shoal of fish of mixed varieties held a mini food festival on the surface, nibbling at the chum and a large piece of tuna tail used as the shark lure. I looked up and could see Graham's shapely thighs in the water. I waited for him to descend the ladder and join me in our aquatic tomb . . .

I waited.

And waited.

And waited.

Inch by inch, he lowered himself, imperceptibly, and around twenty minutes later . . . he *still* wasn't underwater. My fingers were freezing and, although I prayed for warmer waters, I just hoped he wasn't taking a leak in his wetsuit!

I'm not sure if someone pushed him, but he finally slipped under the surface and found the foot loops on the bottom of the cage to anchor himself in. We looked at one another; I shrugged and tried to clear the water from my mask, blowing air from the mouthpiece. Suddenly, Graham pointed. A beautiful seven- or eight-foot great white shark appeared out of the gloom and swam towards us.

The *Jaws* theme tune played in my head. It circled in front of our widened eyes, turned quickly, nosing the tuna and disappeared behind us. I gulped oxygen down and turned in the cage to see where it had gone. 'Clever shark,' I thought. You could tell it knew what we were up to, as it inquisitively watched us from behind and underneath the boat's hull. I looked back; no sooner had the shark vanished than the shoal of fish reappeared and recommenced their watery fiesta. 'Whooo hooo! Hey guys, free food. Yeah, the shark is gone, let's party . . .! SHIT!'

The shoal vanished and suddenly the shark reappeared right by my head. I angled my arm, making sure not to poke it out of the cage, and recorded on my GoPro the shark's every turn and attempt to bite the tuna bait. It was beautiful, majestic and, with the help of my fishy pals, I could tell when he was coming back for a bite.

I looked at Graham and our accompanying camerawoman; we were getting some good footage and Graham had lasted ten minutes underwater . . . before, dramatically, he decided it was enough. Then, vying for a better angle of us, the camerawoman moved back and used her feet to straddle the cage, one leg poking through the gap and her elbow also out of the protective bars. I looked around hurriedly – the fish-party was in full swing. I signed to the camerawoman and gargled in the water. 'Watch out!' (Bubble, bubble.) 'Your leg! Your leg!' (Cough, splutter.) She noticed and swiftly rose to the surface alongside Graham, who had indeed called it quits. I too was turning pale from the icy water and decided it was best not to die of hypothermia.

Safely back on deck, we congratulated ourselves with coffee and a large nip of whisky. 'Well done, mate! You survived . . . again!' I slapped Mr McJaws on the back. Graham sucked down some scalding whisky-laced coffee and grimaced, 'No thanks to you! *However*, that was truly mesmerizing.'

'Yes, it was, wasn't it?' I grinned, feeling elated and refreshed by the cold water. 'Let's just see what's next! Plus, I think I just proved sharks don't like pineapples!'

'Noooooo,' Graham moaned and emptied the flask of whisky into his mug.

GRAHAM

The thing about a shark is he's got lifeless eyes. Black eyes. Like a doll's eyes. When he comes at ya, he doesn't even seem to be livin'. . . till he bites ya, and those black eyes roll over white and then . . . ah then you hear that terrible high-pitched screamin'. The ocean turns red, and despite all your poundin' and your hollerin' those sharks come in and . . . they rip you to pieces. – Robert Shaw as Quint in the movie Jaws.

*[Sam: Urgh! Graham performed this soliloquy **every hour on the hour for the whole day**. I was ready to push him overboard if I heard it one more time . . . Tonight, you'll sleep with the fishes, McT!!]*

Reader, what do you think of when I say: great white shark? I'm pretty sure a lot of you immediately have the *Jaws* theme tune running through your head? Me too! In fact, I can hear it now. Possibly one of the most chilling tunes ever composed. I wonder what John Williams would have come up with if he'd been forced into a shark cage with Sam Heughan. Possibly the sound of nails being hammered into coffins? Prolonged screaming?

People have bucket lists of things like:

- *Swimming with dolphins, which always seems popular even though I suspect the dolphins spend the whole time laughing at us.*
- *Climbing Mount Everest – Sam definitely will have that on HIS list, with the added detail of doing it in a sleeveless top. [Sam: Correct. For once. This is top of my list.]*
- *Seeing the Northern Lights.*
- *Sleeping in the Ice Hotel (God knows why). [Sam: I can imagine you complaining all night.]*

In other words, the cliché-ridden, boring, predictable stuff.

And some people go shark cage diving, people like Sam Heughan and other lobotomized individuals. Personally, I would put this in a different bucket – one with 'Please flush the contents down the toilet' written on it.

Here is my bucket list:

- *Doing a sommelier course. [Sam: I've started one actually. Well, I paid for the course and am drinking wine.]*
- *Buying a Hästens mattress. (Try one. You will cry with joy.)*
- *Going to Iceland (mainly for the spa treatments). [Sam: You do love a spa.]*

You get the picture.

But here I am in Invercargill, at the base of the South Island, about to board a small boat to look for sharks, climb into a tiny cage, lower the aforementioned cage into the water to find them and then know true fear.

There are three things high up on my list of 'The Things I Dread':

1. Enclosed spaces
2. Being underwater
3. Sharks
4. Doing all of the above with Sam Heughan

Between them, Kevin (our director, henceforth to be known as Beelzebub) and Lucifer's ginger helper himself, Sam Heughan, had contrived to combine all three of these things I dread in a smorgasbord of sphincter-clenching ghastliness. The boat had a picture of a great white shark on its side which covered the length of the vessel. The skipper (an excessively jolly salty sea dog) informed us that this was life size. Sam rubbed his hands with glee. I muttered obscenities.

It was time to get onboard. I'm pretty sure Sam tried to rock the boat as I stepped across the gap to board. *[Sam: Oh, how I chortled.]* We then went on a very long boat trip in search of the sharks. Sam took this opportunity to show me videos of shark incidents. One showed a shark getting INSIDE the cage (like a particularly crowded elevator where one of the occupants has multiple rows of razor-sharp teeth and a thirst for blood), another showed a great white landing ON the boat. Yes, you read that correctly.

ON THE BOAT. A shark . . . a boat, and a shark ON IT. He may have shown me a live feed of surfers being dismembered by these monstrous finned carnivores but I had let my mind drift off to a safer, happier place – having a root canal, perhaps, or being repeatedly kicked in the balls.

We arrived at shark central and it was time to suit up. I'm not a big fan of wetsuits; they remind me of a neoprene version of a strait jacket. We stripped down to our swimming trunks, which is when I noticed that Sam seemed to be wearing something stolen from a women's lingerie shop. When I say small, imagine a few strings of dental floss and an eye patch sewn together. On went the suits and yet another chance to force ourselves into giant prophylactics. After nearly dislocating my shoulders, I finally stood wearing a pair of goggles inside a neoprene hood with my beard sprouting from all sides. I looked like a tit. *[Sam: You said it!]*

We wafted around aimlessly for quite a while, me impersonating a beard in a gimp suit while Sam fantasized about being James Bond. It was then I noticed that our skipper (Long John? Bluebeard? He almost certainly wore a hook and a parrot) was dangling a giant dead tuna over the side of the boat. It took my brain a few minutes to process why he might be doing this. He was luring the sharks.

This epiphany was interrupted by a shout from the starboard side. 'SHARK!'

Now, like me, you probably hope to live your entire life without hearing that word being bellowed at you while you're on a boat. He might as well have yelled, 'SHIT YOURSELVES!' What I saw gliding by the boat was nothing short of a vision from Hades. My eyes struggled to process its size but I quickly realized I could lie comfortably next to this leviathan and still have plenty of room for my feet. In other words, it could swallow me whole.

I can't remember what I said. It was probably gibberish, which is my preferred language when possessed by naked fear. As I was still putting my eyes back in my head, Kevin shouted 'Okay, time to get in the water.' Before I knew it, Sam was climbing over the side, regulator in his mouth, sliding into the ocean like an oversized otter. It was my turn. Now, I need to point out I have never worn a regulator, never breathed underwater so it took an eternity for me to just do that. *[Sam: You suggested we use this footage in the show. If we had, the episode would have lasted HOURS!]* I gingerly let my mouth bob under the surface, fighting the urge to rip the regulator out and start swallowing water in blind panic. As my head finally fell below the surface, all I could think of was the roaring of air bubbles as I breathed in and out, my eyes wide open in a silent scream. I turned at the bottom and saw Sam doing his best *Thunderball* impersonation. There was a camerawoman there too, guiding my feet into loops to stop me bobbing to the surface. *[Sam: Which wasn't her job.]*

In front of me was the 'viewing hole'. The crucial thing to grasp is: *it was A HOLE*. A part of the cage with no bars, almost like a welcome mat for great whites and exactly the kind of thing I'd just seen a shark squeezing through in one of those ghastly videos Sam had shown me. I looked around wildly. Partly on the lookout for the shark and partly for pitiful reassurance. Sam began a series of diving signals. You know, the kind of annoying stuff people who dive know and like to demonstrate constantly. I responded with the only signal that came to mind.

And then I saw a shift in the gloomy depths beyond the bars.

Was that . . .?

There WAS something.

Sam gesticulated madly, but I needed no signals to tell me what was approaching.

Almost absent-mindedly, vaguely bored, mildly curious, a gigantic shape emerged from the murky ocean in front of us.

A great white shark.

Jaws come to life. I'd stepped through the movie screen and I was there staring transfixed through what now appeared to be the flimsiest of defences complete with a massive hole, in front of an apex predator that was coming to see ME.

I looked into its eyes.

All I can say is . . . Robert Shaw was right. I was staring at a creature with no empathy, devoid of pity, a moving absence of compassion. And then I stopped staring at Sam and looked at the shark. *[Sam: Touché.]*

And then it drifted down beneath us and away.

Apart from the sudden realization that it could come BENEATH US, I also knew it would be back. I was right, and this time he brought his friends. Suddenly, the cage was surrounded by gliding beasts, all wondering the same thing: can we eat the bearded tit and his friend? Then they saw the tuna. I cannot begin to describe the change in speed. From an idle drift to a full-on maximum acceleration at warp speed. The tuna was torn to pieces. After a few more minutes of this eye-popping spectacle, I decided to call it a day and headed to the surface.

Looking back, it really was amazing. To be in the presence of this mythical creature, an animal summoned by the devil, and to look into its eyes, like staring into the abyss, was an unforgettable experience . . . and then, of course, there was the shark. *[Sam: Chortle, chortle.]*

But fortunately, yet again, I'm grateful I hadn't forgotten to bring a change of underwear. *[Sam: Should have worn pineapple ones like mine.]* In fact, nowadays, even if I meet Sam for a drink . . . I always come prepared.

CHAPTER TEN

The Far North and Graham's Favourite Massacres, Part Deux

'History is a gallery of pictures in which there are few originals and many copies.'
Alexis de Tocqueville, *L'Ancien Régime et la Révolution*

DAY NINE: TRAVELLING DAY

Location: The Far North District, northern part of the Northland Peninsula, Te Ika-a-Māui/North Island

GRAHAM

As our journey takes us by plane to the North Island of New Zealand, called Te Ika-a-Māui by the Māori, I want to spend a little time talking about one of my favourite parts of the country, 'The Far North', and in my experience one of the least visited. *[Sam: It's similar to Mordor. That's why he likes it.]*

The drive northwards along the coast, immediately west of Auckland, is one of the highlights of any New Zealand trip, taking you through the wonderful wild black sand beach communities of Piha, Bethells, and Muriwai. Surfing here is BIG, but I somehow managed to keep Sam off the surfboard and we pushed on up to the very tip of the country, Cape Reinga, where the Pacific and Tasman Oceans meet. This is the place where Māori legend has it that the spirits of their dead leaped into the sea from an 800-year-old Pohutukawa tree to begin their final journey to Hawaiki, their ancestral home.

Nestling on the sheltered east coast is the Bay of Islands. It is incredibly beautiful (even in a country where beautiful has literally become a synonym for New Zealand itself). Unspoilt beaches with barely a soul on them, the quiet coves around the town of Russell are linked by a chain of picture-perfect islands. No wonder it was chosen as the original capital of New Zealand. This region occupies the portion of land that resembles a finger pointing north; on one side is the drama of a 144-km (90-mile) beach and on the other, the sheltered landscape of rivers, bays and subtropical vegetation. I've said before that the country as a whole resembles a child's imaginary perfect island landscape, possessing everything that one needs for adventure and variety. It's always that bit warmer in the north because it's subtropical and Russell itself is a delight. I remember a visit to a particularly idyllic beach called Oke Bay, reached via a vertiginous descent down a long, narrow staircase finishing on a beautiful, isolated beach. My family and I spent the afternoon lazing in the sun with a picnic, the only people there . . .

[Sam: Graham's picnics are actually nine-course tasting menus with wine pairing, amuse-bouche and the necessary condiments, all packed into wicker baskets and served by gentlemen sporting small moustaches and dodgy European accents.]

Eventually, a boat sailed into the bay. A man emerged and canoed to the shore. After a brief spell of sun and sand, he paddled back to his boat, anchored some way off. As he began to head off, he casually called back to us: 'Oh, be careful swimming; there's a group of hammerhead sharks here, babies and mothers, so just keep an eye out.'

The breathtaking off-hand nature of this warning left me momentarily at a loss for words.

It was the kind of tone you'd reserve for recommending a good restaurant, 'Yeah, try the fish and chip place down the road, you might like it.' Except this was imparting a very different meaning: 'Maybe don't go swimming in case you have your testicles chewed off by hammerheads.' Needless to say, the swimming trunks stayed dry. *[Sam: Replace 'trunks' with 'Victorian pantaloons'.]*

Now, even with the hammerhead shark residency, it's hard to imagine that Russell – the favourite destination of tourists, and a playground for wealthy yacht owners and their extravagant clifftop homes – was once known as the Hell Hole of the Pacific.

Why was it so hellish? I hear you ask. Well, it depends on who you asked. Victorian moralists definitely didn't approve, describing it as 'the very stronghold of vice' because it was the principal deep port for whaling ships. The crews would stay weeks at a time and those hard-working whale slaughterers needed their rest and relaxation. This consisted mainly of a staggering number of bars, pubs and shops selling liver-numbing booze (a sort of early franchise of Sassenach whisky), and bringing boat loads of syphilis onshore. The prodigious consumption of alcohol (the kind that would make even Duncan Lacroix blush and call for an Uber) inevitably led to an equal amount of vicious brawling and violent death.

When they weren't drinking and attempting to see how many ships' crew they could send to the hospital, the visitors would be searching high and low for prostitutes. *[Sam: Sounds like a great summer destination!]* With 30–35 whaling ships at anchor at any one time, there were 400–500 crewmen prowling the streets desperate for 'romance'. There were probably around 400–500 prostitutes working in this tiny village. Many of them were local Māori women who would use their wages to purchase muskets and powder for their tribe while tolerating three-week-long 'marriages', often resulting in the lover's name being tattooed on to their arms. Told you they were looking for romance! *[Sam: When are you getting my name on your forearm?]*

Imagine a carousal of whalers, adventurers, deserters and escaped Australian convicts creating a hot mess of drunkenness, with every imaginable kind of vice known to humanity on display – a town full of 500 Black Jack Randalls. And, where there is a multitude of vice, you also find missionaries, and Russell was no exception. It was known as Kororāreke then. They probably changed the name because Russell is easier to say when you're absolutely hammered on the booze and oozing with the pox. The Christians were kept very busy there and the original church still stands to this day. It's well worth a visit.

But Russell was also where the early European arrivals came into contact with the local Māori tribe, the Ngāpuhi. Their chief, Hōne Heke, proved to be very enthusiastic about chopping down flagpoles. It seems Hōne Heke wasn't a fan of a bunch of pissed, sex-mad sailors turning his local village into a modern-day Gomorrah. He had actually gifted the flagpole to the British, but after the Treaty of Waitangi, he began to regard the British as a bunch of thieving bastards who had managed to con the local tribes into giving up the land in return for . . . Well, that's something that is hotly debated to this day. But as far as Hōne Heke was concerned, it was time to take back the gift. This involved climbing to the top of the hill and taking an axe to the aforementioned pole.

Not to be deterred, the British put up another pole. No sooner was it up than it was time for Hōne Heke to take a hike up the hill with his very sharp axe. This happened a total of four times! I wonder if he used the same axe every time, or did he replace the original with an even bigger one? One can almost imagine the local Brits settling down to a night of eye-watering debauchery only to have it disturbed again by the rhythmic sound of wood being slowly chopped into by Hōne Heke's giant blade.

'Have you seen the new flagpole?'

'Yes, it looks nice, doesn't it?'

'I visited it yesterday. Even better than the previous three flagpoles.'

'Absolutely, very sturdy. Very woody.'

'Hold on, what's that bloody noise?'

'Oh balls! It's that bastard, wood-chopping Māori lumberjack!'

You can still visit the flagpole today. At least Hōne Heke definitely had a great view when he was getting busy being Paul Bunyan.

***

No visit to the Far North is complete without talking about Augustus Earle. Most people won't know who he was (I certainly didn't) but he was a prodigiously talented artist from Massachusetts who had an overwhelming need to travel the world and paint EVERYTHING he saw.

Born in 1793, he eventually found his way to New Zealand in 1827, accompanied by his Scottish friend, Mr Shand. Shand remains a shadowy figure. Not much is known about him other than his Scottishness. Something true of many a Scotsman. *[Sam: And that he created a refreshing beer and lemonade drink.]*

[Graham: Very good, Sam!]

Anyway, Earle was drawn to New Zealand by an earlier encounter with Māori in Australia, whom he had already painted on his way across Australia and Brazil at this point. He had resolved to visit the Māori in the Far North, specifically Hokianga, and it was here that he sailed into view in October of 1827. Earle loved the local Māori, and they seemed to love him back. He lived with them for nine months and developed an almost uniquely close relationship with them at a time when Europeans were still relatively rare.

While he disapproved of some of the local Māori customs, he saved most of his ire for the local missionaries. (In reading his diary you can practically feel the hatred of these men leaping off the page.) Of his first encounter with the Māori of the Far North, he noted with an artist's eye: 'They were generally taller and larger men than ourselves; those of middle height were broad-chested and muscular and their limbs as sinewy as though they had been occupied all their lives in laborious employment.' (Well, that's because they HAD, Gus!) He describes their features as small and regular, their hair a profusion of beautiful curls, their disposition one of fun and gaiety. He definitely liked them.

His arrival by ship had provoked an enthusiastic response, with an epic welcoming *haka* being performed. But the joyful arrival was somewhat marred when he got to the village and found the remains of a slave boy being roasted over the fire 'with a number of hogs and pigs feasting upon it'. The unfortunate boy had been guarding the chief's *kumara* (sweet potato) patch from marauding pigs when he'd gone to marvel at the arrival of Earle's ship (something akin to a child seeing a UFO landing on his doorstep).

The chief wasn't impressed, to say the least.

'Where have you been?'

'Watching the ship. Isn't it amazing? So cool! I've never seen ANYTHING like it!'

'You were supposed to be guarding my *kumara* patch!'

'But THE SHIP! Did you see it? Like WOW!!!'

'Hmmmm, I'm afraid I'm going to have to roast you over a fire and eat you.'

'But I was only gone for a couple of minutes.'

'Yes, but the pigs could've eaten the *kumara*, you see. And I really like *kumara*. Maybe I'll cook some as a side dish.'

Earle's encounters with roast dinners didn't end there. When he and some other Europeans arrived back one day after a day's painting, and generally oohing and aahing over the natives, they found a young slave girl that they had grown to like, also being cooked slowly over the fire. So, they resolved to take matters into their own hands.

They insisted on rescuing her corpse and giving her a Christian burial, much to the outrage of the locals, who were no doubt looking forward to a hearty meal.

This prompted the chief to visit Earle and gently but firmly advise him NEVER to do that again.

'You did a foolish thing,' said Te Uruti, the chief. 'Firstly, you could've been killed and, secondly, you didn't accomplish your purpose after all, as you merely succeeded in burying the flesh near the spot on which you found it. After you went away, it was again taken up, and every bit was eaten.' I'm guessing this was the moment Augustus Earle's jaw fell open.

Te Uruti then asked what punishment the English have for thieves and runaways. Earle answered that, after a trial, it was flogging or hanging. 'Then,' replied the chief, 'the only difference in our laws is you flog and hang, but we shoot and eat.' It was an interesting lesson for Earle. To not necessarily apply the customs and morality of one culture upon another. The chief's uncomplicated logic was persuasive in making Earle understand that he'd better accept what he could not bring himself to approve.

It brings me back to the need to avoid 'presentism' and to place the actions of others in the context in which those actions took place. We know how Highland clansmen took feuding to an almost unimaginable level, sometimes over hundreds of years . . . In the same way, Māori custom and tradition dictated that something they perceived as a deep dishonour must be met with *utu*: revenge.

Furthermore, if you were an important Māori individual you were highly conscious of your personal prestige. It's what defined you. It's what inspired men to follow you, sometimes to their deaths. It was imperative. This prestige was expressed in something called *mana*. *Mana* was the spiritual manifestation of this importance; the authority, power and reputation accrued by someone through the actions of their daily lives. It was a reflection of the status they enjoyed as a result of their character and deeds, wisdom and generosity, or ferocity as a warrior. It was accrued with age and experience, and any show of disrespect towards individual or tribal *mana* was a deeply heinous offence. Mess with a guy's *mana* and you're on a fast road to *utu*. Any Highlander would've recognized this very well.

[Sam: Is this a thinly veiled threat? Are you trying to imply you have accrued a great amount of mana *and that I will experience* utu *if I continue to mess with your sensibilities?]*

[Graham: If by mana *you mean therapy, and if by* utu *you mean the bill, then yes.]*

***

Which brings me to what happened when European custom and law met Māori *mana* and *utu*. You knew it was going to lead up to this: massacre, death, vengeance, destruction. If Abel Tasman could be let off for not knowing what he was dealing with, Captain John Thompson of a ship called the *Boyd* really screwed up!

Thompson was bringing the ship back from Sydney. One of his 70 crew members was Te Ara, who happened to be the son of a chief of Whangaroa.

Now, on the voyage, Te Ara showed himself not to be the most dedicated sailor. It was the European custom for someone like Te Ara to work his passage on the boat but Te Ara was not keen on this concept of 'work'.

In other words, he disobeyed orders.

Let's, for a moment, look at this from Captain Thompson's early 19th-century point of view: here is this strapping young man, the son of a Māori chief – I think it's safe to say he wouldn't have been some overweight slob who got tired walking from his cabin. He would've been more than capable of some serious hard work.

Thompson asks him to do some of the said work. Te Ara says, 'Naaaa. I'm all right doing sod all, thanks.'

What should Thompson do?

Laugh it off? Say, 'Fair enough, Te Ara, you put your feet up while the rest of the lads get blisters on their hands the size of pumpkins.'

Nope.

He did what captains of sailing ships of the day did with recalcitrant crewmen.

In other words, the cat was well and truly out of the bag (an expression derived from when the cat o' nine tails whip was taken out of the bag in which it was stored).

The cat o' nine tails was a vicious piece of kit. Te Ara was strapped to the capstan and then given anything from 10–30 lashes of something that would've torn the flesh from his back. *[Sam: Jamie Fraser had 200+ lashes, just saying.]*

[Graham: Meanwhile, back in the real world . . .]

'That'll teach him. Perfectly justified,' thought Thompson.

Te Ara saw it differently. He'd just had his *mana* diminished.

Big mistake by Thompson, but seeing as he'd never met a Māori before, how was he to know?

Not long afterwards, Te Ara happened to mention that he knew a great spot to drop anchor, a quiet harbour with deep water and lots of great kauri trees for them to take back to England (the purpose of their voyage, as giant hardwood trees were of great value and in demand in Europe). Perfect. 'It's called Whangaroa.' Now, the observant among you would've remembered that Te Ara was rather familiar with Whangaroa, being the place where HIS ENTIRE TRIBE LIVED. On arrival, Te Ara probably said he was going to say hello to a couple of friends onshore but once on land he promptly went to visit his dad.

'Te Ara! Good to have you back, son! How was Sydney?'

'Oh, you know, big harbour, lots of convicts.'

'How was the voyage?'

'Not great, actually. The captain asked me to help out on board the ship.'

'And?'

'And I said no.'

'And?'

'And he tied me to a bloody great bollard and flogged me for twenty minutes and didn't give me any food for days.'

'WHAT THE F*#K?!'

Yes, it was *utu* time.

The captain, meanwhile, was blissfully unaware of what was happening. He and four other crew went ashore looking for kauri trees. Instead, they found a sizeable Māori gang with clubs and axes who proceeded to use these to brutally murder the five men. They then proceeded to strip the bodies and five Māori put on their clothes as a disguise. At this point I wonder whether they cared about matching men to the correct size of the clothes. Perhaps the clothes were hanging off them like suits that boys steal from their dads' closets? Or perhaps they were so small that the five disguised Māori looked like they were wearing clothes that had shrunk in the wash. While the five Māori warriors were squeezing into the blood-soaked hand-me-downs, another group took Thompson and his four friends to be cooked and eaten.

Waste not, want not.

The Māori warriors waited until dusk and rowed back to the *Boyd* in their cunning disguises to be greeted by the waiting crew. (I wonder if anyone mentioned the change in the five crewmen on their return.)

'Gosh, Captain Thompson's packed on the beef since he went ashore. He's positively bursting out of his trousers!'

'Hang on, why is he carrying an enormous bloodstained axe?'

Meanwhile, more warriors (presumably dressed in their own clothes) glided alongside and proceeded to stealthily kill and dismember most people on board. Some managed to hide in the rigging and were witness to the savage dismemberment of their pals.

The next morning, the survivors, presumably numb with terror, saw another local chief, Te Pahi, arriving by canoe. They called for help. He took them to shore whereupon the survivors tried to make a run for it along the beach. Te Pahi watched calmly as near all were caught and butchered. A total of five were spared in the massacre including a woman and her baby, the second mate, an apprentice, and a two-year-old who was kept by the chief for three weeks before being rescued. The second mate was eventually killed and eaten when his usefulness at making fish hooks was exhausted.

All in all, not quite the trip they were expecting!

I think it's important to say that we should withhold our judgement here. It is unfair to condemn something, however repugnant to our modern sensibilities, from within our present-day context. When Te Ara (or George as he was known on board ship) refused an order, there was only one path the captain could take. George had to be punished. The penalty for such disobedience and dereliction of duty was public flogging. Just as, according to the customs of Māori life, their notions of *mana* and *utu* meant that the shaming of such an important member of the tribe could also not go unpunished. On their terms, that punishment was death, not just of the perpetrators of the flogging but the witnesses as well. People who saw the affront to Te Ara's *mana* could not escape *utu*. As soon as Captain Thompson flogged the esteemed son of a Māori war chief, his fate was sealed. Any clansmen from the 18th century would've understood this.

The moral of this massacre? Don't drop anchor until you know where the father of the guy you just flogged parks his canoe.

POSTCRIPT: Speed Bonnie Boat

In talking of the Far North, I feel I have to make a short mention here of Marc-Joseph Marion du Fresne, another European, in this case French, who arrived in the Bay of Islands near present-day Russell in 1772.

He stayed several weeks. His crew enjoyed some relaxation and he did a bit of fishing while his ship was repaired.

After five weeks he and his crew were welcomed with a special ceremony.

Four days after that, Marion du Fresne was treated to another special ceremony, in this case having his brains smashed out by the same people who had welcomed him days earlier.

No one knows for sure why a pleasant stay of several weeks turned into a slaughter fest (25 crew were also killed, to which the Europeans reacted by killing 250 locals). It could've been because he ignored several warnings about unfortunate transgressions. It could've been that his crew had violated several sacred spaces known as *tapu*, which roughly translates as 'Don't even think about visiting'. Or it could've been just that they'd had enough of these particular visitors.

Five weeks is a long time when dozens of men are eating all your food. Things got a little strained, to say the least.

'Good welcoming ceremony last night, Dad, for those funny-looking guys on the boats.'

'Yeah, thanks. It was pretty expensive. A lot of *kumara* involved. Several pigs. It was kind of designed as a "Nice to meet you but when are you leaving?" kind of ceremony.'

'But they're still here, Dad.'

'I'm afraid I'll have to invite them to another "special" meeting.'

'Shall I bring my war club, Dad?'

'Deffo.'

A painting made 60 years later shows the scene. Marion du Fresne is sitting on a log on the beach obviously enjoying chatting to the Māori sitting in front of him hanging on his every word. It looks like he's having a great time.

Until he wasn't.

Unfortunately, Marion du Fresne hadn't noticed another figure in the painting, namely a bloody great warrior standing behind him holding a monstrously large war club poised to show him the exit.

I imagine that, to the Māori, he was like that annoying guest (you know the one) that has drunk all the best wine and just won't take the hint that it's time to leave. The host starts preparing for bed, he's doing the washing-up, tidying up the drinks around you, but still he won't take the hint. In the case of dear old Marion du Fresne, instead of ordering him an Uber, they just decided to beat him to death.

One last delicious irony concerning Marion du Fresne is that he was involved in another significant moment in history. A rather famous rescue, many years earlier, from a remote Scottish beach. It was in the Scottish Hebrides. The year was 1746, and his passenger was none other than the Young Pretender himself: Bonnie Prince Charlie.

Twenty-six years later, that heroic rescuer of Charlie boy found himself on another beach, far, far from that Hebridean island. About as far as you can get.

There he sat, chatting away, unaware of the warrior standing poised behind him with a monstrously large war club.

He was probably in the middle of a great story.

You can almost hear him now:

'Did I ever tell you the one about Culloden . . .?'

CHAPTER ELEVEN

Welly Wanging and Udder Adventures

DAY TEN, MORNING

Location: Taihape, Manawatū-Whanganui Region, North Island

**Taihape is the welly boot capital of New Zealand, hosting a
Gumboot Day festival every year.**

SAM

Graham was complaining again about not getting enough
'uninterrupted sleep', apparently I was kicking the sides of the van
like a demented spaniel, which is rich coming from gassy Gandalf.
He sipped his ninth latte sullenly as we headed along the west coast
of the North Island, before cutting inland towards Taihape. Not so
much a one-horse town as a one-boot town, Taihape is where the
uniquely New Zealand competitive sport of gumboot tossing was

born. And, let's just say, Welly Wanging is not a euphemism but an actual pastime, apparently. I've done some strange sports on our *Clanlands* trips – lifted random boulders, thrown a caber or two, hit some birdies and kicked an egg-shaped ball – but this took the proverbial biscuit. I will never toss in public again. It's not worth the humiliation. It is reported that the world record for throwing a rubber welly boot is 165.4m (180yd)! *[Graham: You are COMPLETELY making that up!]* Now, as someone who had been known as a part-time tosser (including the Scots hammer at our impromptu Braemar games in Scotland), that's an impressive distance!

Graham is definitely a tosser. But dare I say, a pretty poor tosser. *[Graham: Remind me who beat you at the hammer throw? Oh yes! That would've been ME!]* Gone is his grace and nimble footwork; as he spins, his kilt tends to fly up and it's just not a pretty sight. Thankfully, we had no spectators to witness this less-than-impressive feat. 'Oh dear God . . .' he moaned as he wanged.

Then came my turn. I questioned myself, 'Why am I doing this? Why wellington boots?'

Named after Arthur Wellesley, the first Duke of Wellington, who famously defeated Napoleon at the Battle of Waterloo in 1815 and had New Zealand's capital city named after him (a real high achiever!), he apparently invented gumboots when he asked a shoemaker to modify his riding boots.

Hmmm, Sassenach footwear . . .?

Our unofficial Welly Tossing guide, Chad, was a good friend of Graham's. *[Graham: His name is Jed! Jed! As I kept reminding you. One of my fellow dwarves from* The Hobbit *and an all-round top bloke]*. Ched assured me that this was indeed a dangerous sport. 'Yeah mate, could get a welly to the face, pull a hamstring, break a nail or perhaps catch a cold while tossing a gumboot.'

Not that it was possible to catch a cold today – it was 40°C (104°F) in the shade and even my sweat objected to the searing heat. We were in the town of Taihape, the gumboot-throwing capital of the world, apparently. This was confirmed by the large oversized sculpture of a wellington boot on the outskirts of the town.

We had arrived at the official tossing area *[Graham: You just love saying 'tossing', don't you?]*, a small gated park next to the local railway line. It didn't appear to be a very illustrious destination for international athletes to come and test their mettle against a rubber boot.

[Graham: It's worth speculating on how such a game was even invented. Chronic boredom? A visceral hatred of waterproof boots? Who did it first? Was he mentally impaired? Why did anyone else do it? And even if others did it, why on earth would you build a giant sculpture to celebrate it?]

Dressed in traditional local attire – a string vest, shorts, pie hat and red gumboots – Cheb *[Graham: JED!]* greeted us with enthusiasm and a selection of worn and slightly smelly boots. The idea was to throw a welly as far as we could, using any technique we wished. Who knew there were so many approaches to welly tossing? The underarm, the run-up, the chucker, the sky-high or the very technical spinning approach, hard to master but effective for a mega toss. *[Graham: See me after class.]*

'Best of three,' Jeg said cheerily. *[Graham: Sigh.]* I suspected he hadn't seen anyone for a very long time and was just delighted to have company. I watched Graham go first, a feeble attempt, 15–20m (16–21yd), which I easily smashed with a spinning lob, hitting the wire fence at around the 30-m (32-yd) mark. Graham tossed again, only slighter further than his last. I winked at Kevin-the-director; we needed to spice this up. I tried the 'up and under', knowing my toss would fall short and put myself and Graham on equal footing (excuse the pun).

As we drew level at 1–1, Graham decided to opt for a large overhand chuck. 'Oooofph, 25m!' (27yd) – Jeb pretended to be impressed; a reasonable throw but really nothing extraordinary. I knew I could beat him easily and, feeling overly confident, I spun and spun and spuuuun! Until I released the welly with as much momentum as I could muster – urghhh! It rocketed sky-high and sailed further and further away . . . until CRUMP!

Silence.

We all looked dumbfounded and confused. A slow, high-pitched whistle began to emanate from Graham's body. 'Eeeeee aaahhhaaaaaZZZZZ! Oh ho ho ho ho, I don't belieeeeeeeve it! Did you do it on purpose? Tell me you didn't do it on purpose?' he pleaded like a trapped animal, his body convulsing and shoulders shaking. I said nothing. Jed looked at the ground, trying to avoid my eyes. The boot had landed on the other side of the fence, slap bang on the railway lines, far out of the designated tossing zone. Yes, you guessed it . . . it was a disqualified toss and Graham had stuck the boot in again and won.

***

DAY TEN, AFTERNOON

Location: Aka Aka, a rural locality on the Aka Aka Stream, a tributary of the Waikato River in the Waikato Region, North Island

SAM
Dressed in our finest bucolic attire (what we thought passed for countryside farming gear), that afternoon we drove through the lush green New Zealand countryside. It was a long drive to the farmyard we were heading for, so we passed the time making cow jokes and considering what would happen if the farm had been taken over by the cows and in fact, if *they* wanted to milk *us!* Shudder. We had travelled to see a herd of cows owned by an enthusiastic farmer who was perhaps even more Scottish than I am. His kilt, ginger hair and authentic Scotch white-freckled skin made him look more suited to the Highlands than the North Island of New Zealand.

I, of course, was driving while Graham made yet another failed attempt to find snacks. The emergency stash hidden in the toilet had been pilfered by Squeezy days before. We knew it was her, as we spotted Tunnock's Teacake wrappers stuffed into her fanny pack and a thin white marshmallow line on her top lip. She kept licking her candy moustache as she drilled us in the finer points of 'bovine safety' but Graham was well versed in that and assured her he 'knew his way around a cow better than anyone'.

I wound the window down to let the air in as we hit a dirt track. The GPS would take us no further and Graham's map-reading skills had been reserved for maritime emergencies only. Just then, standing resplendent astride his quad bike, his thigh-high mini kilt flashing more white flesh than should be allowed before midday, our heroic Scottish-Kiwi farmer appeared in a cloud of dust. He motioned for us to follow him along the dirt road; the old camper van still had some life in her as we gunned along the gravel path, power-sliding round the corners. Even McTavish looked thrilled; perhaps all the previous adrenaline adventures and off-road experiences had toughened him up, or maybe he was just looking forward to seeing a bunch of girls chewing the cud. We parked up next to a rusty red tractor and admired the fields of lush green grass and happily grazing cattle. 'Where are we now?' I asked, looking at Graham, as a wistful smile crossed the Old Dog's face. I felt like things were going to get a whole lot weirder . . .

GRAHAM

When it comes to cows, I have 'form', as they say. I have history. *[Sam: Here it comes . . .]*

As an actor (especially one that's been plying his evil trade for forty years), you have your fair share of low points. But one of the lowest involved a cow. She shall remain nameless, to protect the innocent.

I was asked to audition for a commercial. Now, some actors do really well at commercials. They're *always* doing them, and once upon a time, they paid very well. But I, generally, didn't get them. *[Sam: Very moving.]* So, I approached this particular one with low expectations. The casting director (that special breed of omnipotent gatekeeper who has a bizarre hold over our industry) told me I was a veterinarian inspecting a cow, when suddenly my mobile phone rings (still part of the advert and not my own phone). And people actually get paid for coming up with this drivel!

They had arranged a series of tangled chairs to simulate the cow. I remember placing my hand through a gap in the mess of chair legs as if inspecting the wooden animal.

It all took about three minutes, 'Thank you. Next!'

I never expected to hear another word.

'Good news, darling,' chirruped my agent. Everyone is 'darling' in the acting world. It saves them having to remember your name. *[Sam: You are guilty.]* 'They want you for the phone commercial.'

'Phone commercial?'

'The one with the cow. You fly to Holland tomorrow.'

[Sam: Stop milking it.]

Cut to a farm in the Dutch countryside. I entered a large barn, expecting to see a carefully placed mock-up of a cow's rear end. But, instead, there was a cow (a real one), a farmer (also real) and a gang of expectant film crew, all of whom were grinning . . . at me.

'Gram!' (People outside of the UK are incapable of giving my name two syllables.) 'We loved your audition.'

'*Really?*' I thought, but instead I said, 'Is that a real cow?'

What an imbecile. I think even the cow laughed.

'This is Nils; he's a vet. He's going to demonstrate what you'll be doing.'

Nils was one of that gigantic breed of dairy-fed Dutchman with hands like shovels and a face that couldn't stop smiling (related to Squeezy perhaps?). He then produced a gigantic rubber sheath and, with a practised flourish, proceeded to force his arm into it. A giant glove that reached up to his shoulder. The kind of thing Black Jack Randall probably buys in bulk. 'So you need to pinch your fingers together like this . . . to form a point. Then you gently slide your arm into the cow's rectum. But don't poke! They don't like it when you poke.'

'Well, who would?' I thought.

'You try it!'

I think at this point my dull brain was still trying to grasp what was happening.

I was being asked to put on a giant glove and ram my arm up a cow's ass.

If it wasn't for the fact that I hadn't met Heughan yet, I would've been convinced he'd engineered the entire thing. *[Sam: Can't believe I was beaten to it, to be honest.]*

I slid on the rubber glove and the cow turned its eyes dolefully towards me as if to say, 'Just get on with it.'

I turned to the vet and said, 'I imagine they're used to it, eh?'

'Oh no, they don't like it.'

'Thanks Nils, you freakish perv.' I didn't actually say that but my expression spoke volumes.

The farmer, who was unusually short – almost like a Dutch hobbit – smiled sympathetically.

I performed my bovine entry.

At this point, I want you to pause and ask a friend (you'll need help) to take both their hands and grip your arm firmly. Now ask them to squeeze up and down your arm. That's what a cow's ass feels like. Except it's very warm. *[Sam: Dear God!]* I won't bore you with all the horrific details but it was a very, very long day. *[Sam: No snacks? How about a cheese 'bored' – geddit? Okay, maybe not.]* I became so desensitized to this rubber invasion of this poor animal's privates that I wouldn't even bother removing my arm between set-ups. I just stood there, shoulder-deep in the long-suffering beast as if I'd forgotten where my arm had gone. The whole ghastly experience climaxed after lunch when I attempted re-entry. By this point, it was feeling odd NOT to have my arm disappearing into a cow's anus. I quickly noticed, however, a kind of disturbance, a low rumbling, a boiling, bubbling sensation working around my limb. It was then that I realized the cow had also eaten lunch.

'Erm . . .'

The farmer grinned.

The cow looked back with 'Sorry' etched across its black-and-white brow. The vet said, 'Perhaps you should step to one side.' I'd only extricated myself inches to the left when the star of the show treated us to a volcanic jet stream of projectile cow shit, which actually managed to hit the wall behind me. Any vestige of my own dignity then left the room, leaving me listening to the uncontrollable mirth of the farmer and the crew.

It was with this nightmarish recollection in mind that I approached the farm in the Waikato district of New Zealand with Sam, preparing to wrestle with the multiple teats of 500 relatives of my Dutch bovine victim. *[Sam: Do cows hold grudges, I wonder?]* I've always had enormous respect for farmers. We rely on them utterly *[Sam: yes, udderly]* and yet we often take them for granted. When they wake up at 5am it's not to be driven to work, then brought coffees, and have make-up applied and their hair primped like Sam, myself or any other actor (well, okay, not the hair in my case). No! These people have to be out in all weathers, every day, ensuring we get what we need on our table. And with that admiration at the forefront of my mind, it was time to meet the farmer who was foolish enough to allow us anywhere near his herd.

***

We were heading further towards the west coast of the North Island, in the Waikato district, just south of Auckland. It's a beautiful green expanse (much fought over in the wars of the 1860s, as we'll later find out), and the setting for our first attempts at cow milking. The farmer arrived, thundering in on a quad bike, kilt flapping in the breeze, with two dogs perched on each side. It was quite an entrance. He was even more of a ginger than Sam and wore his obvious Scottish heritage with pride. *[Sam: Definitely a modern Kiwi version of Jamie Fraser, minus the wig and back scars, which he may have had, I didn't ask.]*

He leaped gracefully from the quad bike, his faithful collies bounding over towards Sam (recognizing a kindred spirit perhaps?). After the by-now-familiar handshake of iron (do these outdoor types go to special handshake classes? Do they practise on each other when they're not gripping the unsuspecting teats of hundreds of bovines?), he ushered us up the hill towards the looming vastness of . . . the milking shed.

As we bumped up the farm track and parked up, Kevin soon had Sam and I putting on our 'milking outfits'. Giant aprons, plastic boots, and – you guessed it – rubber gloves. The kind of sight that probably greets Lacroix on a regular basis after an energetic night out.

The farmer offered us some glasses of real milk, straight from the udder, like ambrosia, so delicious, none of this processed crap *[Sam: yeah, it was sooo creamy!]* and informed us that he fed 90 million people a day with this milk. Now, while I appreciate what he's doing, as I have said, I think the cows would have something to say about who's actually doing the feeding. At this point it was indeed time to say hello to the herd.

The cows began to assemble. A lot of cows.

[Sam: Yes, they made their own way from the fields and lush pastures and appeared anxious to be milked; we could sense their anticipation and perhaps fear that McTavish may get carried away and insert his arm somewhere uninvited.]

'How many cows?' I asked.

'Five hundred,' replied our be-kilted Kiwi friend. *[Sam: 2,000 teats!]*

Sweet Jesus, I thought, these poor animals all lining up to have the embarrassment of having their udders interfered with by the likes of Heughan and yours truly. They didn't look happy, as if they knew what we were: bungling amateurs. Quite a few looked . . . well . . . Dutch.

Our flame-haired farmer told us what we had to do. The animals would enter one by one into a giant metal merry-go-round that slowly moved in an anticlockwise direction, thereby successively exposing the cows' rear ends to our gloved advances. 'Take the four mechanical suction cups, clamp them on each teat.' All the while the carousel of cows made its relentless progress. 'Oh, and always look up in case the cow lifts its tail, which is the signal that it is about to take a giant dump on your head,' said our farmer friend. 'And watch out for the ones that like to kick.' Even while my stomach lurched with dread, I was gratified to see Heughan looking equally apprehensive. It was almost worth it. The carnival of milking began. I was up first. The two front suction cups first, followed by the rear two. Or was it rear first, front second? At this point I didn't know my front teat from my rear.

Our farmer had made this look embarrassingly easy. In my hands I resembled a drunken juggler who happened to be wearing rubber gloves. My eyes were constantly darting upwards, alert for any sudden tail movements signalling an imminent 'delivery'. And all the while the carousel continued inexorably moving, like a cattle-filled fairground attraction. I think I managed three udders, then it was Sam's turn and I was gratified to see that his ineptitude matched my own as he gingerly (excuse the pun) placed each cup on each quivering teat. *[Sam: I was udderly useless. Look, I know, I can't help it. I'll stop!]*

As each new cow entered the circle of shame, it was as if they turned to their neighbour, looking at us, and said, 'Who are this pair of giant twats?' The farmer finally asked Sam and me to stop, possibly realizing that to continue would result in night falling before the herd were milked. He then carried on with his own teat application at bewildering speed until one of the milk-heavy beasts tried to kick him. The metal bars around the offending cow saved him but Sam and I visibly leaped in the air. The farmer smiled a sad look of pitiful contempt in our direction and continued manfully supplying food to 90 million people. *[Sam: The cows were certainly relieved that 'McTavish the Cow Whisperer' was leaving.]* Sam and I meanwhile sloped off in our squeaking rubber and plastic outfits in search of a drink. And it wasn't milk.

***

WAIKATO WARS

GRAHAM

While we were in the area, supping raw milk and wrestling with cow teats, my thoughts turned to the war that happened in this area and, in particular, a shameful episode on the part of the British troops. *[Sam: Nice segue, from moos to massacres.]*

Rangiaowhia. It is a place that resonates to this day as, in some way, crystallizing the colonial tactics in dealing with what they saw as 'difficult Māori'. The tiny village sits in the area that we were driving through in Waikato. *[Sam: I was driving. You were probably sleeping or eating.]* Once a thriving Māori settlement, now there is a white Anglican mission church, built in the 1850s, rising like an accusing finger towards heaven amid the empty pasture around it. Looking across these rolling green hills, it was hard to imagine what happened here in 1863. Unlike the Highlands – which still carry a foreboding imprint upon them, a shadow of the clearances, of the ruthless policies of Scottish landowners – New Zealand offers the opposite atmosphere.

When you drive through New Zealand, as Sam and I did, all you are really aware of is its astounding beauty and abundance. Its bloody history lies beneath the picture-postcard perfection, but one doesn't have to dig very far back to see that these green hills were once soaked in blood.

Waikato is also known as 'King Country'. Māori didn't have kings – they had no tradition of monarchy or of a supreme leader. However, when one of the more prominent Māori chiefs, Pirikawau, visited England in 1843, one of the things that he found particularly appealing was the British monarchy. He came back filled with the idea that perhaps this was what the Māori people were lacking – a king. *[Sam: I wonder what they would have made of Prince Harry?]* It didn't really appeal to the Māori back home, presumably not as keen as Pirikawau on handing over ultimate power to one individual i.e., him.

But the idea didn't go away and about ten years later another Māori chief visited Queen Victoria. Tāmihana Te Rauparaha returned very keen on having a unified ruler; it never occurred to them that such an idea might not be so appealing to the British. The current situation of 'divide and conquer' suited the British very well. The idea of a united Māori nation, a nation capable of acting together in their own best interests, would have been a political and strategic disaster for Britain. As a result, they focused their attention on crushing the 'King movement' before it took hold. A movement that thrived in the Waikato, home to the most traditionally powerful *iwi* in New Zealand.

The British decided to build the case for war, citing examples of Māori terrorism and threats to the stability of the region as the excuses they needed. To anyone with the most cursory attention to history, this is an all-too-familiar pattern. Right from the suppression of the Highlands, through Hitler's annexation of the Sudetenland to other more recent examples, politicians (especially those who have a financial interest in fighting a war) have a long and

dirty tradition of finding any excuse to declare war. New Zealand
Governor Sir George Grey was no exception. *[Sam: Not Lord John
Grey, right? No.]*

And so we find ourselves in Rangiaowhia. In some ways it was
a classic example of military outflanking. The main force of Māori
fighting men at Paterangi were bypassed when two Māori guides,
Himi Manuao and John Gage, led the army of 1,200 men past
the warriors at 11pm on the night of 20 February 1864. In a move
reminiscent of the shepherd who guided Bonnie Prince Charlie's
Highlanders along a sheep track to outflank the British . . .
*[Sam: Ah nice, you were in that scene too – The Battle of Prestonpans,
Season 2, Episode 10.]* This massive number of men armed with
swords, muskets, with some on horseback, were able to pass within
1,500m (1,640yd) of Māori lookouts, completely unnoticed.

The next morning, the force was lined up outside the settlement
of Rangiaowhia. What followed has been described by some as
deliberate murder, by others as a tragic breakdown of discipline.
The non-fighting Māori in the village were supplying food to their
front-line warriors and, as far as the British were concerned, the
supply line had to be cut. The advance by the British was met with
some token firing by the villagers; one managed to kill one of the
British commanding officers as well as a couple of other soldiers.
Others took shelter in a church and it was then that the massacre or
breakdown of discipline followed. The church's thatched roof was
set on fire. Some of those fleeing the burning building, including an
elderly man holding a white flag, were shot despite shouted orders
of 'Spare him!' Others were then shot and several died inside the
burning church. Some reports claim casualties on the Māori side
as roughly a dozen, others claim it was well over a hundred men,
women and children.

For the Māori, this was an act of infamy similar to the massacre
in Glencoe. To them, it was a deliberate, treacherous act. For the
British, it signalled the beginning of the end for Māori morale
and the slow collapse of the king movement. Upon such moments
hinges history. The Waikato War fell into an uneasy standoff but
the numbers were on the side of the Europeans: 1.2 million acres

of land were confiscated by the British and the resistance to the tide of European colonization was slowly fading. And so, when the man who was King of the Māori in the 1880s, tired of seeing his people suffer, travelled to England for an audience with Queen Victoria, this time the British saw to it that, on this occasion, Her Majesty was busy.

CHAPTER TWELVE

Between a Rock and a Winery

DAY ELEVEN, MORNING

<u>Location: Rere Rockslide, Gisborne District, towards Gisborne
city, east coast of North Island (six hours east of Aka Aka)</u>

SAM
Just outside of Gisborne is New Zealand's natural water slide – the
Rere Rockslide – a 60-m (65-yd) long waterfall located along the
Wharekopae River, described as 'the best fun you can have for free'
in New Zealand. Hmmm, which I suppose it is if you discount
being eaten by a shark, falling off a cliff or watching McTavish put
on his socks in the morning, etc. In fact, I can think of 100 other
things that are more fun. But perhaps on a boiling hot summer's
day, the chilled water could be refreshing? Perhaps with a large
group of laughing, smiling, adventurous companions, you could

slide down the rocky water slide on a soft mattress or rubber ring, laughing all the way? Perhaps.

But today, it was cold, raining and my companion was miserable. 'Er, guys, best of three?' Kevin-the-director laughed nervously. He and I had read the warning sign on the way down to the river and decided not to show Graham, for fear he would refuse to get in the water. There actually was a very real risk of injury, or even death. Plus, the added 'bonus' that the water often exceeded safety levels of E. coli and could make us very sick. I'll admit, in hindsight, it wasn't the greatest idea. *[Graham: Really??]* But maybe, by this point, the crew had tired of our banter, as they seemed adamant that we slide down the rocks to our watery doom.

Graham held an umbrella awkwardly. 'It's raining, I don't want to get wet,' he grumbled, eyeing the rocky water slide reluctantly.

'Ummmm, you ARE about to get wet!' I replied and jumped into the river.

Now, I'm sure McWhiney will tell you of his dramatic escape from certain death, about how dangerous it was to slide down some slippy, moist rocks, but I can assure you, a six-year-old could do it. As if to testify to that fact, Ben-the-sound-guy, in his bright yellow Crocs and death metal T-shirt, jumped on a boogie board and demonstrated the activity. He bounced and slid down the natural water slide and hit the deep pool at the bottom, slowly sinking beneath its watery surface, leaving his Crocs afloat.

'Three, two, one, GO!' I shouted. My competitive nature kicked in. 'You can't let McTavish win!' it whispered in my ear. This devil on my shoulder kept me up at night, planning ways to beat McBeardy, plotting and scheming new ways to torment my companion in the bunk bed above. 'Yes, my precious, you must win, beat him, BEAT HIM!' I hurled myself down the rocks head first. It was then that I realized my face was in danger of being used as a brake. I gathered speed and momentum, willing my battered boogie board to make it to the bottom, faster than McGrumbly. 'Yeeeeeag-humph!' I hit the pool and went under for a few moments in the murky water. Then seconds later, I surfaced, spraying the bacteria-infused water triumphantly.

'Yazzzzzzzz, I won!' I held my arms aloft for the drone to capture the slow-motion footage of the victor at the finish line. I imagined myself, bronzed and dappled in sunlight, on the top step of the Olympic podium, bathed in glory, receiving my water slide gold medal. But where were my competitors? I needed to gloat. I looked back up the rocks and spotted McTavish, stuck on a rocky outcrop, water gushing over his striped pantaloons. Then, as if given a punt by the water gods, his body jumped the lip of the obstacle and he started to slide down towards me, his boogie board following behind, trying to catch him up. 'Impressive,' I thought. 'Freestyling with no board, he may get extra style points.'

'Mmmph, argh, gah, ouch!' He bounced from rock to rock until he slid gracefully into the pool next to me. I doggy-paddled over, waiting for him to bob up, but there was no sign of McT. I swam over to the bubbles rising from the centre of the pool. It was then that his boogie board arrived, GoPro still attached. I hoped it had got some good footage; perhaps McTavish's last heroic moments? I scanned the water but found no sign of my fearless friend.

Then, rising from the depths, the legendary Kraken appeared! 'GAHHHHHHHHHH!' it screamed, the cry primordial and ancient. Myths and legends spoke of this vast water creature; its tentacles could drown entire ships, barnacles adorned its body, even the striped pantaloons added to the monstrous effect. 'Gahhhhhhhh! My bloody hand!'

I diagnosed that Graham had scraped his hand on the stone and it looked a little bruised. *[Graham: I'm so sorry, I'd completely forgotten that you are an orthopaedic specialist.]* Perhaps not life-threatening, or even warranting a visit to the doctor, he did indeed have an 'owie' and would not be sliding down a geological water feature again.

'Not a F-REEE-KIN chance!' he bellowed, when Kevin enquired about the possibility of a retake.

So, I had won and Graham was still alive. What a great result!

However, Graham insisted on going to hospital. According to him, the injury was quite possibly life-threatening. 'EEEEEeeeehhh-AAAAhhhhhh! It bloody HURTS!' he moaned. I was surprised there weren't flashing blue lights to accompany the McTavish siren.

'Oh no, my hand, it'll never be the same again,' he sobbed in the passenger seat. Poor Scotty, the ever-smiling, latte-delivering, snack-supplying driver, who Graham had commandeered as his own personal chauffeur, gunned the engine of the camper van and sped Graham off to the local Accident and Emergency department. Perhaps he was worried he'd never hold a quill again, unable to write his historical notes by candlelight, or perhaps his fingers would no longer be able to clutch the stem of his regular, overflowing wine glass, the Cabernet dripping over the edge and covering his hand like sticky, red blood. Or perhaps Graham's blood IS actually wine; I wouldn't be surprised.

[Graham: I think that, perhaps, instead of explaining Sam's fondness for writing fiction, I should just issue a general warning that anyone reading his contribution to this book should have a very large pinch of salt to hand.]

GRAHAM

What can I say about our day frolicking on a rockslide other than that it was one of our director's ideas? 'It's going to be great, guys. It's a natural rockslide. You slide down into water, on boogie boards, mattresses, inflatable chairs, yoga mats, and kids' inflatable pools. People come from all over. You're going to love it.' I've lived long enough to know that when someone tells you, 'You're going to love it,' what they really mean is, 'I hope you love it. You may love it. In fact, you may hate it. In short, I have no idea what to expect. Perhaps you'll just die.' *[Sam: I think you may be on to something.]*

It was with this knowledge that we arrived in a remote part of the Eastern Cape. I had never been to this region before and, while I'm sure it has much to recommend it, for most of our drive we passed remote ramshackle buildings miles from anywhere with cars rotting in their front yards and the odd listless dog. All that was missing were the duelling banjos because it was the kind of place where no one can hear your screams, and I had a feeling that I was definitely going to be screaming . . . yet again!

By this point in the trip, I was in no doubt that Sam and Kevin, like a pair of diabolical twins separated at birth, were determined to break me both physically and mentally. Having screamed myself hoarse all over New Zealand, I was promised that this one was going to be easy.

I have visions of members of the Spanish Inquisition whispering to their sobbing, broken victims, 'Don't worry, this next one is going to be easy.' *[Sam: Any excuse to drop in another accent!]* We descended some steps towards where the crew were assembled. (I wonder why so many of these descents and climbs always put me in mind of a journey to the scaffold into the waiting arms of the hangman?) By the time I got to the bottom I half expected to see the crew wearing hoods and leather aprons, with a single drum beating out a sombre tattoo of death.

I think Sam bounded down the steps like some kind of freakish goat on heat. After all, he is never happier than when I am facing some kind of buttock-clenching terror. *[Sam: True.]* We passed a sign on the way down which may have had some letters highlighted in block capitals against a red background accompanied by many exclamation marks. *[Sam: Yes, don't bother reading that, nothing of importance, look over here! Ahem.]* Hmmm.

I could hear the sound of rushing water as we got closer (or that could've been coming from my underwear), and then I saw the rockslide. Now, I think it's important to say at this point that I love water parks. You know the kind of thing: twisting tubes plunging you downhill or dropping into darkness as you hurtle towards the sun-drenched pool at the bottom, the echoing whoops of joy as you zip down the serpent-like coils. Great fun!

What I saw before me was a natural rockslide. For the word 'natural', substitute the word 'uneven' and for the word 'rock' substitute the word ... 'ROCK'. As in that word you use immediately before the word 'hard' to describe something so unyielding as to be the likely cause of blunt-force trauma. *[Sam: Yes, it was a dead giveaway.]*

Kevin could see my trepidation. 'It's totally safe. I've just seen a six-year-old do it,' he chuckled. I managed to hold back my non-existent mirth and resisted the urge to point out the bloody obvious, namely that I am 61! *[Sam: Ancient.]* One of the crew demonstrated the descent on a boogie board. He resembled a rag doll being thrown into the sea. *[Sam: Oh no! If Ben had died, who would have recorded Graham's screams?!]*

Now it was our turn. So many times, I have stood next to Sam on this journey with a voice screaming in my head, 'What are you doing? You can just say no. Walk away! Have a coffee. *[Sam: And a snack.]* SAVE YOURSELF!' But instead, I find myself walking trance-like, as if someone is shouting, 'All those seeking possible doom, come this way.' Kevin attempted to direct us over the roar of the waterfall. 'I'll count down from three, then GO!'

We were given GoPros, which were attached to our boards. I'm pretty sure Sam would have one permanently attached to his head if he could. Come to think of it, perhaps he does. *[Sam: Naughty.]* Getting out into the middle of the cascading water was bad enough. Slipping around on the treacherous rocks, basically walking like I'd just pissed myself. Which at this point, I'm almost certain I had done. By now I should always be wearing adult diapers when I'm out with Sam, just in case. The countdown began and we were off! Well, Sam was off. I was stuck, like a turd that refuses to be flushed. *[Sam: Beautifully put. So graphic.]* It's as well to remind you that EVERYTHING Sam does is a competition, so he was determined to beat me to the bottom. I'm pretty sure he'd compete to see who could be fired farthest from a cannon, or who could hold his breath the longest while being strangled. *[Sam: I think I'd win that.]*

Sam was already halfway down while I struggled like some ageing beached seal to get going. The kind of seal that the rest of the seals just feel sorry for. I scrambled to get purchase and push myself forward. 'Why?' I hear you ask. Vanity? Pride? Mental decrepitude? Finally, I found myself moving. It was then that I perhaps realized for the first time what I was actually doing. I was pushing myself down an uneven rockslide at a 30-degree angle for about 60m (65yd) on a boogie board the size of a postage stamp, wearing a gossamer-thin top, swimming trunks and a GoPro, towards a freezing-cold pool of unknown depth. While this passed through my harrowed amygdala, I simultaneously realized I couldn't stop. It was happening. What an idiot!

I lost sight of Sam. Too busy concentrating on holding on to the board with whitening knuckles while images of air ambulances flashed through my mind, it was then I hit 'the bump'. Like one of those vicious speed bumps that you get on residential streets, except this one was positioned on a rockslide that I was hurtling downhill at speed, while clinging to a ridiculously small piece of foam.

Boooomphf! I was thrown off and watched the board leap forward and skate down the slope in a whimsical devil-may-care way, the receding GoPro looking amusingly at me, while I followed. The giant turd finally going down the pan. It was then I realized how comfortable the board had been because now I was being subjected to 'chest shave by rock'. As I felt every crevice of rock tear across my arms, chest and legs, not for the first time I wanted to scream abuse at Sam, who was now bobbing in the pool at the bottom grinning maniacally and waving at me. Why was he waving? In case I couldn't see him? To signal that he was actually drowning? Or, most likely, to say goodbye as he saw my nipples bouncing off solid rock. [Sam: I was trying to say, 'Don't drown!']

This rock, allegedly smoothed over centuries, still managed to treat me to numerous impacts as I continued downwards. First the left knee, then a crack against my hand, until finally I piled into the pool like some kind of Mayan human sacrifice. I struggled to the shore where I think Sam was saying: 'Wasn't that great?' To which I probably replied, 'Where are my nipples?'

My left hand was throbbing in pain, my knee was wincing every time I bent it, but we finally made it back to the top to the waiting Grand Inquisitor himself, our director Kevin. 'Are you okay? Shall we do one more?' I won't transcribe my exact response but Kevin was left in no doubt that I would rather stick needles in my eyes than do it again. Come to think of it, 'needles in Graham's eyes' was probably on tomorrow's call sheet.

When I finally reached the top with Sam, we passed the sign that I hadn't bothered to read on the way down. It read: 'Warning!

Serious Risks. Serious injury can occur when using the rockslide. Rocks can be sharp and slippery. Drowning has occurred. Bottom of pool up to 4 metres deep. Water does not meet health requirements. Swimming here may cause illness. DON'T DO IT!'

Okay, I made the last bit up, but still! As I passed it, pitifully grateful that I had survived yet another day with Heughan, a local man who resembled a cave-troll approached, nodding and smiling as he saw me nursing my swelling hand. 'You're lucky! There was a bloke here a month ago your age. Went down the slope, the rock tore open his nut-sack and his balls trailed him all the way to the bottom.'

I think he laughed. I reached for the diapers. *[Sam: Ah, so that's what I found, floating around at the bottom.]*

***

After hauling myself into the passenger seat, we drove on through the winding narrow roads of the region. While Sam rambled on about our most recent dice with death, my mind turned to the story of when death really did pay a visit to this area.

Apart from being the scene of my near castration, the Rere Rockslides was also the scene of an infamous massacre. Somehow, everywhere the Scots go, massacres seem to follow:

'Hey Jock, do ye remember those great massacres back hame?'

'Aye, I do.'

'I miss them. We could do with some here!'

'Dinnae fash! Give it time!'

The infamous massacre in question here was the one at Ngātapa in January 1869. A hop, skip and a jump from that diabolical rockslide. It has been described by modern historians as a 'stain upon New Zealand history'. But, like Glencoe, Culloden and many other historical events, we must look a little further back to give context for what followed.

The dominant character of this slice of history is Te Kooti Arikirangi Te Tūruki of Rongowhakaata. He had been arrested for rebellion in 1865, then re-arrested, and finally sent to the Chatham Islands in exile. Now, while the Chathams are a lovely spot, I'm told, they are a long way from Te Kooti's home in Gisborne and he wasn't allowed to leave. A little like Sam's MIQ experience, except at gunpoint and with the threat of death.

But Te Kooti was obviously a man who liked to keep busy, even in exile, so he promptly set about starting his own religion called 'Ringatū'. This was enthusiastically embraced by about 300 of his fellow exiles. Now it is definitely worth mentioning some of the teachings of Te Kooti's new religion as described by one that was there. I'll paraphrase, but this is the gist. Te Kooti would wake up and call his followers to prayer (seems pretty straightforward). He would begin by quoting the 32nd and 34th psalm that begin respectively:

Blessed is the one whose transgressions are forgiven,
whose sins are covered.
Psalm 32

Evil will slay the wicked; the foes of the righteous will
be condemned. The Lord will rescue his servants; no one
who takes refuge in him will be condemned.
Psalm 34

Now, one could be forgiven for interpreting this particular selection of morning psalms as a 'Get Out of Jail Free' card. They roughly translate as 'I can pretty much do what I like and you'd better agree, or else.'

Then Te Kooti would tell his men to get busy hunting for wild pigs. If you were the tribal member who came back empty-handed, well, Te Kooti didn't like them much, and he'd deny the offender another chance to hunt as punishment. A service was held four times a day, the final one being the prayer for sleep. Then it was lights out, no talking, no moving about, no nothing. And I mean nothing. Again, if someone so much as farted, Te Kooti would get a tad upset.

'I can't hold it in.'

'Shhhh. Te Kooti will hear you, and then we'll all be in the shit.'

'It was the beans.'

Phhhhhaaaaarrrrrrrp!

'WHICH ONE OF YOU BASTARDS WAS THAT?!!' bellowed Te Kooti.

Our friend would often get up early to hunt, not returning till evening. He would carry a decoy parrot on his shoulder like Long John Silver (I'm really not making this up) and explain to his followers that his missions to murder and plunder were all messages from his 'Atua'. Yes, basically God told him to do it.

Sometimes he would wake up in the middle of the night and tell his followers that Atua had told him to get a man, or food, or a woman (Atua was apparently a little vague on which of these exactly he wanted), but if those he sent out returned empty-handed, well, it was time to be tied up and left without food for days on end. Seems fair.

When Atua wasn't telling Te Kooti to murder or plunder, or to search for something, he was often telling him to have sex with his followers' wives. If some foolhardy husband didn't fully embrace Te Kooti's amorous intentions towards his wife, well, Atua had a solution for that too. That husband was obviously a traitorous bastard who needed to die.

Te Kooti: 'Ah, there you are. Just had a quick chat with Atua and he told me I had to jump on your wife for a wee bit of houghmagandy!'

Baffled husband: 'Ahh, sorry, chief, me and the missus are a bit sensitive about other blokes having sex with our wives so we'll have to pass. Tell Atua we appreciate the offer though.' This would then be followed promptly by the sound of the husband being clubbed to death.

The sound of thunder was also bad news for Te Kooti's followers. He would gently explain that this meant there were traitors among them who obviously had to be, yes, you guessed it, clubbed to death. So, all in all, here was a guy who was basically the Reverend Jim Jones/Charles Manson of the Chatham Islands.

And it was he who, along with those of his followers that were still breathing, escaped and headed to Poverty Bay on the mainland. Te Kooti had 100 of his men descend upon a settlement called

Matawhero in the dead of night, no doubt after a quick word with Atua. By dawn, they'd killed 60 men, women and children. Some were shot, but to avoid alerting the neighbours, most were either bayoneted, tomahawked or, of course, clubbed to death, no doubt while quietly humming the tune to Psalm 34. This has been described as *utu* (our good friend vengeance) against those who had exiled him and who had refused him safe passage to his home in the North.

Those Europeans that escaped the slaughter were able to alert the government forces, while hundreds of local Māori joined Te Kooti with various degrees of enthusiasm. Once alerted, the British pursued Te Kooti and his followers across the North Island led by one Colonel Lambert (no relation to my horse in *Outlander*), Captain Westrup, a Lieutenant Preece and many government troops, including around 370 Māori. (It is important to note here that many Māoris fought alongside the British for their own reasons.) They fought battles along the way, finally cornering Te Kooti, his remaining followers, and presumably Atua in the mountain *pā* (fort) of Ngātapa (not far from the delightful Rere slide). Within the *pā*, Te Kooti had around 300 fighting men, along with women and children.

The first attack on 5 December 1868 was led by 300 Māori troops divided between Lieutenant Preece and the Māori leaders. It was a formidable defensive position and Preece and his Māori leader counterpart Ropata were awarded the New Zealand Cross for their conspicuous gallantry. Ropata in particular deserves mention here. He was another John Rambo type, with balls the size of melons and hands that constantly itched to either be throttling his enemy or firing guns until they practically melted in his hands. He once attacked another Māori who merely had the temerity to defy him. Thinking himself safe from Ropata's homicidal urges, the poor fool stood on one side of a ravine taunting Ropata with any number of really, really, really upsetting insults (many of which, no doubt, questioned Ropata's legitimacy as well as the sexual proclivities of his mother). With veins bursting in his temples, Ropata promptly went across the ravine, armed only with an unquenchable thirst for death. He then proceeded to beat the guy's brains out while men on both sides stood with jaws hanging open, asking for a change of underwear, while making a mental note to NEVER EVER piss Ropata off.

He rarely carried a weapon apart from a pistol and a walking stick ('Because I'm not weak!'), the latter coming in handy when some of his men proved reluctant to follow him during one of his many attacks on anything that remotely looked like an enemy. He proceeded to thrash them with said walking stick until they saw the error of their ways.

In short, an absolute beast.

Despite this first failed attempt to total the fort at Ngātapa, the combined British and Māori force staged another attack in early January with men who volunteered from the armed constabulary along with more Māori troops recruited by Ropata. The siege continued for three days and nights with repeated assaults on the high walls of the fort, including a group described charmingly as 'the forlorn hope'. I don't know what's worse: that they actually had this name for such a group of volunteers or that people volunteered for something so named in the first place!

'Morning Jim, you're part of the forlorn hope today. Good luck.'

'Oh, sir! Jolly good! Sounds very exciting! I hope we succeed!'

'I doubt it, Jim. That's why it's called a forlorn hope.'

'Oh.'

'Yes, Jim, pretty much certain death.'

'Death?'

'Certain. Hence the word "forlorn". Almost futile to the point of stupidity. Now! Off you go!'

Needless to say, a few more New Zealand Crosses were awarded for bravery that day. Eventually, Te Kooti realized the position was hopeless and planned an escape under cover of darkness. They lowered themselves down the sheer 18-m (60-ft) cliff on vines cut from local trees. (Fortunately, Sam wasn't aware of this or no doubt he would've suggested we try it!)

Some escaped, but many did not. Those that were captured were women and wounded men too weakened to escape. It is now that

Day one of shooting, top of Bob's Peak, minutes before
throwing Graham down the mountain in a go-cart.

Completed isolation jigsaw of famous authors –
took me most of my incarceration to finish…
Imagine if we were on it, Graham?!

Keep your distance! Daily exercise, 45mins of walking clockwise, in a car park, with mask.

McT promised me kiwi food was amazing…day one proved otherwise.

Maybe McT is planning a prison break?

FREEDOM! Finally allowed to explore New Zealand.
And what a view! On the shores of Wellington Harbour.

On a walk through Omaru, Steam Punk capital of
the world. I wonder if we can catch the train next time?

Gone Fishing. All the gear, no idea.

Two thespians star in new movie 'Sharkbait'!

I survived. No sign of McTavish.

100m-high zip line. Contemplating whether this time I'd pushed McT too far...

Getting the band back together! An incredible day, welcomed into the Marae (Māori community complex).

Groin the dwarf. Known for his extensive use of obscenities and hair-care products.

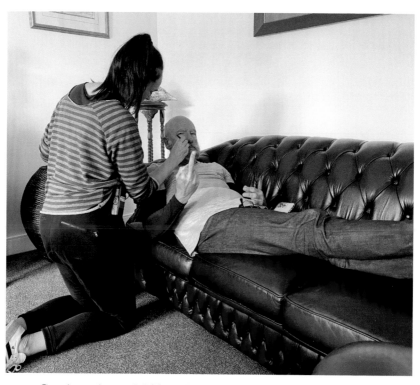

Caught in the act. McTavish's daily grooming, for which he insists he must be lying down or still in bed.

Kārearea the Falcon moments
before she escaped.

A bit drafty! Can be dangerous
riding a helicopter in a kilt.

The boys on spa day. No sign of
fluffy dressing gowns.

The first men in commando, on a glacier, in the southern hemisphere (allegedly).

Wine o'clock! Pre-wine tasting, why we are in a good mood?

The healing water of Hell's Gate. Sodom and Gomorrah, respectively.

Formula 1's new addition to the grid.

Upgraded the camper van to something a little more sporty... 'Graham?!! You Ready??!'

'You TIT!' Someone left the handbreak on. Again.

Ditched McTavish for my dolphin-spotting
friend, Albie.

Veritable feast at Fleur's Place.
The excitement (and copious
amounts of seafood) clearly got to
my friend, falling asleep mid-chew…

Holmes Warf. No relation
to Sherlock.

'the stain on New Zealand history' rears its head. The men were taken to the cliff edge, where they were summarily shot and their bodies tipped over the edge. It was a ruthless, brutal, savage act.

It is hard for us now to understand the actions of those men at the time. Those followers of Te Kooti who killed sleeping men, women and children because of a forced exile. Also those soldiers who took unarmed men after a battle, who posed no threat, lined them up and killed them in cold blood before hurling them over the cliff near Rere falls. It is easy to condemn them, to indulge in that new word 'presentism', which judges everyone based on what we know now, unfortunately resulting in everyone in history being consigned to the same thought: 'Should've known better'. But, of course, those people in the 1860s only knew what they were exposed to. They wanted *utu*. They wanted revenge, whether it came from Te Kooti's voice of God, or the barked command of a British officer.

I'm sure some of those men were haunted by their actions and that there were some who weren't at all. But when we are looking for stains in history, it's as well to make sure we see all of them.

Te Kooti himself continued to fight against the government for a further three years until his eventual surrender, at which time he sought the protection of the Māori king, Tāwhiao.

And, while those followers of Te Kooti rotted at the foot of that fateful cliff, and soldiers of both Māori and European origin lay buried where they fell trying to defeat him, what happened to Te Kooti himself?

He was given a government pardon in 1883 and lived another ten years until 1893, whereupon he died peacefully in his bed.

***

DAY TWELVE
[Sam: And time for some wine!]

Location: Hawke's Bay/Te Matau-a-Māui, east coast, North Island

Hawke's Bay is the second-largest wine region in New Zealand after Marlborough. It was named by Captain James Cook in

honour of Admiral Edward Hawke. The region has a hill with the longest place name in New Zealand, and the longest in the world: Taumatawhakatangihangakoauauotamateaturipukakapiki maungahoronukupokaiwhenuakitanatahu.
(Source: 2009 Guinness Book of Records)
[Sam: Try and say that after several glasses of Chardonnay!]

SAM

As we drove south the next morning, after Graham had engaged yet another medical professional to examine the 'owie' on his finger, which truly was but a wee scratch, he sat in the passenger seat, his finger encased in Elastoplast, moaning about his poor little hand. 'It will never be the same, you know,' he said anxiously, keeping his arm elevated for most of the journey, save for the occasional root about in the glovebox searching for snacks. The director and I decided today was the day to give the Old Dog a treat, so we were heading to Black Barn Vineyard in Hawke's Bay. Graham's beard bristled with excitement when he learned of our destination, his life-threatening injury soon but a distant memory. It certainly didn't hamper his ability to hold the stem of a wine glass. Or twenty. Maybe that was part of his rehabilitation, or his finger physio regime? On doctor's orders, of course!

GRAHAM

It was with great pleasure that we left the treacherous rockslides in the rear-view mirror and made our way south to a favourite region of New Zealand: Hawke's Bay.

I have been coming here every year for about 12 years. It has a fabulous climate, mile upon mile of beautiful rolling hills, a stunning coastline and one other thing that draws me back year after year. The small region boasts a mouth-watering 200 vineyards, 70 wineries, and 30 'cellar doors', where you can devote a day or more to sampling every possible combination of grapes and varietals. Best traversed by bicycle so that, if you fall off completely stocious on booze, you'll simply collapse unconscious onto one of the many wonderful cycle paths built just for this purpose.

My personal favourites are Elephant Hill, Linden Estate and Craggy Range, although unfortunately the latter's restaurant and cellar door appears to have been designed by a Stalinist architect – the utilitarian building is so ugly and forbidding.

But my absolute favourite has to be Black Barn. It was here that Sam and I, in our four-wheeled Kazakhstani eyesore, approached, our palates at the ready. My lips were literally twitching to sample that first glass of Sauvignon. Only opened in 2000, it has developed into not only a fabulous winery and restaurant, but it is also home to some truly epic accommodation. It was in one of these delightful homes that Sam and I were going to spend the night.

The region itself has been pumping out the booze since 1851. Considering the country had barely anyone living there at the time, it showed where their priorities lay when one of the first things the local settlers did was start frantically planting vines. These first grapes were planted by missionaries. I'm actually enjoying a glass of their Chardonnay as I write!

A bit like Wētā, I had built up Black Barn Estate to Sam in increasingly glowing terms.

At first, I just said, 'You'll love it.' Then it was, 'They have incredible wines, and the houses to rent on the estate are something special.' As I could see his appetite for a luxury retreat experience growing, I leaned heavily on each villa having an inexhaustible supply of wine and beer. 'Forget the mini-bar, think mini-cellar!' By the time we were approaching the vineyard, as the afternoon sun played across the acre upon acre of ripening grapes, I was confident enough to say: 'You will weep with joy. It will be a religious experience. You will barricade yourself in the villa and refuse to leave.'

It was with this endorsement ringing in Sam's perfectly formed ears that we pulled up in the Kitsch-mobile, musical bagpipe ornaments a gogo and grotesque stuffed Highland cows bouncing on the dashboard. 'Welcome to Black Barn!' said our host and winemaker Dave McKee. (Why is everyone called Dave?)

To which I wanted to reply, 'Show me the booze.' Instead, we had to do all the long setting up of cameras, drones, rocket satellites and whatever else we were using to film our little show. Simon (our daredevil cameraman) busied himself with lenses.

Kevin-the-director and he huddled in a corner with Squeezy-of-the-fanny-pack plotting how we were going to shoot it.

Sam and I, meanwhile (being of one mind about this sort of thing), immediately set to work securing a pair of wine glasses and urging Dave to uncork the nearest bottle.

Actually, New Zealand doesn't do corks. They are a screw-top nation. Which, at first, I regarded with enormous suspicion being, in my opinion, only one up from the blasphemous wine box. I have since, however, been converted and like nothing more than repeatedly unscrewing the tops of New Zealand wine bottles.

Dave had a wonderfully dry wit (looking back, I don't understand how he wasn't permanently half drunk. I mean who wouldn't be? Constantly surrounded by stacks of screw-topped booze just waiting for a twist of your wrist). He was a positive fount of information about all things wine-related. I tried to pay attention, knowing from today's call sheet that there was a wine competition coming.

Vineyards hold a special place in my memory. I had once worked on one in Switzerland when I was 18 years old, high above the shores of Lake Geneva. I had no interest AT ALL in picking grapes but I thought being trapped on a farm with several attractive young foreign girls sounded like a perfect way to spend an October. Unfortunately, when I arrived, I found a farm filled with a bunch of Brits, all of whom happened to be boys. I remember us all staring at one another in disbelief, almost as if looking hard enough would magically transform several of us into beautiful young foreign girls. But no, just a collection of similarly deluded British boys, all of them no doubt harbouring the same teenage dream as me, and consequently feeling the same bitterness about being stuck on a remote Swiss farm with a load of other Brits of the XY chromosome type in the sweltering heat.

We were out in the fields working at 6am. I remember we would have hot sweet tea brought out to us by one of the farmer's brutish-looking sons. However, this gave us all the opportunity to cast our eyes upon his assistant, the only saving grace of the entire experience: the au pair, Daniella.

She was Italian, with dark hair, a winning smile and a figure built for speed. I can confidently say that our group of hormonally raging 18-year-old boys only had one thing on our minds, and it wasn't the grapes. We worked till 6pm each day with an hour for lunch back at the farm where we had the midday pleasure of having our food served to us by the local Monica Bellucci. (I've always had a thing for Mediterranean women.) The combination of the heat, the back-breaking work, a cruel reminder of all that was missing from our farm, and the realization that we would NEVER escape each other's sweaty, exceedingly British, exclusively male company, eventually pushed us to make a break for it.

We had heard (on the grapevine – sorry – I couldn't resist!) that there was a farm 10km (6 miles) away that had only young girls working on it. Such was our fevered state that we didn't even think twice about leaving straight after dinner on a forced march to the aforementioned farm. We covered the distance in just over an hour, in the pitch black. Yes, we were desperate. At last! This was what we had come for! This is why we had volunteered for this gulag under the Stalinist rule of the farmer. (He was like a Dickens character, just not one of the jolly funny ones.) We were finally going to hear the tinkling laughter of people of the opposite sex, allowing us to imagine, if only briefly, a future beyond the *Vorkutlag*. We knocked at the door.

God knows what the farmer thought at the sight of a dozen panting young men standing on his doorstep in the dark. Come to think of it, I know exactly what he must've been thinking seeing as we were probably the sixth such gathering of priapic teenage boys to darken his door that week. I think one of us actually uttered the words, 'We're here for the girls,' which would obviously have sounded very alarming, especially delivered by some spotty teenage boy breathing heavily into the night air.

'The girls? Oh . . . they've gone.'

'Gone?' I muttered.

'Away. Yesterday. Left.'

'Yesterday,' we all thought simultaneously. 'Left,' we digested this bald statement. The simple truth that, whatever respite – by way of conversation, beauty, or just the very fact they weren't *us* – had gone. Joy had left the building. Joy was far away. Joy didn't live here anymore. Since yesterday.

I think we stood in numb silence for a while. He may have offered us a drink, out of sheer pity, or perhaps cyanide pills. I have no idea. All twelve of us simply turned away in shock and began the 6-mile walk back. There may have been talk of a suicide pact on our long walk home, or perhaps it was conducted in aching silence, each of us alone with only one thought: what might have been.

All of this was running through my mind as Dave promenaded us through the rows and rows of vines, but all I actually said was, 'I once did grape-picking in Switzerland.' Little did they know the tale of woe, despair and disappointment contained in that simple statement.

The sun was slowly setting as Sam and I began our tasting. It brought back memories of that very first stop we made on our first *Men in Kilts* series at the Clachaig Inn, working our way through a bevy of cask-strength whiskies. Just like then, this tasting quickly turned into more of a 'gulping', followed by a 'finishing', and then an 'asking for more'! During this professional draining of Dave's supply of Black Barn wines, Sam managed to remember the plan for yet another wretched competition.

SAM

Ah, yes, the wine competition, which Graham took VERY seriously indeed. Our guide and sommelier asked us to take notes as he told us in detail about each wine before I downed the sample. I never spit, it's rude. As we reached the end of the tasting and began the quiz, Graham was the most competitive I've ever seen him, his nose positively quivering. As a wine connoisseur, he was in his element, showing off like a pretentious peacock and by the middle of the quiz he wasn't even waiting for the questions to finish, he was literally jumping in mid-question and getting the answers right. It was like a wino's version of *University Challenge* and I was on the losing team. I had to stop him winning, so Kevin and I did something I'm not proud of . . . (it was Kevin's fault, honest! Okay, I dabble on the dark side when it comes to McT). We rigged the last questions so I'd win and he would lose. And lose he did, because he didn't know about residual sugars in a Riesling and I did (thanks to Google). Ha-ha!

GRAHAM

In terms of drinking, of course, there is no competition. Sam wins. Hands down. His drinking arm takes on an almost mechanical quality as he downs glass after glass of whatever is put in front of him. The only discernible change in his appearance is a developing faraway glassy stare as reaches for another full glass of anything alcoholic. I've never actually watched Sam sleep but I suspect his right arm is always just about to pour an imaginary glass of the amber nectar down his thrapple.

This is, of course, why he has devoted so much energy to creating his own spirits company. First whisky, then tequila, now gin. It can't be long before he launches the Sassenach lighter-fuel collection, or the Sassenach antifreeze 'collector's edition'.

All because he simply can't risk being without a steady supply of the loopy juice at any moment, even if it means making it himself from potatoes.

We were tied in the wine knowledge competition. Dave had poured us generous measures of each variety of Black Barn wine (the Sangiovese was a particular winner). Sam was doing his usual impersonation of a sommelier, ramming one nostril into the glass and then doing that annoying twirly thing people do with their wine glasses. You know the kind of thing: gripping the stem of the wine glass between forefinger and thumb and spinning the glass around, causing the liquid inside to swirl. Apparently, it's supposed to release the 'nose' and flavours. To me, you just look like a pretentious twat. This may, however, be due to the fact that somehow, I have never mastered this action. When I do it, it's likely to end up with me sloshing the contents over the rim of the glass like a chimpanzee. I'm just jealous.

Then came the tiebreaker. I can't even remember the question, something about sugar content, blah blah blah. All I know is, Sam got the question right. He had won.

He, of course, proceeded to caper about like a drug-crazed bellbird doing a mating dance. Much fist pumping and general crying out with sheer joy. I meanwhile consoled myself by downing the contents of all the half-drunk glasses arrayed in front of us.

We thanked Dave and realized it was time to retire to our villa, leaving Dave to inspect the sheer volume of his wine that had disappeared in little under an hour. We left the life-sized Lego vehicle that masquerades as our camper van and were dropped off by the alarmingly sober Scotty. (As a side note, we learned that Scotty seems to work out for approximately 18 hours a day. He's ridiculously fit. He has probably devised a way to work out while driving.)

I cooked dinner. Well, I heated up some rather delicious pre-cooked moussaka, and we set about diminishing the stock of booze in the cellar. We ended the evening on the patio outside sampling some of Sam's tequila. He had brought a bottle with him and I couldn't help noticing that over half had already been consumed. *Does* he drink while he's sleeping? Intravenously? Suppositories?

It was delicious. I've got to hand it to him, the man knows how to make hard liquor.

Then it was time to retire to our respective bedrooms. It was a three-bedroomed villa, but I'd ensured that our rooms were as far away from each other as possible. I'm not saying I actually built a barricade in front of my door but it crossed my mind. I finally fell asleep but not before I heard that unmistakable sound of a hand twisting around a bottle top.

Sleep well, Sam.

SAM

And now it is my turn to question Graham's memory. Because what actually happened was, we retired to our cottage at Black

Barn, which did indeed have three bedrooms, but which also had been supplied with yet more bottles of every single variety of wine produced at the vineyard. And the G-Force and I stayed up all night drinking them! Maybe he was too pished to remember? We didn't finish them all but we certainly did test our knowledge of wine.

Sláinte!

CHAPTER THIRTEEN

Ab'Zorbing the Culture

DAY THIRTEEN, MORNING

<u>Location: Rotorua, southern shores of Lake Rotorua, Bay of Plenty region, North Island</u>

SAM
All hail the Zorb god! We had headed north to Rotorua, the original birthplace of: Zorbing. Zorbs are strange creatures. Spherical beings from another dimension, they are mostly harmless but occasionally they have been known to herd together and creep up behind unsuspecting humans and try to crush them. Thankfully, they're mostly filled with hot air, water, occasionally beer and the odd, bearded, screaming human being, so, pretty harmless as I said.

'Is it necessary to get lubed up?' I asked while our Zorbing

instructor and centre co-founder, David Akers, explained the
origins of this peculiar 'sport'. *[Graham: Is Dave the official name
for every man in New Zealand?]* Graham paused.
*[Graham: Yes, I did pause, Sam. So did the guy running the Zorbing
centre. In fact, so did the instructor later on when you repeated your
question about 'lubing up'. You could hear the proverbial pin drop.
Many questions spring to mind here. Why? Do you think lube is a
frequently asked-for accessory in this situation? Were you imagining
applying the said lube to your entire body or just selected spots? So many
questions.]*

I looked down at David's hairless legs in Kiwi board shorts and
wondered if he shaved them specifically? I shuffled nervously as
he continued to tell us more about the origins of Zorbing, which
was created in New Zealand in 1994 by two Kiwi brothers. It is
the unusual practice of rolling down a hill or slope inside a large
transparent bouncy ball or orb. This particular site, overlooking
the picturesque lake and mountains, has developed over the years
and now has multiple options for the keen 'baller' *[Graham: I think
you're confusing this with something else]*, or orbist, orber, Zorbist,
Zorbian or just madman, to climb into his chosen sphere and
roll in multiple directions. There are slalom courses, speed tracks,
jumps and obstacles, but we had opted for a straight dragster race
down the hill.

'Lube . . .?' It's not necessary but perfectly acceptable,' replied
Andrew, one of the original brothers who had created the practice.
*[Graham: He completely made this up, presumably to deflect from the
weirdness of his actual question.]*

'We fill the middle of the orb with water, so you'll slip down
nicely,' he said with an enthusiastic smile. Graham shifted
uncomfortably again. 'One guy once filled it with beer but it stung
his eyes,' Andrew continued.

'Ahhhh, maybe not,' I replied. I had been considering filling the
Zorb with whisky but decided better of it. Zorbing and drinking,
at the same time, probably wasn't the best idea. We climbed the
hill, dressed in our sporty workout gear, Graham in a fancy pair
of slippers I think he'd stolen from the hotel spa, to be greeted

by a friendly chap at the top who guided us into our respective balls. I was feeling nervous; my knee hadn't quite healed and I didn't want to do myself another injury but then the spirit of competition gave me a kick in the Zorbs and I realized this was further opportunity for me to THRASH McTavish at another sport. Albeit a rather peculiar one.

The interior of the Zorb was warm, humid and moist. All sound was muffled and distant. The southern hemisphere sun heated the water inside and I was overcome by drowsiness. It was like being inside the stomach of a large see-through animal, slowly being comforted to sleep, or digested.

'Three . . . two . . . two and a half . . . one!' Our manic, smiling friend counted us down and we were off! I pushed forward, slipping on the moist surface, and landed flat on my face. The Zorb refused to move; perhaps I'd left the handbrake on again? Or maybe I just need to speak nicely to this Mother Zorb. Large, fulsome and majestic, my Zorb looked down the hill at the waiting crew below. Graham was having no luck either.

'Expelliarmus!' I yelled, '*Vamos, schnell, allez, gie it laldy!* Please, please Mr/Mrs Zorb! I have to beat him!' And I pushed hard again. Perhaps the Zorb gods heard me because my imposing bouncy sphere began to roll downhill, picking up speed as it went. 'Yeeeeeeees!' I screamed and slipped onto my back, spinning down the hill, a few feet ahead of McTavish's now-rolling wet ball. 'Ha-ha, yes Zorb, go, go, go! Beat that McTavish!'

We raced down the hill, my screams muffled by the thick interior, bouncing towards the finish line. Apparently, these strange ground-living balloons can travel at up to 48km/h (30mph). Whatever speed I was going, Zorb and I passed the finish line a good few metres ahead of my bearded companion. The transformation was complete. I had been baptised, lost my Zorb-ginity, been welcomed into the Zorb community as one of their own. I unzipped the bottom of my Zorb and was birthed back into the world. I was now a 'Zorbist'! I beat McTavish. No lube required.

***

DAY THIRTEEN, LATE AFTERNOON

GRAHAM

From the playground of the Zorbs to some suspended walkways slung between redwood trees. We took a leisurely drive and arrived around dusk. Food had been sparse at our last stop so I demolished the contents of the glovebox in between supportive snoozing. The best time to experience the 'Redwood Walk' is apparently after dark. That's when a host of twinkling lights pop up all over the forest canopy. I suspect the main purpose of this visit was to, yet again, have me dozens of metres off the ground precariously suspended on a series of walkways wide enough for only one person so that Sam could then bounce up and down like an angry chimp as I made my way, inch by inch, across, causing me to revisit my all-too-familiar second home: vertigo. All of the above were indeed accomplished by my scheming camper companion.

SAM

Redwood Trees. Night time (after McTavish's bedtime)

McTavish was having NONE of it. 'No. No, I've done it before and it's going to look rubbish on camera,' he grumbled inside the passenger seat of the camper, refusing to get out.

The mosquitos were circling and the crew were restless. It had been a long day of filming. A long few weeks, in fact, and McTavish had reached his limit. It was late, he was hungry, it was past his bedtime and he didn't want to be anywhere high up. Especially not 20m (65ft) up on a rickety wooden platform, high above the forest floor on a series of beautiful and occasionally daring walkways that had been constructed in the foliage of these mighty 75m- (246ft-) high redwood trees. These eco-designed roped wooden bridges and platforms were built into the trees, each one higher than the other, creating an Ewok-style village in the trees. Or perhaps a Robin Hood village, the Kevin Costner one, or *Mad Max* . . .?

'Or the Three Little Pigs . . .' Graham added. He was huffing and puffing like the great wolf, perhaps hoping to blow down this wooden village, but Squeezy the safety officer assured him it was all stable and insured. 'Get her away from me,' he grumbled again and sneaked out the back of the camper by the side door, only to be caught by Ben-the-sound-guy, who deftly attached a microphone to his woolly sweater. 'Now we can hear you complain from the treetops,' Ben smiled and then beat a hasty retreat, lest he have the microphone thrown at him from a distance. McTavish trudged up the wooden stairs and gingerly began the climb into the treetops.

Night had fallen and then, out of the darkness, the foliage began to light up. Hundreds of skilfully placed lights illuminated the forest until it resembled the underwater scene from *Aquaman*. At 700m (765yd) long, with over 28 swing bridges, it was a psychedelic experience and I half wished I'd brought some of my mushroom friends along, or perhaps licked a frog . . . or two. Though I wouldn't recommend it, especially if you don't know the frog personally; they tend to get a bit grumpy when kissed uninvited. Perhaps it was the long day or lack of sleep, the miles travelled or the wine consumed, but I lost myself in the trees. The kaleidoscope of colours and patterns that played on the redwoods was beautiful and mesmerizing. I raced forward, looking to explore each new bridge and observation platform.

Time stood still. The colours blended and melded into different universes; the dappled trees welcomed the explorer and I lost myself – my mind expanded, and my consciousness was stretched by the ever-changing patterns. 'Awwweeesome,' I sighed, taking a huge breath in and then letting it out slowly, 'Aaahhh.' Or perhaps it was the extra oxygen emitted by these guardians of the earth, but I instantly felt more chilled and relaxed. The redwoods help clean the air by removing carbon dioxide and mitigating the effects of climate change. They store more than five times the amount of carbon than other forests and live an average of 1,000–1,200 years (almost as old as McTavish). Being high up among these ancient guardians was a stark reminder of the need to protect these incredible trees and I thanked them for such an awesome trip . . . once my feet were firmly back on the ground.

Back in the camper, McTavish was waiting. 'Where've you been?' he asked incredulously, 'We've got a dinner appointment!'

'Yeeeah, what a trip!' I replied. 'I've definitely got the munchies, time for dinner.'

I just hoped mushrooms or frogs weren't on the menu.

***

DAY FOURTEEN, MORNING

Location: Hell's Gate/Tikitere, between Lake Rotorua and Lake Rotoiti in the Bay of Plenty, Rotorua, North Island

GRAHAM

The next destination for the 'strange vehicle resembling a van' was Rotorua. Now, no offence to that fine town, but Rotorua smells. Of rotten eggs. So we drove with the windows rolled up, breathing through our mouths. I may have added some potpourri to the camper's interior (trying to avoid lavender of course . . .). The reason for this pervading odour (depending on the wind direction) would soon become apparent.

SAM

Graham's last visit to a 'spa' had been traumatic. He appeared on set during our first few days of shooting with a large fresh gash on top of his hairless barnet. I had proposed that all he needed was a sticking plaster or perhaps some glue, but the local Kiwi doctor had prescribed several stitches. I forget how many. We had been shooting in Queenstown, the natural home of adrenaline sports, and I was sure the medical team had seen a great many worse injuries – perhaps someone garrotted by a rampant kayak, maimed by a mountain bike or even a squeezie water bottle lodged in the eye? So how had Graham sustained this apparently life-threatening scratch on the bonnet, I hear you ask? He had been spending the day in A SPA recommended by Kevin our director (no doubt wearing a silk dressing gown and sequin slippers to match) and had bent down to pick the towel up and hit his head on the towel rail, thus grazing his noggin. Or that was his alibi? I'm sure the truth was a lot darker. Perhaps as he bent down to pick up the soap, another 'guest' had taken this as an invitation to begin exfoliating his back? The truth, I fear, may be too base and foul even for this publication. Whatever the real reason for Graham's first of many 'owies', our make-up artist was on hand and covered up his scratch for the duration of the shoot. I wonder, if he'd had hair, it would have been easier to disguise . . . you get my point?

Which brings us to Tikitere, or 'Hell's Gate' as it's also known. In the Te Puia region lies Whakarewarewa Valley, where let's just say Kevin and I had organized another little surprise for Graham, one that he couldn't refuse.

A day out to the spa!

However, this particularly R&R spot involved bubbling mud pools and a 30-m (98-ft) Pohutu Geyser, which erupts (like McTavish does) many times daily! Given his recent spa injuries, soaking in sulphur pools and mud baths at New Zealand's most active geothermal reserve could be risky! But there could also be unexpected benefits . . . as the man standing before us, Paul Rayner, the operations manager, explained. Wearing board shorts and a tight T-shirt, he had the most luxurious mane of hair I've ever seen. It fluttered and waved in the breeze as if moving in slow motion. 'I used to be bald before I started working here!' he cheerfully smiled, his hair partially hiding his face. I thought I could see it growing as we spoke, quickly covering his eyes and nose then reaching down to his ever-smiling mouth. He flicked it back over his shoulder, like a supermodel in a shampoo commercial. 'Really?' we said in unison, Graham's eyes full of hope . . .

'Nahhhh, but the mud does hold healing properties.'

Sorry, Graham.

'The geothermal mud and sulphur mineral water have been used by local Māori for over 800 years,' Paul continued, his hair wafting in the wind like a 1980s Timotei advert, as if taunting my follicularly challenged friend.

'Traditionally, people believed the ammonia from urine could help sterilize and heal a wound. The local Māori realized that these pools had magical properties and started bathing in these Ngawha Springs, with their sulphurous mineral waters, to heal their wounds quicker.'

'Oh, oh, oh! Graham has a wound!' I volunteered.

'Oh yeah? I could piss on your head if you like!' our surfer dude replied.

'No, I don't think so.' Graham shifted uneasily in his sandals, trying to put some distance between himself and our eager tour guide. However, there wasn't much room to escape; we were on a small dirt path, surrounded by molten hot mud pools. One step off the path would mean certain death, the pools violently bubbling and occasionally erupting with temperatures of up to 122°C (252°F). Upon entering the pool, one's whole body would be boiled in seconds, leaving only your bones remaining.

'I thought this was a spa?' Graham moaned, peering around, hoping to spot some fresh white towels and perhaps the approach of a stocky masseuse with thick forearms. 'I can see why it's called Hell's Gate!' Just then he jumped backwards as a volcanic burst erupted from the 'Steaming Cliffs', the hottest of all the pools.

'Ah, that name was given by one of your Scottish friends. In 1934, the playwright George Bernard Shaw coined the phrase that "it could be the very gates of hell".' Graham and I looked at each other silently; we hadn't the heart to correct our hairy tour guide that G B Shaw was actually Irish. Despite his cheerful demeanour and luscious locks, we were aware that provoking an enthusiastic tour guide in full flow could very well result in an early bath . . . so we remained quiet and followed in his sandalled footsteps.

'It's not just a spa, it's a very sacred place,' our hairy guide continued. 'From cooking pools and land coral to the largest hot waterfall in the southern hemisphere, the surrounding region is steeped in legend.' Our guide led us along the path, explaining the ancient Māori history. 'Over 650 years ago a Māori princess, named Hurutini, lived within reach of where we are now. She was married to a Māori chief whose mistreatment drove her to kill herself by throwing herself in one of the boiling pools. When the princess's mother found out, she cried: *"Aue teri nei tik"*. This cry was shortened to Tikitere, the sacred Māori name of Hell's Gate.

'The treacherous pools provided a source of heat to warm the local tribe, and the Māori village could also utilize the steam to cook or bathe, much as they still do today in the modern town. It also acted as a natural defence; any attacking enemy wouldn't know the secret paths and routes between the boiling pools and would meet their end.

'The bubbling geothermal activity you see is a sign of the power existing below. Rūaumoko is the God of earthquakes, volcanoes and seasons. He is the son of the sky father, Ranginui, and the earth mother, Papatūānuku; his legend begins with their separation. It is said that with every movement he makes, Rūaumoko's heat boils the earth above . . .'

BrrrrrrrARP! At that moment, Rūaumoko had a very large movement, blowing some escaped gas and mud sky high. 'Must have been something he ate,' Graham replied, as small pieces of sulphurous-smelling mud spattered around our feet. 'Urrrgh!'

'Sodom and Gomorrah,' our guide presented proudly. No, he didn't mean us, two reprobates that would soon be burned for their sins, but two natural geysers, which regularly expelled Rūaumoko's gaseous stench skyward. I couldn't tell which was which; I think Sodom was the smaller and more active of the two, Gomorrah having a low grumble but not much action!

'Ah finally.' Graham breathed a sigh of relief. 'The spa!' We were standing by a group of buildings and naturally heated pools. 'Yes, my friends,' said our guide beaming with pride, our tour completed. 'Time to rub each other with this magical mud, benefit from all its minerals and healing properties.'

Graham looked confused. 'Rub? Each other?' he repeated.

'Well, whatever makes you feel comfortable,' our guide continued. 'Enjoy your spa time!' and with that he wandered off, slowly evaporating as if he himself were made of steam.

'Yes, don't pretend you haven't been to one of THOSE kinds of spas, McT!' I laughed and ran full tilt, diving into the mud.

McTavish gingerly tiptoed into the muddy lagoon and started to
bathe himself in the sulphuric sands. I tried to swim, front crawl,
backstroke and doggy-paddle but, alas, couldn't get very far. I
flipped over, belly up to survey the scene, and there I witnessed
the God of Volcanoes himself covered in mud, dressed in his 1940s
swimming shorts and plimsolls, conducting his ablutions. Then, as
he bent down to pick up some more mud, a tremendous amount
of gas escaped McTavish . . . bbbBLUUURP!

The geysers answered in unison . . . pppppPPPARRRRP!
Delightful.

***

DAY FOURTEEN, LATE MORNING

Location: Te Pā Tū (previously Tamaki Māori Village), Rotorua,
North Island

SAM

That afternoon, Graham and I booked in to learn about the culture
and heritage of the Māori people at Te Pā Tū, a Māori village. We
were standing opposite a large wooden building as a small group
of traditionally dressed Māori faced us in silence. The wind played
with the bottom of our kilts and the sun felt hot on my back. I
started to sweat. This was a great honour. We had been brought to
the local 'marae' (meeting ground) in Rotorua, a fenced-in complex
of carved buildings and grounds that belonged to that particular
iwi. Even Inia, our jovial Māori guide, remained stoic and silent
in reverence. The Māori see their marae as their tūrangawaewae – a
place to stand and belong. It was a great honour and I really didn't
want to mess up.

Graham stood firm and proud; he'd partaken in this ceremony
before, so I decided to follow his lead. He was the elder (MUCH
elder) and therefore was required to be our spokesperson. I felt like
a time traveller (less Outlander, more like James Cook exploring
the Pacific) encountering the local Kiwi population for the first
time. A female in the group broke the silence with a cry, then the

rest of the tribe joined in a powerful and moving song. A lone warrior approached tentatively; he wielded a *taiaha* (a spear-like weapon) and appeared to be inquisitive of our intentions. I glanced at Graham, who also looked rather intimidated, perhaps owing to the warrior's challenge or his impressive physique. He laid down a small branch and waited for Graham to pick it up. I hoped that the warrior wouldn't judge us by the size of our puny muscles. I stiffened my back and tried to look more worthy. Graham bent down to pick up the branch. 'Mmmmph,' he let out a small groan; perhaps his back twinged again, but thankfully he stood upright and managed a smile. We received the branch as a symbol that we came in peace, at which point we were invited inside and the main ceremony began.

We had been welcomed into the *wharenui* or carved meeting house, which we were told resembles the human body in structure and represented a particular ancestor of the tribe. There was a carved figure on the rooftop in front of the house, which depicted the head, and large doors which were the arms – held out in welcome to visitors. The main speaker of the *iwi* introduced us to the family's history, citing their forefathers and connections to the land, then our hosts smiled and sang some more. It was at this point we were invited to present ourselves and my bearded companion and I rose to the occasion. 'Oh, flower of Scotland . . . when will we see yer likes again?' My voice cracked on the top note; I realized I'd only really ever sung our national anthem while slightly drunk. I also realized it was less singing and more enthusiastic shouting. Graham and I tried to make our voices more powerful to finish the song, 'Aaaaannd sent him homeward, tae think, agaaaaain!' The Māori all smiled, perhaps out of sympathy or relief that our rendition was over. *[Graham: It was definitely an awkward moment. I was proud that we had sung that song together but no one would want us to sing it twice!]* The ceremony, too, was over.

A visitor who has never set foot on a *marae* is known as *waewae tapu*, or sacred feet, but the ceremony had removed the *tapu* (sacredness). We had now become one people with those of the *marae*. The warrior approached me, shook my hand firmly and pressed his nose to mine. He smiled and winked, 'Now you get to become a true Māori warrior,' and he placed his spear into my hands.

Graham loves to fight. Or should I say, he loves to pretend to fight. Lots of sound and fury, but deep down he's a pussy cat. One of those hairless ones. We stood in line and were shown the basics of the Mau Rākau – a martial art which uses almost bird-like movements to wield the Māori spear, the *taiaha*. Our warrior friend had such perfect timing, balance and coordination and made it look easy. He was powerful and strong. The *taiaha* was a long wooden staff, about the same size as us, maybe 1.8m (6ft) long (Graham really was too tall for a dwarf), with carvings at one end to represent a tongue. It was sharp, made from jade stone (a highly valued stone used for ornaments and weapons), which could be used for stabbing an opponent. The other end was flat, like the blade of an oar, which could be used to strike or parry. It was a very versatile weapon and had a collar of feathers that could distract the opponent when shaken. The Mau *taiaha*, the ancient form of stick fighting, went back hundreds of years and reminded me a little of other martial arts found around the world, like fencing or kendo, the Japanese martial art. 'Hyaaa! Gahhh!' Graham and I shouted as we swung the spears and stabbed our imaginary opponents. On *Outlander*, I have been accused of making too many sound effects during fight scenes, like 'Pah! Oof! Urgh! Yazzz!' Which may be true, but when firing a flintlock pistol that sounds like a ray gun, it really doesn't help . . . 'Peow, peow!'

Our warrior friend perhaps took pity and commended us for our 'enthusiasm'. 'Here's something you can try; even the kids can do this and you won't hurt yourselves either,' Inia laughed and handed us some furry pompoms. They looked like the kind of fluffy dice you get to hang on your car's front mirror. (Do people still do that? I must get Graham a set for his shiny new midlife-crisis American Muscle Car.) *Poi* are two balls attached by a long string and were used initially by warriors to gain wrist strength and develop their wrist flexibility for the use of hand weapons. The choreographed spinning routines are now used in performances across the world.

I imagined Graham at Burning Man Festival, spinning his fire *poi* or glow-in-the-dark sticks, dressed as a shaman and high on mushrooms or just life itself!

But no. He was rubbish. So was I. I can juggle balls, apples, even clubs and knives. That's a Steiner education for you – you should send your kids, Graham! *[Graham: I need to see this! Why has this been kept from me? Like your legendary red nose clowning skills?]* But the *poi* eluded us and we kept getting our balls in a tangle . . . so to speak. 'Gah we are RUBBISH!' Graham bellowed from behind his Gandalf grey beard.

'Hmmm, not bad boys,' Inia smirked. 'You might just be better at making a lot of noise though. Follow me!'

Inia led us to a large grassy field, 'I'm going to teach you the art of *hauora*, the breath of life into the heart and lungs.' As the sun set, steam rose all around us from the ground. Like the previous day at the thermal spa, the earth itself began releasing *hauora*, which the Māori harnessed, using the geothermal power to heat their homes. The boiling water or steam even bubbled in people's back gardens, and the Māori were known to cook on these natural barbecues.

The *hauora* filled my lungs, I breathed deeply, feeling energized and more connected to my surroundings. As we finished our *hauora* breaths, the summer sun was dropping and we had hit the 'golden hour' after a long day at the Māori meeting grounds. Graham and I had been welcomed by the Māori people and introduced to a slice of their culture and heritage, but before we left, we were given one last treat: a *haka*.

The most famous *haka*, one that I'd witnessed, was the 'Ka Mate' performed by the All Blacks rugby team before each match. Although many other Pacific Island teams also have their own *haka*, each one is individual and tells a different story or challenge. Inia was responsible for teaching the famous All Blacks their Māori dance, which tells the story of Te Rauparaha (whom we met earlier on in our tale) hiding from his enemies in a *kumara* (sweet potato) pit. As they drew near, he muttered, *'Ka mate, ka mate'* ('It is death, it is death'). Concealed from the Tohunga – a rival *iwi* – he was protected by the spiritual powers of both food and a woman who was helping him. Te Rauparaha was not discovered and, as the searchers passed overhead, he muttered '*Ka ora, ka ora*' ('It is life, it is life'). When the warriors finally departed, Te Rauparaha was able to climb up out of the *kumara* pit chanting: '*Tenei te tangata puhuruhuru nana nei i tiki mai whaka whiti te ra.*' He had escaped the darkness of the pit and was greeted by the light of the sun.

The *haka* definitely brought us all closer together, and we thanked and hugged our hosts. Even the Māori warrior, now looking less fearsome and intimidating in his civilian clothing, gave me a huge bear hug with his enormous arms.

It had been a long, intense day and I felt blessed and very honoured to have been given these insights into a proud and vibrant people.

***

DAY FOURTEEN, LATE AFTERNOON

TĀ MOKO

SAM

I looked down at my arm. It looked like a mermaid or talisman, an object with religious or magical powers, or a potent person. Swirls of the hammerhead shark and fern leaves made up the vivid outline of the temporary *moko* (the European name, from the Tahitian, would be a 'tattoo'). This one had been drawn on my forearm first in yellow marker then in black biro and I loved it. It represented my story and my life so far.

We arrived at 'Moko 101' in Rotorua, a traditional *moko* parlour, having come straight from the Māori village, as usual, tight for time. Our host was Hohua. He was tall, perhaps even taller than Graham or me. At first, I was intimidated, his whole body and face covered in *tā moko* design, but as we shook hands his warm smile and soft eyes welcomed us. He wore a T-shirt and shorts and looked cool as hell.

He described *tā moko* as a process that reveals the character of an individual hidden beneath their skin, denoting an individual's link to their family, heritage and themselves. After a fascinating and electric day being welcomed and then immersed in Māori tradition, I was tired and raw. The welcome ceremony to the *marae* had been intense but joyful and the *haka*, weapons training and waka race (Graham and I had raced each other in the traditional Māori canoe – I had beaten him easily, of course!) had tired us out. At least falling in a couple of times during the race meant that I no longer smelled of rotten eggs – from the hot mud bath, days before.

We were welcomed into the parlour and admired the pictures of traditional artwork. It occurred to me that the Scottish Pict warriors had been described by the Romans as 'the painted people', covered from head to toe in traditional hand-drawn tattoos. It felt as if, despite being halfway around the world, the Picts and the Māori had very similar traditions.

We were invited to lie on the bench and talk to Hohua in a very intimate manner. As the cameras rolled, I listened to Graham begin to open up about his family, his parents and his difficult relationship with his father. Silence fell upon the crew as we were all drawn into his story and moved deeply by the outcome. His *tā moko* was strong, dazzling and suited him greatly.

Then it was my turn. I felt nervous and flushed – my face was bright red. Did I want to share my secrets with a stranger? Did I want to talk openly on camera about subjects I'd kept to myself

for my entire life? As I started to talk, Hohua listened, his tone reassuring. He asked the occasional question, digging a little deeper in order to try to understand the journey I had been on. I talked, as if in therapy, of my father's absence, my brother, my mother's care, my fears and hopes. I mentioned the guilt I felt about a recent death in the family and some of my more intimate relationships. Hohua listened as I talked, quietly sketching a design on a piece of paper. Unable to see what was being drawn, I continued to unpack my life. He then picked up my left forearm, turned it over and began to draw in marker pen.

Maybe an hour later, I sat up from the table, moist from sweat but feeling relieved. It felt good to talk, to share, to lay some things to rest. And there on my arm was the most beautiful temporary design. Hohua had chosen my left inner forearm because the left side is feminine and I had spoken about my mother a lot. A single parent, she had raised me and my brother well. It was on the inside of my arm, close to my heart and hidden, being something that I kept sacred and didn't want to openly share with the world. The design pointed towards my head and heart: 'Your mother's advice travelling to your ear, so she can always guide you,' he explained. The two hammerhead motifs symbolized my brother and me, and the large gap in the design was the absence of my father. There was also a talisman to remind, comfort and remove any negative thoughts. Fern-leaf edges represented the opportunities and travel that I hoped for in the future. There, on my arm, was a deeply personal representation of my inner thoughts and feelings to carry my family with me and remind me of where I was from. Yet, if I didn't want to, I wouldn't have to explain the meaning; to a casual observer it just looked like a unique and pretty design.

I loved it.

***

Sam: Incredible experience. I love this *tā moko*. I'd really like to get one done before I leave but I doubt we have time. I leave at 10am? Best wishes, my friend and thank you. Sam.

Hohua: Nah sorry, my bro, I'm in Hastings for a *kauai* (chin *moko*) and *mataora* (facial *moko*). Ratz – if u could wrap up earlier, I might have been able to fit it in tonight.

Sam: Decided I'm coming back and getting a proper session when I eventually finish shooting *Outlander*, add it to the story . . .

Hohua: All good, my bro, I hope you both can travel back one day. Thank you for sharing your stories with me, I know that this can be difficult at times, especially when it's things that are quite personal. Was awesome to meet you both, travel safely and remember, we are all connected through the *rahu* (pigment).

***

Unfortunately, there was no time for me to have my *moko* made permanent. We were leaving the next morning and Hohua was in huge demand. I didn't wash my arm for days and every time I caught a glimpse of it under my sleeve or in the New Zealand sun, it comforted me and made my heart a little bit prouder. I was desperate to keep the design and as it faded away, I felt sad to have lost the story. But then I realized that my life and journey are always changing. Even this trip to the southern hemisphere could become part of a new design and my friendship with a certain bearded latte drinker could be captured too. I realized I had been on the greatest adventure and still had a long way to go, so I promised myself that, if it felt right at the time, once I had completed my work on *Outlander* (so far living almost a decade as Jamie Fraser in Scotland), I would return to Moko 101. I wondered what other stories and experiences I'd be able to tell Hohua that would enrich my *tā moko* further . . .

GRAHAM

In the interests of full disclosure, I have to say that I have never had any interest in getting a tattoo. For a brief, fleeting nanosecond (about the time it takes for Sam to come down from one adrenaline rush before seeking the next), I thought about getting one to commemorate the birth of my first child. But just as quickly (like Duncan downing a whisky), it was gone.

I've just never understood it. When I was growing up, the only people who had tattoos were sailors and, well . . . convicts. Now it's more unusual NOT to see some Eastern symbol of meditation nailed to someone's lower back, or a favourite cartoon character adorning someone's arm. Don't get me wrong, I loved Bugs Bunny, but I wouldn't want to see his toothy grin PERMANENTLY on my shoulder.

And there are those ones called 'sleeves'. I have a friend who has the entire history of Tottenham Hotspur Football Club tattooed all over his body. I like football, but if I tattooed the history of the England football team across my torso it would just be a lot of missed penalties and images of copious weeping. Then there are the leg ones. One calf is tattooed while the other is spared.

I was once shown by a *Hobbit* fan a tattoo on her thigh of my face as Dwalin. By the time she gets to 85 years old, Dwalin's face will resemble that of Jabba the Hutt, because, COME ON, what about when you get old? When that face you had tattooed on your chest starts to resemble a bag of spanners as your skin slowly starts creeping downwards to your knees. Or the neck tattoos? I only have one question – why? Necks don't age well, and the tattoos on them are going to end up looking like the drunken doodlings of a five-year-old. I'm told by those who have them that they are addictive. But then, so is crack.

My eldest daughter (she's 16) announced her intention to get a tattoo when she turns 18 to celebrate her favourite K-Pop band. I tried to smile and nod but I think I ended up looking like I was having a stroke (which is probably what the tattoo would end up looking like eventually). So, in a nutshell, no tats for me. That is, until I went to Moko 101 in Rotorua.

As Hohua began to draw my *tā moko* onto my forearm, it all made sense. First of all, *tā moko* is NOT tattooing, a mistake I myself made before Hohua gently corrected me. This was *tā moko*, and *tā moko* is already within us; it is the job of the *moko* artist to draw it out. And this he did by subtly probing my history. Like all the best therapists, (and believe me, that is what Hohua is), he got me talking about my father, and reflecting upon the similarities in our lives and how I was trying to learn from my father in relation to spending more time with my own children. In talking about them all, I felt a great combination of sadness, relief and pride. I have always known I miss my father, that I regret not asking him more and that there are conversations that I wish we had had, but this conversation with Hohua as he drew on my arm felt, in some way, as if I was communicating directly with my dad. By the time he had finished, I felt that both my father and I were in that small *moko* parlour in Rotorua together and that our lost communication was there, etched upon my arm. It was a beautiful design, reflecting my love for my children, their connection with their grandfather, and the lessons that he taught me, all combined into a flowing, connected tribute to the legacy of ancestry that we all carry. It was a genuinely moving experience.

Sam has spoken of wanting to return to get it done permanently. Would I? I'm not positive I would, but I certainly know where to find Hohua if I need him. I feel as if, after our conversation, he has added my father to the host of stories that he carries within him as the great *tā moko* artist that he undoubtedly is and, if the time came, he would be ready for me.

CHAPTER FOURTEEN

Valentine's

DAY FOURTEEN, EVENING

SAM

Valentine's Day (well, it was in New Zealand, a day before everywhere else in the world).

The server at the smoothie shop smiled sweetly and disappeared behind the counter. Or at least I think she smiled beneath her N95 mask. She had winked at me *[Graham: could've been the beginnings of a seizure?]*, the only possible form of communication with a surgical mask, and she had given me extra protein in my shake. For free! So I hoped she liked me and wasn't just feeling sorry for me and my disarming odour. (I'd popped back for another mud spa and hadn't hosed myself down properly in the rush to the next location. Graham was so repulsed he kept the camper van window down all morning on principle, convinced that perhaps there was something wrong with the toilet or that we had dropped an egg making breakfast – such was the ripe sulphuric smell filling the camper van interior.)

I believed she had very beautiful eyes (doesn't everyone wearing a mask?!) *[Graham: no, they don't]* and I swore to myself I'd ask her out for coffee (or a smoothie? Though that was perhaps overkill seeing as she served them all day?). But after sucking down the ice-cold banana nut drink, I couldn't catch her attention. She made herself busy by cutting strawberries and shaving ice. I wondered if she had perhaps caught a whiff of my freshly exfoliated pores and would hurriedly leave the shop before I blasted my ass trumpet. *[Graham: It's like reading an undiscovered manuscript by Noël Coward, isn't it?]*

So it was Valentine's night and I had no date, but the evening off work. I walked back to the romantic lakeside hotel we had been treated to by production. It was our last day in Rotorua and I'd been upgraded to a one-bedroom suite. I pictured myself and my imaginary partner sharing some fine wine, a delicious dinner and then making use of the hot tub, overlooking the shimmering lake as it reflected a lonesome full moon. Instead, I sighed and settled down to order room service and have a quiet night in.

Brrriiing. The phone shattered the balmy summer evening. The local sheep, grazing peacefully halfway down the grassy slope towards the still lake, looked up in disdain.

'Oi, bastard. What are you doing? I've booked a table. Get your ass over here and stop feeling sorry for yourself.' Graham hung up and I sighed again; at least I wouldn't have to be alone on Valentine's night.

Red rose petals were scattered around the hotel restaurant, on the floor. A rather surprised waiter led me to a secluded wooden booth. Heavy red velvet curtains provided some privacy from the other couples sharing an intimate moment. There, sitting waiting and tapping his fingers impatiently, was Graham, my date for the evening.

Again.

We had dined at this very table a number of times. I stifled another sigh and sat down. Graham silently pushed a large red rose in front of my face. 'Happy Valentine's!' he said. 'Now let's order some of that expensive wine!'

My mood brightened. 'Ah yes!' I thought. 'Maybe we can finally go halves, split the bill!? Go Dutch? After all, it IS Valentine's! Let's get a bottle,' I replied. 'Or two!' Pegasus Bay Del Canto 2017. Oh, it's nectar from the Greek gods, perhaps created by Aphrodite herself, the god of love. *[Graham: Goddess. Sorry to be such a stickler for the gendering of the ancient divinities.]*

The label had a picture of Pegasus, the mythological flying horse. 'I hate horses,' Graham reminded me, 'but this one tastes good,' he added. A dry Riesling from New Canterbury, New Zealand, I had actually tasted this back in Scotland and LOVED it. A slight fizz on the tongue, citrus with dry apples and with only the slight oiliness/heavy mouthfeel of a Riesling, it was delicious. So delicious, we ordered another before our main meals arrived. The waiter looked slightly nervous; I think he was confused as to whether we were staying at the hotel together or TOGETHER. I thought it best to playfully continue his dubiety and order a further two glasses of champagne. 'We're celebrating, aren't we, darling?' I clinked Graham's flute.

'Mmmmm,' Graham agreed, barely looking up from his roast venison haunch.

In reality, we were; we had almost finished our journey around the islands of New Zealand and, more importantly, we were still friends, still speaking to one another (if you can call the odd grump or groan from McG 'communication'). Indeed, our relationship HAD developed further; we had travelled the length and breadth of the islands and supported each other in some very precarious moments. I'd even seen Graham cry a number of times: upon waking, upon finishing the contents of the snack box, zip-lining, speed-boating, receiving the check after dinner, and falling upside down attached to me. We had slept in a rickety camper van and travelled hundreds of miles and were now sharing a romantic and intimate Valentine's dinner – albeit we were forced to as neither of us had secured a more appropriate date. We certainly now shared a mutual love for all things Kiwi (especially the wine) and I thought our Greek god friends would approve. Cheers!

'Want to come back to mine for, erm, a nightcap?' I said quietly.

Graham stopped mid-chew. The waiter, pouring the last of the wine, stopped and vanished backwards behind the heavy curtains.

'What kind of nightcap? What have you got stashed away?' He spat pieces of honeycomb across the table. 'We've got an early start tomorrow,' he swallowed.

'Oh, just a little . . . bottle . . .' I winked. 'If you get lucky?'

Graham rolled his eyes and pushed back his chair. The other couples all looked up from their candlelit dinners and watched us leave. I made sure to hold the door open for my date as we left.

'We'll see you for breakfast.' We waved to the waiter, who waved back holding the red rose we had given him.

'Ah, I see I'm not the only one you've invited back tonight.' Graham stopped at the open door to my suite; I had left it ajar and the lights were on. 'I'm a little upset, I thought I was special, but you've literally invited hundreds over for a party. No, thousands!'

Graham was right; instead of a quiet night in, I had somehow allowed the entire lakeside population into the superior suite bedroom, and the party was in full swing! 'It's a bloody orgy!' Graham exclaimed and looked at the mass of bodies writhing on the floor. And the ceiling.

And the walls.

The lights and open door had allowed the infinitely vast community of marsh flies into the room and they were going at it with abandon. 'What do you expect from a creature that only lasts one night? It's going to live its life to the max!' I replied, staring in disbelief at the vast bacchanalia before me. The flies were partying in every room, hundreds of thousands of them in an epic lakeside pool-party bender. They were going to party hard all night until they literally dropped dead.

'Oh well, if you can't beat them, join them,' I said and poured us both a large double wood Oamaruvian whisky and we settled down on the couch together and marvelled at the night sky among the slowly dying, debauched local insects.

VALENTINE'S DAY REDUX

GRAHAM

I realize that some of you reading this would like nothing more than a Valentine's Day dinner with my waxed companion (I only know this waxed fact from spending far too much time cheek by jowl in a camper van around the country with him, and NO! I don't know quite how far his depilating is taken).

However, not all Valentine's evenings are created equally. In this case, this bore about as much resemblance to a romantic dinner for two as my room bore to the expansiveness of Sam's lakeside suite. We had arrived at the hotel and sauntered towards a gigantic bungalow with a veranda the size of a small apartment – a structure laughingly referred to as 'a room'. It was a room in the same way that the Taj Mahal could be described by a realtor as a detached house. As I prepared to dump my bags in relief, after a day of Zorbing without lube, the porter politely pointed out that this was 'Mr Heughan's room'. I followed him out feeling the scorch marks of Sam's mocking grin on my back. I was then led into what appeared to be the entrance to a bomb shelter. The walls were heaving with insects (were they expecting the midge-whisperer himself?). They were literally coating the walls, and after a couple of turns through sweating dark corridors I was ushered into my room. While it had a bed and a toilet, it was there that the comparison with Sam's accommodation ended. It looked like someone had forgotten to tell my room that the rest of the hotel had been upgraded some twenty years earlier. It stubbornly refused to give up its fading decoration and reminded me of the interior of a bad 1970s sitcom.

We had three nights here during which we experienced multiple adventures, but our last night was, indeed, Valentine's night.

Once more, at this point, I need to remind the reader (or listener) that this book shows two very different sets of remembrances: Sam's, the ramblings of a man trapped in a self-made fantasy, and mine, the accurate recorder of all that occurred, mainly because it has been seared into my cortex like the kind of trauma that a therapist's second home is made of.

I did indeed summon Sam to dinner. I had actually forgotten that it was Valentine's Day (strangely, my romantic mind was not up to speed that day), so I was somewhat surprised when I was led to a secluded corner table and there, lost in the white linen expanse of tablecloth, was indeed, a single red rose.

'Odd,' I thought.

It was then that I looked around the other tables. Ours was the most secluded, almost hidden. The others were filled with couples gently sipping champagne under the soft amber glow of candlelight, fingers entwined, eyes brimming with . . . 'Oh God,' I suddenly realized. 'It's f#@k*!g Valentine's Day!'

At that moment, my date chose to arrive. As the waiter poured us two glasses of Sam's excellent wine choice, for a moment all the other couples paused in their mutual adoration and raised their glasses, as if to say, 'That's so sweet. The two of you are finally enjoying a quiet evening together. The fact that you choose to do so in a secluded corner table on Valentine's Day, with velvet curtains, soft candlelight, and a single red rose is just a weird, totally unanticipated coincidence and NOT the final declaration of love that it so painfully appears to be.'

All of this ran through my mind quite as if the entire room had spoken this out loud in unison. We both smiled valiantly. I think we both tried to convey in our expressions a careful mixture of 'It's really lovely to be here on this special night, but really, the red rose wasn't my idea, we are, in fact, mainly thinking about what "our team" had planned for the morning (not something I'm bouncing up and down with joy about), and frankly I'd rather be having dinner with virtually anyone on Valentine's night than the person you see seated opposite me. Cheers!'

After the waiter had finished pouring the wine, he left us to our own turbulent thoughts. I think he may have winked as he left. No wonder we ended up drinking so many bottles of that Riesling. By the time we left, I'm pretty sure we were the last 'couple' there. Or perhaps we left early, the eyes of the room following us in approval at our burgeoning romance. Either way, it's true, we ended up back at the Taj Mahal and yes, indeed, a party of tiny flesh-eating insects was in full swing. It seems that Sam wasn't going to be the only one enjoying a lakeside view that night. I finally left him to his miniature house guests, no doubt reminiscing together about midge nets in the Highlands of Scotland, and retired to my bomb shelter, surprised that I still had that single red rose in my hand.

CHAPTER FIFTEEN

A Swing Made for Two

DAY FIFTEEN, MORNING

<u>Location: Near Queenstown/Tahūna, Otago, back on the South Island</u>

GRAHAM

Before I sat down to write about this final, climactic tale of horror, I thought I'd do a quick Google search of the ten scariest things you can do. Now obviously everyone's list varies. Some would include being trapped in a room full of spiders, being stuck in an elevator with ten other people, or a Friday night with Duncan Lacroix, but this is what immediately came up:

1. Shark cage diving. (Yup!)
2. Bungee jumping from the highest bungee jump in the world. (It's in South Africa, if you have a thirst for testing the limits of your sanity, but are you detecting a pattern?)

3. Class 5 white water rafting on l'Imbut at the Gorges du Verdons. (Where is that you ask? To which I respond, I DON'T CARE!)
4. Crocodile cage diving. (I'm not making this up.)
5. Survival training. (A Friday night with Lacroix DID make the list then.)
6. A very, very long incredibly high zip line. (Yes . . . I see.)
7. Caving. (Did that in my teens. NEVER again, and Sam – don't even think about it.)
8. Skydiving. *[Sam – see above.]*
9. Ice diving. (Serious doubts about the mental health of anyone who does this.)
10. Rock climbing. (Nope, been there done that.)

Yes, it appears Sam may have consulted this list before travelling to New Zealand.

I mention all this because it brings me to the climax of our trip, the deus ex machina of *Men in Kilts*, the circle of hell that even Dante refused to write about: ladies and gentlemen, I give you **the Nevis Swing.**

[Sam: The very exciting, wild and screamy climax, or as I like to call it the 'Grimax'.]

SAM

Through it all, the old bugger had survived. Graham had kept up with me on this epic journey and at times, surpassed me. Not only that, I'm ashamed to admit, he'd beaten me on several sporting occasions. Back in 2020, we had shorn sheep, swum naked in the Atlantic (well, I had), traversed the barren battlefield of Culloden in the Highlands of Scotland, and now we had travelled halfway around the world to continue our adventures here. In these magical islands in the southern hemisphere, we had learned about the Māori culture, witnessed the varied animal life, sampled the extensive Kiwi cuisine and laughed a lot. Through all our travels, Graham and I had barely fallen out, in fact, not once. We remained firm friends, bonded by the experiences shared together. Even Squeezy's safety meetings hadn't worn down our resolve.

As I stood on top of the Nevis mountaintop, just outside of Queensland, back on the South Island for one final hurrah, I realized it was not quite as high as its Scottish namesake. I studied my unsuspecting companion struggling once more with his adult's baby harness; he puffed and groaned as he tightened the belt and shoulder straps. I thought back to us sharing a dram on the final leg of our journey in Scotland. Graham's eyes had welled up as he toasted our first adventure together and he uttered the words: 'I really do hope we do it all again.'

'He's only got himself to blame,' I thought to myself and couldn't help smiling.

Over the past few weeks, I'd slowly pushed my risk-averse companion further each day. I think the cumulative stress and adrenaline overload on his brain finally pushed him over the edge, so to speak! In fact, McTavish was currently displaying definite signs of Stockholm Syndrome, happily strapping (though struggling) himself into his harness. I'd go as far as to say, he was in a good mood . . . for now.

'So, mate, what are we doing?' the bearded one asked expectantly; so far he'd zip-lined off a 100-m (328-ft) cliff, been driven in a speedboat, flown in a helicopter over snow-capped peaks and even slalomed down a mountain in a child's go-kart. 'Oh, not much. Just walk over this little bridge then sit on a swing,' I replied, reading the sign at the entrance to the walkway. 'You know, Graham, I'm really proud of you. You've learned to fear less and live more.'

Like a frightened gazelle sensing a pride of lions stealthily approaching in the tall grass, Graham stopped in his tracks. His nose twitched, smelling the scent of predators on the breeze. The man could sense danger a mile away, but I had hoped by now I'd managed to dull his instincts. I remember filming with him in the presence of a rampant Highland cow, back in Season One of *Outlander*. Back then he had resembled a meerkat, ears pinned back, lip trembling, planning the quickest escape route over the drystone wall and out of sight. 'Uuuuhh, errrrr, I don't like him, mate, not one bit. You've always got to have an escape route!' he had mumbled, more to himself than to the accompanying actors, dressed as Scottish Highland warriors. Duncan Lacroix and I smiled at each other. 'Ah, the brave war chief,' we sniggered. Nothing had changed.

So here he stood, on the precipice of a long suspended walkway, high above the valley floor, dressed in a safety harness and sporty clothing (hopefully waterproof, should he soil himself during the activity).

'Wait, wait, wait. WHAT are we doing again?' he asked over his shoulder, staring directly ahead, not daring to look down. The penny had dropped. His brain had finally woken up. The sedative I had gradually supplied – a toxic mix of extreme adrenaline, frothy caffeine, zero sleep in a cramped camper van and copious amounts of Sauvignon Blanc – had failed to suppress his survival instinct after all. 'No, wait. I don't want to do this. What are we doing?!' he asked again, his life flashing before his eyes. I thought it best to keep him calm so, in my softest voice, I gently coaxed him further.

'It's fine, buddy, just keep walking, we're almost done. It'll all be over soon.' I carefully manoeuvred him forward onto the suspension bridge. 'We are just going to walk over there and sit on a little swing,' I continued. It was painfully slow but he started to walk, a trembling hand holding on to each side of the bridge. 'It's just a little swing . . . and a . . . *terrific* view!' I said, looking down at the valley below.

The Nevis Swing, the highest in the world, has a platform (the one we were standing on) 160m (525ft) up and the swing itself carries passengers over a huge 300-m (984-ft) arcing drop, just metres above the valley floor, at speeds of up to 120km/h (75mph)!

We were quickly strapped in and, by now, Graham had gone silent. Normally in these terrifying situations he breathes heavily and swears a lot. This time, total silence. For a brief moment I felt pity for him . . . but then thought better of it. 'YES, MATE!' I shouted, to encourage him and hide the nerves rising up from the pit of my stomach. It really was high, and we were about to plummet together backwards, upside down with only a harness to catch our fall.

'Three . . . two . . . one . . .'

Then there was nothing and the world fell away . . .

GRAHAM

The Nevis Swing. It doesn't sound too bad, does it? I mean, it has the word 'swing' in its name. Who doesn't like to swing? (Unless it's at the end of a noose.) But don't be fooled. It is the product of a satanic imagination, and the person who would think to introduce this as part of a New Zealand camper tour is on definite first-name terms with the ginger imp himself. In other words, Sam Heughan.

I knew what was planned which, of course, made it worse. I knew the show was to climax with one of us being flung from a cliff side on a swing seat suspended by a piece of dental floss to plummet straight down before arcing across a gigantic canyon until eventually either the swinging stopped, or your heart did.

Let me set the scene: the Nevis Swing is the largest canyon swing in the world.

Suspended high above a yawning canyon, it drops you the length of an Olympic running track until you reach terminal velocity, then swings you across the gaping maw of death below you for another 300m (984ft). You reach it by crossing a suspension bridge, wide enough for one person, onto a platform not much bigger than a doormat. It was this diabolical creation that I found myself walking towards on a sunny day near Queenstown. I was very unsure I could do this. I had voiced my concerns (terror) to our esteemed director, Kevin, back at the reception area. (Yes, hell actually has a reception.) He told me that they had already done reconnaissance and several of the crew had really loved it. 'Did you do it, Kevin?' I had asked.

'Er, no.'

'Who did?'

'Well, Simon.'

Of course, Simon had. He was probably doing it again while

we were talking, perhaps with some slow fuse dynamite strapped to his body just to add to the thrills.

'Anyone else?'

'I did it!' piped Squeezy. 'I loved it. So serene. All you hear are the sounds of the birds.' She smiled as she said this, of course. I almost believed her.

One of the staff, Doug, came over to reassure me. 'Hi. I'm Doug. Nice to meet you. Are you nervous?'

'How can you tell?'

'Don't worry. It's really not scary.'

I looked at this young man with a healthy, outdoor complexion, winning smile, and encouraging nod. 'Doug. Do you go upside down at any point?' I asked, because for me this was the deal-breaker; the idea of falling upside down was just too hideous to even entertain.

'No, absolutely not. It's a swing, so you . . . you know, swing. It's very peaceful,' said Doug helpfully. I felt Kevin's eyes upon me, as well as those of the entire building we were standing in. Sam had announced that he was going to join me on the swing. As I'm sure you can understand, this did not reassure me. The equivalent of Jeffrey Dahmer saying, 'You must come over for dinner.'

Sam caught my eye, Squeezy smiled and Doug gave an encouraging nod. 'Just as long as I'm not upside down,' I repeated.

'You won't be,' reassured the baby-faced Doug.

And so, I was strapped into yet another harness. The number of harnesses I've been strapped into on this trip would make even Black Jack blush. Once gripped by the nylon straps and carabiners, it was time to take the long walk to the distant platform floating above the canyon. I'm told that when people were to be taken to be hanged, the executioner could get them from their condemned cell to the trapdoor and pull the lever in ten seconds. This walk took a little longer, mainly because I was shaking uncontrollably on the bouncing suspension bridge. The crew had gone on ahead, determined to record every moment of my sphincter-clenching fear. Sam walked behind me. I won't repeat what he said but suffice to say it was the exact opposite of helpful.

Finally, we arrived on the platform. It was absurd! At least ten people were crammed onto a space that was about equal to something you'd step onto climbing out of a bath.

Simon was hooked onto the side of the platform leaning out into the void, grinning like a maniac. (I was beginning to hate him.) Another prepubescent member of staff checked my S&M harness. I asked again if I would go upside down.

'Oh no, not at all. It's a swing,' said another baby-faced member of staff. 'Okay, I'm going to hook you on, Graham.'

I think Sam started muttering words of encouragement. Things like, 'You're fucked, mate,' and 'Please shit yourself downwind of me,' but I can't be sure. The reason I can't be sure is that all I could hear was the blood pounding in my ears and the sound of my tortured, terrified breathing. I think I kept repeating the words, 'Oh shit, oh fuck, oh no,' like some unholy mantra.

'Okay, Graham and Sam,' announced the preschooler who was helping us. 'I'm going to ask you to walk backwards to the edge of the platform.'

Okay, let's pause here. I'm on the equivalent of a yoga mat suspended over a canyon, sitting on a bar that resembles a large toothpick, clipped onto some giant piece of rope next to a notorious adrenaline junkie/sadist, and I was being asked to walk BACKWARDS TO THE EDGE OF THE PLATFORM.

WHY? Why would I do it backwards?!

'It's actually less scary. People prefer it. That way they can't see what's coming,' said the cherubic assassin.

Rather like wearing a blindfold at your own execution?

By this point, my nerves were so shredded, my brain so scrambled that he could've said, 'Because that's what I've been paid to tell you but it's complete bullshit and it'll be way worse than going face first,' and I would have just meekly nodded and gone, 'Yes, please, sir, just make sure that the guillotine is nice and sharp.'

So it came to pass that Sam and I edged backwards until our feet were on the very micron edge of the platform. We were then told to sit in the seat. (The very idea of calling something that you would use to stir a cocktail a 'seat' was ludicrous.) Sam began to sit, which forced my own inevitable descent into a recumbent position. We were now dangling over the edge like a pair of Pooh sticks that you are preparing to drop into a river far, far below you.

'Good luck, mate,' said the man in the sleeveless top.

I think I may have uttered the heart-warming response, 'I hate you.'

'We're going to pull you further out now,' which just sounded like, 'Just making sure our guns are loaded.'

'Okay, on five.'

'Five . . .'

'Four . . .'

'Three . . .'

'Two . . .'

'One . . .'

There are things in this world that are so terrifying that, rather than utter a sound, your mouth freezes in a silent scream. Not the excited scream of a rollercoaster, or the fright of a scary movie. No. This was something else. This was naked, balls-out terror.

We felt the release of the swing and then . . .

My feet.

All I could see as I rushed downwards towards the earth, my scream trapped in my throat, were my feet.

I was upside down.

I was upside down, falling downwards at an alarming speed . . .

SAM

A rushing, shrill wind filled my ears, or was it the screaming from my companion? Or maybe me? 'That's strange, is that supposed to happen?' I thought. The ground was now above us. We had inverted and were falling headfirst at an incredible speed. 'Perhaps this is it? I've pushed it too far?' My brain questioned whether this had actually been a mistake; if we didn't fall to our deaths, smashed to pieces by the rocks below, we could probably die of a heart attack or a broken neck due to whiplash. I thought it best if I recorded our demise on camera for posterity and future lawsuits. I angled my GoPro at the limp body next to me: totally lifeless. Graham was a deadweight.

GRAHAM

The gravity of the earth pulls you at a constant acceleration of 9.81m per second per second (32ft per second per second). Which means that you fall 9.81m per second faster every second. So, at a speed of 9.81m per second during the first second, and 19.62m per second the next second, and so on until, basically, you hit the ground.

This was a 100-m (328-ft) drop. Just take a moment to let that sink in.

My brain, while at the same time gazing in horror at my own feet above me, was telling me in no uncertain terms: 'You're about to die. This is what death feels like. You're welcome.' One other thought managed to surface through the harrowing frontal-lobe miasma I was enduring. *They had me face backwards so they could record my facial expression as my ass remained suspended briefly in the air while the rest of me plummeted straight down!*

The freefall was long enough to become on first-name terms with true fear. There was no way my brain was going to be able to rationalize this; instead it was screaming inside my head, 'You are upside down hurtling towards your imminent fatal end.'

SAM

Then suddenly: GAHHHH!! The swing caught at the end of the rope and spun us back upright; we swung high up again and out over the valley. 'Yeeeesssss, ha-ha-hah!!!!' I shouted and we became a human pendulum, rocking back and forth across the vast Nevis gorge.

GRAHAM

Meanwhile, of course, Sam was whooping and bellowing like some demented hippopotamus. But I can assure you, the one sound I definitely could not hear was the sound of birdsong. We finally reached the bottom of our fall only to feel ourselves curving backwards in a harrowing arc of pant-staining endlessness. At that point, my stomach chose to join me (it was about two seconds behind the rest of me, desperately trying its best to catch up), and my feet were finally facing forwards (well, backwards, but below my head!). As we couldn't see where we were going, it felt like at any moment we were going to splatter like bugs on a car windscreen as we said hello to the canyon wall.

As we reached what felt like the limit of the known universe, we began to go back in the other direction. It was then that I found my voice; I couldn't hold it in any longer. No, not screaming, I simply burst into tears. I'm not ashamed to say that I was so pathetically grateful to not actually be dead that the emotion just exploded out of me, partly out of relief that nothing had exploded in my underwear. I turned to Sam, suddenly feeling an overwhelming fondness for this monstrous architect of terror, and started telling him how glad I was that he was there. Yes, I really was that out of it!

SAM

'What a view! What a ride! What a journey!' I smiled and looked at my friend. 'Thank you, buddy! What a way to end it!' Graham was smiling and laughing, too. No . . . he was crying.

'Oh, ho, ho, ho! Thank you, mate. Thank you. I couldn't have done it without you. I was soooo scared!' he sobbed. Tears of joy, I think.

GRAHAM

Clearly, I had experienced some kind of psychotic breakdown. It was then that I became aware of the GoPro in Sam's hands. Yes, he was filming me as I wept. Sam was concentrating on getting the best camera angle to record my wracking sobs. Is there no depth to which this man will not sink? No moment of pain and humiliation too private not to chronicle for the twisted pleasure of others? Apparently not.

Finally, the endless back and forth of the hellish contraption came to an end.

SAM

We were pulled back up to the platform and released from our straitjackets. I whipped out my flask, filled with delicious Sassenach whisky (that I'd somehow saved the whole journey), and we toasted our adventures and having cheated death. 'Cheers, buddy, thank you for inviting me to New Zealand. I've had such a great time!' I passed the flask over after taking a celebratory swig. Graham stood shell-shocked.

'The torture. Panic. Fear. Surprise. Cliff edges . . . where did it all go wrong?' he jabbered and took a swig after each word, finishing the bottle in seconds. The adventure was over, BUT he was still alive.

GRAHAM

I could see Squeezy smiling. I think Simon was probably base-jumping off the side out of sheer boredom. I think the crew were clapping. I think we had whisky to celebrate. I think I survived!

But all I was really thinking was . . . 'Where's that BASTARD DOUG?!!!'

CHAPTER SIXTEEN

Remembering

'Any historical narrative is a particular bundle of silences . . .'
Michel-Rolph Trouillot, *Silencing the Past*

DAY SIXTEEN

Location: Auckland/Tāmaki Makaurau, North Island

Situated between the Hauraki Gulf (east), the Hunua Ranges
(south-east), the Manukau Harbour (south-west), and the
Waitākere Ranges (west and north-west), the Māori name
means 'Tāmaki desired by many', due to its natural resources and
topography. Local *iwi*: Ngāti Whātua, Tainui, Ngāti Ākarana
(pan-tribal).

GRAHAM

After terror comes quiet reflection. Not only for my own brushes
with death while on this epic journey, but also, inspired by the War
Memorial in Auckland, the city where our adventures end, the
extraordinary sacrifice of those New Zealanders who endured the
horrors and lost their lives in the First and Second World Wars.

When war was declared by Britain in August 1914, New Zealand
was very different. Even today it can feel very isolated and far from
the world – especially if you travel around the country in a camper
van. In 1914, it must have felt like you were on a distant planet.

It was only around 50 years since the bloody Waikato Wars, and
33 years since the infamous invasion of Parihaka in 1881. This was
the decision by the colonial government to send 1,600 troops into
an area in Taranaki in order to break what had come to symbolize
the peaceful resistance by Māori against the confiscation of their
land. People remembered it. People definitely had relatives who
remembered only too well.

So, the response from the Māori population was mixed, to say
the least. One can imagine the reaction of someone whose relatives
were killed by the very people now asking for their help. People
who may have lost grandparents, cousins, uncles. I expect it was
the Māori equivalent of 'they can go f*#k themselves.' The views
of *Pākehā* and Māori were deeply entrenched, and there was little
mixing among them. Most Māori still lived in rural areas. Some,
whose bloodlines had benefited from the individualization of land
titles, lived in modern European-style homes, but at the other
extreme those who had lost everything through land confiscation
had three or four generations living in a cramped two-room tin hut.

Māori were blamed by many *Pākehā* for the smallpox epidemic of
1913, which resulted in Māori needing to show proof of vaccination,
and many restaurants banning Māori from their premises. (This is,
perhaps, one reason that many Māori resisted the more recent call
for mass Covid vaccination, many reminded of something similar
100 years earlier when they, along with other non-vaccinated New
Zealanders, were denied entry to restaurants.) For their part some
Māori believed the Europeans were using it all as a pretext for

discrimination. So when war came in 1914, not all the Māori rushed to serve. As one warrior put it, why should we fight for the British king when we already have a king of our own? It is interesting to note, however, that New Zealand's first foreign adventure in the war was when 1,600 men were sent to invade Samoa, then a German colony, as a 'great and urgent Imperial service'.

As well as some understandable reluctance on the part of some Māori, there was also resistance from the British government to what they called 'a native contingent'. But, after much lobbying by Europeans and Māori alike, and after the formation of the Indian Corps, the government finally relented. Eventually 2,227 Māori and 458 Pacific Islanders fought in the First World War as part of the Māori contingent out of a total male Māori population of around 26,000. They set sail for Egypt, enthusiastically doing rifle and bayonet practice on the way, throwing messages in bottles overboard, optimistically hoping they would reach loved ones. They arrived literally champing at the bit for action. Instead, they were told they would be a garrison force in Egypt protecting the *Pākehā*. NOT what hundreds of hard-as-nails descendants of fearsome warriors wanted at all.

Then Gallipoli happened. To call it a gigantic cock-up from beginning to end is oversimplifying it, and offensive to all cock-ups before and since. Like other notable military disasters, it began with the best intentions: seize control of the Dardanelles Strait, off the coast of north-western Turkey, exposing the Turkish fleet to bombardment, safeguarding the Suez Canal and generally bringing about a swift end to the war. One of the principal enthusiasts behind the plan was Winston Churchill, who went some way towards redeeming himself by leading Britain against the Nazis 25 years later.

However, in 1915, it all went to proverbial shit. The sea campaign failed; the next option was an amphibious landing on the Gallipoli peninsula. There followed eight months of slaughter on an epic scale, resulting in the eventual abandonment of the peninsula by the Allies after 250,000 casualties fell on both sides. It was a defining moment of national consciousness, an awakening for New Zealand

(and Australia) and also for the Māori population whose brave men went to fight on behalf of this fledgling nation. As one veteran put it, 'It took travelling thousands of miles to a distant war to help Māori and *Pākehā* see each other properly for the first time.'

Māori veteran Rikihana Carkeek said in his war memoir: 'It was the first time the tribes had united to fight a common enemy.' So impressive was this body of Māori warriors that one old grey-haired chief was heard to comment, 'If I only had this army of men under me, I could conquer New Zealand!'

These were the guys stuck playing babysitter to the British in Egypt. And then Gallipoli started to unravel, casualties were increasing and they needed men. The announcement was made by the commanding officer in the mess hall of the Māori battalion, 'We're going to fight the Turks.'

Now you or I might have met this news with, 'Actually, I'm quite enjoying Egypt, thanks.'

But not this lot; they went crazy with joy. They couldn't have been happier. If the commanding officer had said: 'After you've finished eating, we're going to take you over to some hell-hole where half of you will almost certainly die,' their response would have still been the same.

The assembled men threw their plates, cutlery and food in the air in raucous celebration, positively screaming for blood. Basically, the 1915 equivalent of 'F*#K YEAH! Show me who to kill first!'

They arrived and it wasn't long before they got their wish. Many Māori had already arrived in Gallipoli as part of the provincial infantry battalions. People like Watene Moeke, who became the first Māori casualty, killed on the very first day of the campaign on 25 April 1915.

The Māori battalion was accommodated in ledges cut into the hills in what became known as Māori Ridge. It was then that they received their orders. The Turks had deployed barbed wire across the foothills on the ridge above, called Chunuk Bair. The battalion were tasked with clearing that barbed wire, while at the same time removing the Turks that were defending it. They were given two and a half hours to do it. Just before those 500 men charged up that hill, their chaplain, Wainohu, gave them these words of encouragement:

Fellow members of a brave family . . . you are the descendants of . . . warlike ancestors . . . I know that some . . . now here will never again stand together with us. But it would be better for us all to lie dead in these hollows and on the tops of mountains than for a whisper of dishonour to go back to the old people at home.

Roughly translated as:

Do what your ancestors would've done, kill everyone with a Turkish accent, and by the way, don't think about surviving if you do anything remotely embarrassing to the family back home. Now off you go and sharpen those bayonets and good luck!

So off they went. They destroyed those in the first seat of trenches that night.

It reminds me very much of Prestonpans and what the British must've felt when they witnessed hundreds of barefoot screaming Gaelic warriors tearing towards them with only one thing on their minds. The Turks, tucked in comfortably behind barbed wire, armed with machine guns, must've thought a horde from Hades itself had descended upon them.

After they had bayoneted, shot, clubbed and generally set about the Turks, the Māori battalion stood in those trenches and performed a giant *haka*. The same one that the All Blacks perform today at rugby matches, 'Ka mate, Ka mate, Ka ora, Ka ora . . .'

Only this time, it was 500 Māori, who weren't there to run around with a ball; 17 Māori were killed, and 89 were wounded. We don't know how many Turkish soldiers died but the ground was thick with bodies while the victorious Māori battalion bellowed out their blood-curdling war cries.

The fighting continued for months until eventually the Allies abandoned the peninsula. By the time those brave Māori soldiers left Gallipoli, of the 16 officers and 461 ordinary soldiers, only 132 were left, along with two officers. A British officer was later heard to remark, 'Of all the men who fought at Gallipoli, the fiercest among them were those Māori.' One of those officers was Colonel William Malone, who exhibited extraordinary bravery during his time on Gallipoli and worked hard to protect his men. He became one of Gallipoli's casualties on 8 August 1915 when he was accidentally killed by Allied supporting artillery fire. But in that great way that history inconveniently reminds us of its complexities, he was also one of those 1,600 men who had invaded Parihaka in 1881. It is, therefore, likely that he stood and died alongside some whose Māori ancestors had been the victims of his own actions 33 years earlier. History is never simple, nor straightforward.

One of the Māori casualties was Lieutenant Thomas Grace, a renowned rugby player and cricketer. He commanded his men on how to bowl grenades into the trenches of the enemy, and specialized in stalking and killing Turkish snipers. Of the 760 members of the Wellington Regiment who fought that day on 5 August 1915, he became one of 711 casualties. It truly must hav e been awful; a day of unspeakable loss. Thomas was a descendant of Horonuku Te Heuheu Tūkino IV, the paramount chief of the Ngāti Tūwharetoa tribe. One of those ancestors for whom honour was upheld but at the highest cost, and who found his final resting place among so many other brave young men, Māori and *Pākehā*, Australian, British and Turkish, on those desolate hills in a small peninsula far, far from home.

ANZAC day, on 25 April, is the day in Australia and New Zealand chosen to honour their war dead, among them, this great Māori warrior.

When I reflect on these brave men and their sacrifice in both the First and Second World Wars, along with their *Pākehā* brothers in arms, it brings home how far New Zealand had come in less than 100 years. In some ways it was out of this terrible crucible of fighting, particularly the First World War, that New Zealand was born.

THAT'S A WRAP!

GRAHAM

Wrap parties, for those unfamiliar with the world of film-making, are those occasions when the producers/studio splash out on a party to celebrate the end of filming.

I have been to a lot of wrap parties. They vary in extravagance and they definitely vary in enjoyment.

The best ones were while working on *The Hobbit*, with a small village in New Zealand taken over for a 'halfway through filming' wrap party. It was an epically long shoot so production sensibly decided to give everyone a morale boost. We were even all given commemorative sweatshirts showing how many days we had shot (it was already in three figures), and the locals were encouraged to abandon the village. My memory is hazy (which probably indicates how bacchanalian it was), but I do remember trying martinis for the first time. I liked them so much that I kept drinking them until I lost count, along with the ability to speak coherently. My last memory was bellowing for 'more drink'! I also remember one of the producers locking themselves out of their room, naked, and having to resort to pulling down a curtain in the elevator lobby in order to cover their modesty.

The final wrap party was truly wonderful. Peter Jackson is one of the most generous, thoughtful people I've ever worked with. Along with our weapons, we were all given paintings done by one of the late Queen's portrait artists, as well as our own Lego figures (with which I was childishly delighted). The party continued with us taking over a whole arena in Wellington with every part of it filled with a dizzying variety of activities.

SAM

Allow me to jump in here. Ahem. Over the course of seven seasons (soon to be an eighth and final season, imagine the party we'll have then!) *Outlander* has held a party each year (bar the Covid-ridden Season Six). The venues have varied but they have always been a blast. Highlights include a mini funfair (on which I was first on the dodgems), a fresh seafood bar (consumed my bodyweight in scallops), arcade machines, several free bars, including a Sassenach Spirits bar where we provided delicious whisky-based cocktails such as highballs, Rob Roys and my favourite, whisky sours. There have been live bands, burlesque dancers that bathed in baked beans and, most recently, I managed to organize the famous Scottish DJ GBX George Bowie to play some bangers!

Every party has been a total blast, with several of the cast and crew arranging to meet beforehand to 'lubricate' ourselves in advance. On one memorable occasion, Duncan Lacroix, Marina Campbell (my Leòdhasach friend), Ron Moore (the *Outlander* showrunner) and I finished a bottle of vodka making home-made martini cocktails. Unfortunately, this meant Duncan had enjoyed himself so much that he didn't make it to the actual party, or at least, left after half an hour! It would be remiss of me to say that Lacroix was the only fatality of the party as virtually every cast and crew member partied until they dropped. It's a long, tough job and by the end of the season everyone is barely able to stand, even before they start on the appletinis. Even my co-star Ms Balfe had to be put in a taxi after the Season One party, due to her 'enthusiasm'.

GRAHAM

Then there was the *Rambo* wrap party. Any detailed mention would need to be completely redacted to protect the innocent, and the guilty. *[Sam: I've heard, actually. All I can say is that Stallone DID pay for 'everything'.]*

Another one was the wrap party for *Family* – a TV miniseries I was in – which ended with karaoke, and the single most disturbing rendition of 'Edelweiss' I have ever heard. Put it this way, you would have run screaming from the theatre if this version had made it into *The Sound of Music*. I also managed to lock myself out of my hotel room (a seemingly popular feature of wrap parties) and had to resort to descending in the elevator stark-bollock naked and ask the appalled receptionist for a replacement key.

Which brings me neatly to our *Men in Kilts 2* wrap party in Auckland. As with most wrap parties – hence why I've only managed to list about five out of probably dozens that I've attended – my memory is sketchy. My principal memory is Sam and I singing 'I'm Gonna Be (500 Miles)' by the Proclaimers. Given the lyrics, this was a decidedly ironic choice – some folk may wish to walk 500 miles to fall down at Sam's door, but I would probably be walking 500 miles in the opposite direction, most likely to the nearest airport.

Karaoke is one of those love/hate things. Some people love it and then there are those that would rather gargle broken glass than listen to another karaoke version of 'YMCA'. I'll leave you to guess my own feelings on the matter. The ones that love it tend to be those who believe they can sing. I don't suffer from this particular delusion having had my singing ability roundly condemned by everyone from family members to professional musicians, even passing toddlers. Others have managed to skip through life without anyone telling them the truth and as such there is always one person at a karaoke party who just won't stop singing. Maybe they will pause for the odd song to allow a couple of other people a chance, mainly just to draw breath, but generally they will glue themselves to the microphone and warble incessantly while the rest of the party guzzle alcohol to drown out the noise. At the *Men in Kilts* party, it was the soundman, Ben, who decided to be the Karaoke Dominatrix of the day. During the shoot, he had been a warm, friendly, reliable presence. A good guy. Nothing was too much trouble. But it was as if all that lovely, warm cuddliness was a cunning ruse to give him licence to own the karaoke. The machine had barely been switched on before he bounded up and began a series of performances that would have made most singers pass out with exhaustion.

I can't remember how many he performed, but I have a vague memory of begging Sam to knock me out just to put an end to the marathon music mangling. My mood was not helped by the scarcity of anything to eat. By the time I arrived, the tables had nearly been swept clean as if a biblical plague of locusts had gate-crashed the party. I can't be sure who were the main culprits but let's just say Squeezy's fanny pack looked unusually heavy.

SAM

It's at this point that I forced Graham to have a drink. 'Shots?' I asked. 'No, no, no. A glass of Sauvignon, if they'll even do that,' he replied grumpily. We managed to secure him a bottle of plonk and I double-fisted a couple of local beers; it'd be rude not to! As I discovered early on in the trip, Wellington is the craft beer capital of New Zealand, and Tuatara and the Garage Project quickly became my favourite Kiwi breweries. I continued to force McTavish into 'the spirit' of things, or should I say continued to force spirits down his throat. He agreed to some local whisky and then I spied my moment as Ben-the-singing-soundman paused for breath. 'Right, we are up next!' I pulled Graham's arm and headed for the makeshift stage.

'Wait, what? What are we doing?' he protested, spilling his third or fourth glass of plonk on the crusty dance floor. 'Walk with me,' I called out over my shoulder as the intro music started up. 'Walk . . . 500 miles?' Graham looked lost. The Proclaimers, two Edinburgh boys, had sung this famous song years ago, but now two Scottish boys were going to get the real party started! 'And I would walk 500 miles, and I would roll 500 more . . .!' I clutched the microphone and tried to encourage the bewildered, tired crew to join in the chorus.

'Dahlalalala da da, dahlalalala da da, dudrum da da da daaa!' Even Graham's reluctant baritone, which could wake the dead, had no effect on our beleaguered team. Or perhaps it was the frozen pizza slices and mini party sausage rolls arriving that stunned them into silence. We finished our rendition of the popular Scottish song and returned the microphone to its rightful bearer. Ben-the-sound-guy cleared his throat and broke into some caramel Frank Sinatra, possibly his favourite party piece, with the clear intention of showing up our pathetic attempt. At least we had given it some gusto and passion, like our singing of the Scottish national anthem when welcomed by the local Māori *iwi*.

The next day I woke up with a start. 'Ugh, what happened?!' I groaned and fumbled for some bottled water beside my hotel bed. Where was my bottle? Where was the crusty camper van and my snoring, bearded companion? I looked around the clinically clean hotel in vain, hoping to spot one of Ben's mics, or perhaps Squeezy's fanny pack – it's always the weird little things I'd miss from a trip with Graham and those were the ones lodged in my mind following our road trip down under. Last night had become a blur; we had ended up in Ben's hotel room, singing yet more show tunes and emptying his mini bar until the early hours of the morning. I'm not sure how, but I had made it back to my bed, thankfully alone! But I felt very alone. After several weeks on the road with our crew and travel companions, I realized I missed them already. I now longed for Kevin's infectious laugh, the open road, and another death-defying adventure. Our trip had come to an end and our extended *Clanlands* family had moved on. As I boarded my flight from Auckland to London, via Dubai, I even missed the McGrumpy wrap party.

Slightly.

[Graham: We LOVE New Zealand!!!]

Postscript

<u>Location: Borthwick Castle, Scottish Borders, 19km (12 miles) south-east of Edinburgh</u>

6 JANUARY 2023

SAM

Wedding bells! Almost exactly a year to the day, I sat at the back of the great hall in Borthwick Castle and watched my trusty travel companion tie the knot. For the second time. Garance Doré, Graham's fiancée, had agreed to marry him and, boy, did they know how to do it in style! The newlyweds had organized a week-long extravaganza to celebrate the historic day. I'll let Graham supply you with the details of the truly incredible event, but let me just add that, even after organizing many of the stag-do activities (despite him employing not one but TWO best men) I wasn't invited to stay at the castle, or with the stags during our rather McTavishesque stag weekend!!

I had planned a historical private tour that Graham refused to do, a whisky tasting, personalized sporrans for all the stags, lunch at the oldest pub in Edinburgh with a competitive game of skittles (which I, of course, won) and also had secured a relative of Squeezy's to come and do a sexy striptease for the groom. Unfortunately, Roly-Poly had cancelled at the last minute due to a double booking – she was very busy – and we had to make do with a late-night game of movie-based Trivial Pursuit. I admit I was rubbish at this, but 1950s films are not my strong suit.

I suppose I was a wee bit jealous seeing Graham marry; it felt like I was losing my travel buddy all over again. As the pipe band finished playing in the dining hall, the ceilidh had cleared the floor of any stragglers and there in the middle of the floor was the beautiful, happy couple dancing. Graham, content, proud and dapper in his kilt and impressively oversized sporran and Garance looking radiant and beautiful in her stylish white evening gown. Circling them, Graham's children danced and cheered. Duncan Lacroix bounced past, playing air guitar with an inflatable cone upon his head, much to the amusement of a group of enamoured nine-year-olds.

Numerous guests from the first season of *Clanlands* all busted out their best moves on the dance floor and I shook my booty, too. What a wedding! Our *Clanlands* family had grown. We had made many good friends both here in Scotland and now in New Zealand and I knew, on Graham and Garance's special day, both sides of the world would be celebrating with them!

GRAHAM

Ah yes! The wedding. It was indeed an epic event. I love organizing things, as a result of having to organize my own birthday parties, having been born on the shittiest day of the year: 4 January.

It was a gathering of my nearest and dearest, and yes, that included Sam. His description is accurate, down to and including my oversized sporran. I decided to dwarf any sporran in the room. (I had hoped for a giant haggis nailed to my loins but it was out of season!) Duncan's tremendous gyrations were surrounded by ebullient nine-year-olds. And my beautiful wife, Garance, dazzled me every time I looked at her. How did this happen? I felt very, very lucky.

And, of course, my children, Honor and Hope, who were part of the bridal party and made me so proud, along with our dog Lulu (dressed in McTavish tartan). Yes, I really did go a bit nuts.

My wife is Corsican and they would give the Scots a run for their money when it comes to clannishness. A wonderful, formidable, generous extended family who couldn't stop weeping when a group of Corsican singers (who had flown in especially) sang deeply emotional songs from their homeland.

But when it comes to the accommodation, I have to confess I feel bad. I had promised Sam a room – we had after all filmed there – but when one of the Corsicans unexpectedly decided to come, the local boy had to make way for family. Sorry, mate! As for the stag-do. It was a memorable four days. Sam organized some wonderful stuff, but I had already done the tour he'd organized, and when I learned of Roly-Poly, the thought of what I narrowly avoided haunts me to this day.

One of my final abiding memories of the evening was when Sam kept insisting on getting the keys to the roof of the castle, coupled with a desire for me to join him there. Thankfully, the keys were not to be found (I think I ate them just to be safe). But I shudder to think what fresh hell he planned to introduce me to on that cold, wintery night on top of those Scottish castle battlements. Knowing him as I do now, it could only be a combination of two things that awaited me.

A bungee cord . . .

. . . and the waiting arms of Roly-Poly.

***

REFLECTIONS

GRAHAM

We've come a long way. Yes, in the geographical sense, but we've come even further than that together since our first meeting in that hot, cramped office in Soho. I've always said that Sam bears a strong resemblance to his character in *Outlander*. His generosity, his open-hearted approach to life, and his courage (sometimes to the point of insane recklessness!).

I'm not sure if Diana Gabaldon ever described Jamie Fraser's love of scaring the living daylights out of his friends and putting them through screaming terror, but I suspect it's only a matter of time.

Even with all that I have written about my sufferings at the hands of my friend Mr Heughan, he remains above all exactly that – a friend. And a good one at that.

It seemed impossible at so many moments that Sam and I would get to do this trip together. At one point it seemed like the gods were against us and then, suddenly, those Fates were firmly on our side.

I talked of those qualities that make Sam and Jamie similar. One, perhaps above them all, is that when he says he'll do something, he does it! And he brings booze.

We had made it. We were in New Zealand together with a full tank of petrol in the camper, an equally insane crew at our side, and a tenuous grasp on common sense.

It gave me such pleasure to have him join me in my adopted homeland. To see him laughing with my wife and children at the dinner table, and to embark on another adventure together beyond anything that we could possibly have imagined.

When we finally stood side by side singing badly into a microphone together at that wrap party, murdering a perfectly good song by the Proclaimers, it wasn't just 500 miles that we'd gone together. It was thousands.

And I, for one, would do it all again.

SAM

Last time we wrote a book together, we were on opposite sides of the world. During the Covid pandemic, we had written the first *Clanlands* book online, discussing and disagreeing over our experiences on a road trip around Scotland. This time, Covid (and the NZ visa system) had again very nearly sabotaged our adventures but ultimately, like the southern cross in the night sky, the Kiwi stars had aligned and we were able to explore the whole of New Zealand (and perhaps our dysfunctional relationship). The journey had bonded us closer together; it's incredible how much you learn about someone when you're locked in a camper van for a few days. Not only that, but we had shared experiences that were truly personal and touching. I travelled halfway around the world to see my good friend, spent time with Graham and his wonderful children, his exceptional new wife – a gorgeous family. We had intimately shared our hopes and fears – then immortalized them in traditional Māori *moko* (I'm going back for mine!). In unison, we (almost) soiled our wetsuits, shared romantic dinners (he even got the check!) and – like some strange ritualistic wedding ceremony – we screamed together as we fell backwards off a cliff . . .

'EeeeEEAHHHFfuuuuuuuuuuuuuu . . .'

This book is a reflection of an epic adventure around the islands of New Zealand, with the best travel companion you can find, a very, very dear friend.

I would consider you, the reader, our third mucker and compadre on this epic adventure – who knows where we will all go together next . . . Graham?

SAM & GRAHAM (IN UNISON)

Here's to the next adventure, friend. Cheers!

FX: Clinking of glasses.

Acknowledgements

Sam

I thoroughly enjoyed recounting and writing this third book in the *Clanlands* series. A huge thank you to the people of New Zealand who shared their magical islands with us. Especially to our Māori guide Inia and the community of Rotorua, who made us feel most welcome. To the Radar/Octopus team – in particular Briony, our ever patient and accommodating editor. To Charlie, who worked tirelessly to help shape and correlate our ramblings, Scotty for the snacks/banter and laughs, Squeezy, and of course, my fearless companion McT. What a pleasure, buddy!

Graham

A big thank-you to everyone we encountered on this lengthy road trip in New Zealand, from the baristas who make the best coffee in the world to the folk who care for the precious unique wildlife of Aotearoa, to our fabulous Kiwi crew and the kind people at countless venues who generously let two rogues like Sam and me into their lives. To Sir Richard Taylor, Ri Streeter, Danielle Prestidge, Peter Lyon, and the rest of the fabulous Wētā Workshop team; to Paul Tobin for his beautiful illustrations, Sir Peter Jackson, Jed Brophy, Black Barn Vineyards, Moko 101 in Rotorua. Thank you to the gang at Octopus Books and the ever marvellous Briony Gowlett. Thanks to Zoe Ross and Olivia Davies at United Agents, to Charlie who has the patience of a saint, and to Scotty who made me laugh, kept me fed, and put up with us all over NZ. To my wife Garance, and my children Honor and Hope, who accompanied us on some of this crazy journey and put me to shame by doing the zip line with no fear whatsoever. And finally, to all the people of New Zealand who showed us such kindness and helped introduce my wonderful travel companion Sam Heughan to their very special land.

Charlotte

I would like to thank Sam and Graham for being so fabulous to work with. They are as funny, wise and wildly attractive on Zoom as they are on the telly.

Thank you to Briony for giving me the opportunity to work on all three *Clanlands* books and for her continued faith in me. To my agents at A. M. Heath, Becky Ritchie (and her new baby, Kip) and Tom Killingbeck, who is embarking on one of the most exciting non-fiction journeys with me!

And to my lovely parents who were the first to believe in me and accept that a 'proper' job wasn't really going to work. To Tallulah and Matilda, my funny, bright and fabulous daughters, I love you; to Ed, my husband, rock and the most annoying person I have ever met, whose fan letter from Afghanistan praising my humorous column in a country magazine dropped onto my doormat 13 years ago . . . Reader, I married him.

Author Biographies

Sam Heughan is an award-winning actor, producer, entrepreneur and philanthropist, best known for his starring role as Jamie Fraser in the hit TV show *Outlander*. From his early days at the Royal Lyceum Theatre Edinburgh, Sam has enjoyed a career in theatre, television and film spanning almost two decades. He is the author of a bestselling memoir, *Waypoints*, and co-author of two previous books, *Clanlands* and *The Clanlands Almanac*, all of which appeared on the *Sunday Times* and *New York Times* bestseller lists, with *Clanlands* becoming an instant NYT #1. Due to his outstanding contribution to charitable endeavours and artistic success he was bestowed with honorary doctorates by the University of Glasgow and the University of Stirling in 2019, and by the Royal Conservatoire of Scotland in 2022.

Graham McTavish has been acting for nearly 40 years in theatre, film and television. On film and TV he is best known for his roles as Dougal MacKenzie in *Outlander*, the fierce dwarf Dwalin in *The Hobbit* trilogy, Ser Harrold Westerling in *House of the Dragon*, and the extravagantly named Sigismund Dijkstra in the Netflix hit series, *The Witcher*. He was lucky enough to portray the Saint of Killers in AMC's cult show *Preacher*, fulfilling a childhood dream of playing a cowboy, and he is the only actor to have performed opposite Sylvester Stallone as both Rocky Balboa and Rambo, in the movies *Creed* and *John Rambo*. He has performed in theatre all over the world, from the Royal Court Theatre in London to the Metropolitan Museum of Art in New York. Graham is co-author of the worldwide bestselling *Clanlands* and *The Clanlands Almanac*. When he's not acting, writing, drinking lattes or being with his family, Graham enjoys waiting impatiently for his luggage to appear at various airports around the world.

Charlotte Reather is a leading country lifestyle journalist, columnist, author and comedy writer. She is the co-writer of the *New York Times* and the *Sunday Times* bestselling *Clanlands* and *Clanlands Almanac* by Sam Heughan and Graham McTavish and the international bestselling *Extreme Fishing* by Robson Green. She lives in West Sussex with her husband, Edward, two daughters, Tallulah and Matilda and labrador, Douglas.

charlottereather.com / @charlottereather